Jane Conway

MARY BORDEN

A Woman of Two Wars

Published by Munday Books 2010

First published in Great Britain in 2010 by Munday Books

ISBN 978-0-9563297-0-7

Cover design by Tim Foster

Printed and bound in Great Britain by
CPI Antomy Rowe, Chippenham and Eastbourne

This book is available through:

www.maryborden.com

*For my parents Hope and Paddy
and
Steve, James, Dominic and Sophy*

Contents

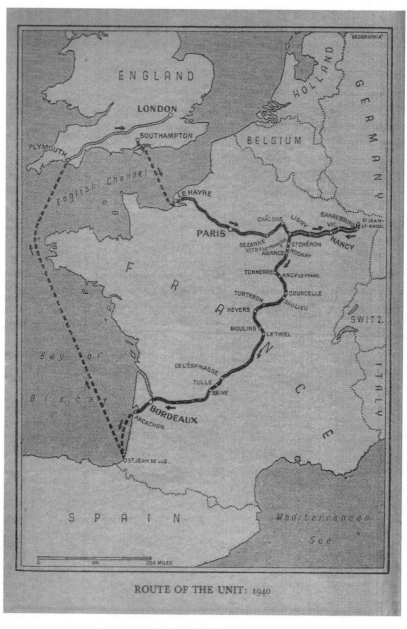

ROUTE OF THE UNIT: 1940

Route of the Hadfield–Spears unit 1940.

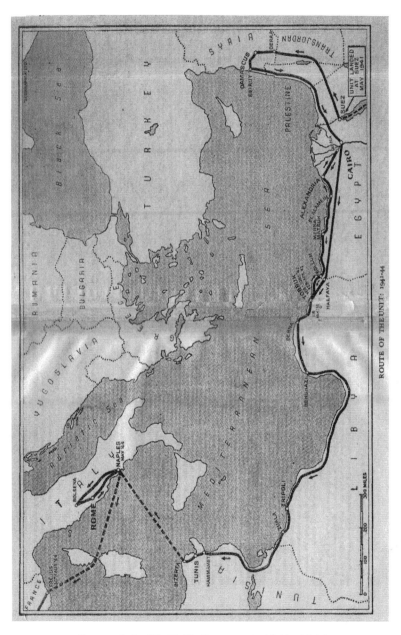

Route of the Hadfield–Spears unit 1941–1944.
Original maps appeared in Journey Down a Blind Alley

1

A London Party

In May 1914, London society was surprised and intrigued by the circulation of an invitation, sent anonymously, requesting guests to attend dinner at the Pall Mall Restaurant to celebrate the 357th wedding anniversary of Mary, Queen of Scots. Their curiosity aroused, a large number of people turned up to the event. The food was excellent, the wine well chosen, and those present, if not already acquainted, were pleased by the opportunity to make agreeable new friends. The party was off to a lively start, and yet to begin with the identity of the host or hostess remained a mystery.

Suddenly, attention was diverted towards a petite, attractive young woman, escorted by a tall gentleman, standing on a platform to deliver a speech, in a strong American accent.

'Friends,' she began. 'Today is my birthday. I was in London and lonely. I wanted you all to dine with me. But I knew you would none of you dine with me if I said "Please come and dine with Mary Borden Turner on her birthday". So I looked in the calendar and found it was the wedding anniversary of another Mary.'[1]

With this cleverly orchestrated publicity stunt, May, as her friends and family knew her, announced her arrival upon the centre stage of the literary scene, and ensured that in future she would have no need to resort to such tactics to entice guests to her parties. She was celebrating her twenty-eighth birthday and the man at her side was her husband, George Douglas Turner. In the words of the writer Ford Madox Ford, who was one of the guests, this occasion 'immediately established her as a popular London hostess.'

Two months earlier, May and Douglas had moved to London from the Far East where they had been living, on and off, since their marriage, a life which May had become increasingly weary of and was determined not to return to. As a couple, theirs was a somewhat unlikely union. She was an American heiress, with a sizeable fortune of her own. He was a Scottish missionary who, at the time of their first meeting, had been living in self-imposed poverty in Lahore. May herself was something of a contradiction, having been brought up by parents who each had a very different outlook on life. Her father, William Borden, was a man of worldly ambitions who enjoyed the privileges his wealth afforded him, while her mother, Mary, was God-fearing and increasingly withdrawn from earthly riches. No less of a contrast was that between May's own life as a missionary's wife in India and her role as a literary hostess in London, where she was establishing herself as a writer. By the time of her birthday party she was already being talked about as an up-and-coming novelist, with two books published.

Ford was again the guest of the Turners when, at the end of July, they held a large house party at a shooting lodge which they had rented for the summer in Berwickshire in the Scottish borders. Others invited included Ford's partner Violet Hunt, author of *White Rose of Weary Leaf*, and the Vorticist artist Percy Wyndham Lewis. It was one of many literary gatherings that took place that summer season, and it would remain in the collective memory of the final, charmed days of pre-war peace. People relaxed with games of golf or sat on the lawn in the garden, where they took turns to read aloud. Ford read from the proofs of *The Saddest Story* (*The Good Soldier*) which was appearing in the newly established journal *Blast*, of which Lewis was the editor. May herself read *A Portrait of the Artist as a Young Man*, which was being serialised in *The Egoist*, introducing Ford to the work of James Joyce. Ezra Pound, one of the contributors to the short-lived *Blast*, was expected to arrive later.

E. M. Forster was staying with friends nearby, and joined the party for dinner on the Monday evening. He found May in apathetic mood, 'most languid and peevish', though looking pretty and wearing 'an outré gown of white, high on the shins, low in the back, and shimmering with rainbow hues round her milieu.' [2] Forster liked Douglas a great deal, but he did not care for May whom he blamed for taking her husband away from his missionary work in India. He did, however, consider her efforts at writing worthwhile, describing her first novel as rather good.

If, as Forster's description suggests, May was feeling out of sorts that Monday evening, one reason may have been the somewhat strained relations between herself and Wyndham Lewis, with whom she had had a brief and stormy love affair. The painful confusion of her love life, however, was about to be eclipsed by the infinitely greater chaos of the First World War. May herself seems to have had no premonition of the impending catastrophe. Only that morning at breakfast she had been in dispute with Ford, insisting that a Liberal government would never declare war, and arguing her point so emphatically as to impress Lewis with her knowledge of political affairs.

When one week later, on 4 August, she found herself proved horribly wrong and in a country at war, her response, like that of many other women of her generation, was to seek to make a contribution – a decision that threw her into an altogether different world, and one in which she would need all the toughness of spirit of her pioneering ancestors.

* * *

The Bordens are now scattered around the globe, but many of those alive today are the direct descendants of Richard and Joane Borden, who left their home in Headcorn, Kent, in the 1630's and sailed to America with their five children, settling in Portsmouth, Rhode Island. According to Quaker records, their third son, Mathew, was the first English child to be born there. Five generations later, Richard's great great great grandson, Gail Borden, invented condensed milk. His discovery that milk could be prevented from spoiling if it was boiled at a high temperature proved timely. Used as a field ration during the American Civil War, this new commodity created a demand that outstripped supply. His insistence on hygienic techniques revolutionized the dairy industry, and made him a fortune. Success, however, came only after a number of disastrous inventions. These included a giant refrigerator in which to treat patients with yellow fever, which, he had observed, struck only in summer, anticipating Walter Reed's discovery half a century later that mosquitoes carry the disease.

The company Gail founded continues to thrive to the present day. For many children growing up in America in the nineteenth and twentieth centuries, the name Borden was synonymous with milk and Elsie, the cartoon cow, who grinned out at them from the label with the slogan 'If It's Borden's It's Got To Be Good'. Nowadays, though, the name is more likely to be associated with the infamous Lizzie Borden, also one of Richard's descendants, whose father and stepmother were both found brutally murdered one sultry August morning in 1882 at their house in Fall River, Massachusetts. Suspicion quickly fell upon their youngest daughter who was at home when the crime took place, and although her guilt was never proven, she became immortalized in the verse:

Lizzie Borden took an axe
And gave her mother forty whacks.
And when she saw what she had done
She gave her father forty-one.

If Lizzie's notoriety sullies the Borden name, its fabled French origins imbue it with romance and mystery. Richard Borden was one of a long line of Bordens to live in Headcorn, beginning with one Henry Borden, born in the 1370s. Before that the family lived twelve miles away in the village of Borden, where for many generations it was said by the family that there were important family documents immured in the wall of the parish church. One of Richard's descendants, Lavinia Cook, claimed to have discovered these when she was on her honeymoon in the village in 1869, having crept with her husband into the church at night and removed a stone bearing the Borden coat of arms. They found it was hollow and contained a cylindrical leaden box. Inside, wrapped in a yellow cloth of well oiled linen was a parchment manuscript prepared in 1220 by Robergia DeBourdon, who with her husband is believed to be buried in the churchyard, giving details of her French lineage and her mother's Saxon grandfather, Ethelwulf, who was killed at the Battle of Hastings.

From these distant origins, May's great-grandfather, John, left Rhode Island as a young man and sailed down the Ohio in search of silver mines. When silver eluded him, he redoubled his efforts to find fertile land to farm, settling down with his wife, Lydia, in New Providence, Indiana (later renamed Borden in memory of his son, a well-known geologist and philanthropist). John's second son shared both his christian name and youthful adventurous spirit, deciding to leave the family farm to study law at college and after graduating, set up a practice in Chicago to become one of the most prominent lawyers of his time.

His son William seemed destined to follow in his footsteps, but after entering the University of Michigan at the age of fifteen to take a law degree, he observed the potential for making money in the gold, silver and lead mining craze. Showing an unusual degree of patience and industry, he travelled to Europe to study engineering at the then-celebrated School of Mines at Freiburg, and from there went on to Heidelberg, where the scientist Robert Bunsen was at the height of his fame. When William returned to Chicago three and a half years later, at the age of twenty-one, he had turned into a self-possessed young man, sporting, to the surprise of his friends and family, an elegant beard and moustache. As a fully qualified mining engineer, and with his sense of purpose emboldened, he shocked some of his family's more conservative friends when he became swept up in the mining fever and took himself off to Leadville, one of the most famous of the Wild West camps in Colorado at the very beginning of its silver boom.

Here, he grubstaked a prospector nicknamed Chicken Bill and managed to secure an interest in a silver mine he believed was worth developing. Fortunately, his father had useful connections: his friends and business associates, Marshall Field and Levi Leiter, joint owners of the prestigious retail firm, had enough faith in John's son's venture to provide him with the fifty-thousand dollars he needed. His geologist uncle joined him in Leadville as a consultant and struck up a partnership with Colorado's legendary 'Silver King,' Horace Tabor, whose rags to riches story was remarkable even by Wild West standards; but having owned mining property worth millions, he eventually died penniless after the fall of the value of the metal in the 1890s.

William was wiser and more level-headed with the success that came to him as a prospector. He promptly sold his mine in New York city for $4 million, and taking his quarter share of this record-setting profit, he invested almost all of it in downtown Chicago property at a time when the market was depressed, later once more quadrupling his fortune. Where others might have been tempted to gamble further, he was content to call it a day, having made more than enough money to retire, although still in his twenties.

William was thirty-three and still enjoying the life of a bachelor, when one evening, embarking from his schooner in the Upper Great Lakes, he came ashore at Mackinaw; he climbed the steps of the clubhouse where a dance was in full swing, looked through the window and was immediately captivated by the sight of a beautiful young woman. Upon the spot he determined she would become his wife, and this taciturn man, with a brusqueness of speech which some found intimidating, persuaded her to marry him and then swept her off to Europe for a year-long honeymoon. Mary de Garme Whiting, eleven years younger than William, was a student at an art college in Chicago at the time she caught his eye, and was thought to have considerable talent as a painter, a leaning her new husband took seriously. In Paris they studied the work of the great masters, and developed a particular fascination with the Barbizon School, buying several of their paintings, including one by Corot, a number of Daubigny's, and from Rousseau's widow, one of her husband's pieces and a collection of Millet's pencil sketches.

Mary Whiting was born in Detroit and her ancestors had an even earlier claim to American soil than the Bordens. No fewer than six of them had arrived on the Mayflower and were among the signatories of the covenant of the Pilgrim Fathers. Coming from a long line of prominent magistrates, preachers and physicians, Mary's father, John, was known for his indefatigable efforts to improve shipping on the Great Lakes, and for developing the rich copper and silver mines in Northern Michigan. He and his 16-year-old bride, Mary Sophia, had begun their married life at a lonely outpost at Sault Sainte Marie, on the Canadian border, where mail was delivered only once during the long winter months. From here John would sometimes walk hundreds of miles in snowshoes in the freezing temperatures in the course of his work.

When William and Mary were married in Detroit on 28

William and Mary Borden

December 1883 at the Jefferson Avenue Presbyterian Church, and began their own life together on the shores of Lake Michigan, the world was much changed. In a single generation, the frontier community built on the marshy lowlands around the lake had grown into an urban metropolis. The transformation of Chicago had been accelerated by the great fire of 1871, which having broken out in a barn on the west side of the city, quickly spread to the centre where the predominantly timber-framed buildings and houses fuelled the inferno until there was little left to burn. When the fire was finally subdued by rain two days later, nearly one hundred thousand people had been made homeless, and Chicago lay in ruins.

Yet only a few years later, the town had become the most important trade centre of the West. The city skyline grew higher by several storeys and commercialism flourished with the mushrooming of new hotels, factories and businesses. It was a time of turbulent change, bringing fears that life in the city was veering out of control, with the newspapers regularly reporting crime and violence in China Town and the French Belt.

For May and her three siblings, however, the unruliness of the city seemed far removed from the peaceful surroundings of the grey stone chateau-style house their father had built on the north corner of Bellevue Place and Lake Shore Drive. He had secured one of the first plots of virgin lakeside land in what, by the early 1880s, was becoming the most desirable and exclusive residential district, a status it still carries to this day. When the Drive first began to be developed in the 1870s, it had quickly lent itself to being used as a raceway for horse drivers, a sport that became so popular it had to be restricted. Once established as home to the elite, it was where the city's finest horse-drawn carriages could be seen, and one of May's early memories was of her father's carriage approaching their house along the Drive in the winter snow.

Mary and William had five children, one of whom, Frederick,

died in infancy. May, born on 15 May 1886, occupied the middle position between John, two years older, and William, two years younger. In photographs of her as a young girl she has an oval face, framed by fair wavy hair, often worn in plaits or pigtails. Her best features were her large and expressive grey-green eyes, which as an adult would sometimes give her an air of fragility. She adored her brothers, looking up to John with due respect as the head of the sibling group and missing him when he was away. She considered it perfectly natural to do everything her brothers did, accompanying them on fishing and sailing trips with their father, or for games of golf, another favourite pastime. She was just as ready to join them in the more boisterous pursuits of gang warfare waged daily between the 'Hot Push', made up of boys from the local private school and swelled in numbers by their sisters and sisters' friends, and 'the Micks' from the public school next door, with the vacant lots between the mansions on

*May with her father and brother in the garden of
their holiday home in Camden, Maine*

the Drive serving as the fields of glory. The fiercest exchanges were over the right of way to a German bakery a few blocks distant, with the result that many a pumpkin pie was wrestled to the ground.

Although quite a tomboy, she was also interested in the latest fashions of clothing, and made her own designs in a miniature book with special attention paid to millinery, showing a preference for elaborate feathered hats. As an adult she was a stylish and original dresser (at one time holding the title of 'best-dressed of English hostesses') and would often complete an outfit, formal or informal, with a large beret or flamboyant hat. From an early age, she showed a particular interest in drawing and painting. During her adolescent years, she contemplated becoming a professional artist before the desire to be a novelist took a firmer hold, and in later life she returned with renewed vigour to painting as a means of expression.

She was a precocious reader, devouring the classics as a child, and the early influences of writers such as the Brontës, Dickens, Thackeray and Trollope, encouraged her natural instinct for composition and a self-identity as a writer. Her brothers were an eager, if patient, audience for her story-telling; one epic she managed to stretch out over an entire year. She started writing when still in the nursery, her earliest effort a poem inspired by the 1896 Presidential election.

When she was eleven, there came an unplanned addition to the family with the birth of a baby girl, christened Joyce. May celebrated her arrival with a short poem entitled 'Baby's Hands', and hand-painted roses on a cradle William had made for the new infant. This joint effort was sturdy enough to carry four generations of Borden offspring and to still be in use to this day.

In spite of the privileges of wealth and status, May's childhood was not dominated by the conventions of social etiquette, or one in which children were expected to be seen but not heard. If anything, they ruled the roost. Growing up on the water's edge, the Borden young were allowed to run wild and enjoy the freedom of outdoors. In those days Lake Shore Drive was still so empty of traffic and people that May could sail down the sidewalk on her roller skates for a couple of miles and bump into no one. On the other side of the Drive, a sea-wall took the full force of the crashing waves and the wind. Built as a defence against the elements, the wall also had the unfortunate distinction of acting as a magnet for people desperate enough to choose to end their lives by jumping from it into the water– a frequent enough occurrence for the family to keep a coil of rope and a kitchen chair to throw as a lifeline. For the Borden children, though, the lake and its immediate surroundings were places of limitless possibilities, providing a wonderful adventure playground which changed with the seasons. In May's early childhood, the sea-wall was taken away and a raised concrete beach built in its place; at first this was for the exclusive use of those who lived on Lake Shore Drive, but when May was nine, the beaches along the lakefront opened for public use. So as not to offend the sensitivities of those residents whose windows faced the beach, swimmers were required to wear decorous attire.

In the winter, besides tobogganing and ice-skating at the city rink, there was also the excitement of playing on the frozen lake. This was strictly forbidden and the potential dangers of breaking the rules were brought home one day when, after a few days of warmer temperatures, a boy from the local school fell through the ice and drowned. When storms raged across the lake, the children could watch from the safety of the house, their faces pressed against the window panes. It was not unusual to witness a ship running into trouble in bad weather and the lifeboats racing to the rescue; occasionally, after floods, bits of wreckage were strewn across the drive.

During the summer the family left their artificial seashore for the real sea, heading east to Camden, on the coast of Maine, where William had built a holiday home overlooking the bay.

There were also visits to the grandparents at their large estate on the Mississippi in Indiana.

Having grown up in a beautiful home, with the security of a close and loving family, May looked back on her early childhood years as supremely happy. Yet they were overshadowed by an event which had a profound and lasting effect upon her. When she was not much more than eight or nine, her mother became a member of a fundamentalist Church, founded in Chicago by Dwight Lyman Moody in 1864, which with its worldwide evangelistic campaigns was rapidly growing in reputation and influence. When Moody and his singing partner, Ira Sankey, embarked on their revival campaign in 1876, thousands filled the meeting places wherever they went. Moody and Sankey became household names, and when the gospel hymns Sankey had written were printed, they became overnight best-sellers.

Mary Whiting had come from a family of clergymen and missionaries, a side she seems to have inherited with an intensity of fervour. Tormented by the conviction of guilt, she believed her family to be damned, and feared the outside world, which she equated with sin. Whether the cause or effect of the conversion, it is likely that she experienced some form of breakdown or post-natal depression. Her daughter Joyce later recalled how as a small child, whenever she was naughty, she was made to sing 'There is a fountain filled with blood drawn from Emanuel's veins', a hymn whose imagery she found horrifying. On another occasion, when she had done something wrong, her mother forced her to her knees in a small dark room in the Moody church and commanded her to give herself to Jesus, which had sent her into such a paroxysm of physical protest, kicking, screaming and biting, that she was able to break free.

May rarely spoke about this rupture in her sheltered family life, but she repeatedly made women of extreme Christian beliefs figure in her early novels, and the theme of religion became a central and evolving preoccupation throughout her later writing.

When at the age of twenty-five she came to write her first novel, *The Mistress of Kingdoms*, she relived her experiences through the heroine Barbara, whose mother also converts to an evangelical church, and who recalls:

> the memory of a glowing woman seated before the lights of the dressing table in a shimmering coral pink gown, a million jewels glimmering in her hair ... but after the coming of that thing – the conviction of sins, there had been no jewel mother. There had been instead a wan, white faced woman, who spent much of her time in a closet on her knees and wept terribly over her sins and the sins of those she loved.[3]

After her conversion, Mary sold all the jewels that William had given her, and bit by bit stopped wearing her made-to-order, French brocaded satin dresses, clothing herself entirely in black or white. May observed the changes in her mother with a terrible sense of helplessness. She believed in God, but a benign one, and although she willingly took part in the ritual of saying her prayers each night, she wanted nothing to do with the Moody Church, later giving vent to her feelings on the subject in her third novel, *The Romantic Woman*, in which she was fiercely critical of the theology practised by Revivalists. Strongly autobiographical in parts, particularly in its evocation of an American childhood in the fictional town of Iroquois, clearly based on Chicago, the novel centres on Joan Fairfax, an American heiress, whose father owns a palatial house on the shores of a lake as big as a sea. Along with the many details borrowed from May's own childhood, there is the gentle and childlike mother, Mrs Fairfax, a victim of her own religious fervour, who discovers the Ebenezer Sprott Church, 'a furiously militant Protestantism'. The 13-year-old Joan is made to confess her sins at a prayer meeting:

> My miserable little soul was stripped and exposed to their sanctified curiosity ... I can see myself now, a quaking, shivering little girl, rising up in the midst of that heated

congregation and confessing my sins in a trembling voice, with a thousand pairs of eyes devouring my shame and my tears; a thousand minds in a state resembling intoxication, praising God for my utter and disgraceful loss of self control.

For May, the highly emotional atmosphere of the prayer meetings was abhorrent, and she never hid from her mother her antagonism toward the Moody Church, but in the end it was easier to give in to her religious dictates, on the surface at least, just as she observed her father doing. The children watched him becoming more and more silent and withdrawn as a result of the irreconcilable differences between himself and his wife. To comfort her, he would read the Bible with her, but he did not give up the things in life which he enjoyed, and did what he could to alleviate the changed circumstances of his children's lives.

May was sometimes made shy by her father's profound reserve, but when she had the courage to break through his silence, she was rewarded by the sudden warmth of his smile. As well as taking her to concerts, he possessed an extensive collection of books on a range of subjects. Under his wing, May was able to cultivate her taste for art, literature, politics and philosophy, and through the books that she found to read in his library, she aspired to the discovery of greater knowledge and learning.

To begin with, May was taught at home, in the schoolroom, by French and German governesses, but it was her father's input she most valued, sitting with him in his library each evening while he helped her with her studies. At fifteen she was sent as a boarder to Rye Seminary on Long Island, New York, owned by Miss Harriet Stowe and her sister Miss Mary Stowe, whose emphasis on a classical education, with a rich variety of extra-curricular activities, had earned it the reputation of one of the leading preparatory schools in the country.

It was a wrench at first to be uprooted from family and home and transplanted to the surroundings of the Seminary, but May was determined to overcome her homesickness, seeing hard work as the cure. Her subjects included Latin, prose, geometry, French, English, Greek and Roman History, for which she set herself high standards. In one of her letters home she described her state of terror at the thought of her impending exams: 'I positively tremble to think of them. I might just as well not pass at all as not get above ninety and I'm afraid I can't do it ... Latin is what worries me most my hands grow clammy at the thought and it seems as though I never would be composed enough to even write what I know.'[4]

It was not all hard grind, however, and there was plenty of scope for more leisurely diversions in the quiet sea-coast village of Rye, with its rolling countryside and magnificent sandy beach on Long Island Sound. The girls were regularly allowed out for walks, and even bicycle rides. May hired a brand new bike, an expense she felt it necessary to justify to her parents, pointing out that her old one would cost almost as much to repair. Besides, she reasoned, showing her father's eye for business acumen, she could rent her new one out to other pupils when she was not using it. She was good at sports, although her request to start a baseball team was refused on the grounds that there was no space except for the lawn, and if they played there they would attract too big an audience.

Now and again the pupils were allowed to travel by train to New York City, some thirty-two miles south of Rye, where they liked to explore the shops for trinkets and the latest fashions in clothes. May coveted a particular red golf jacket of a type worn by some of the girls at school, and in a moment of impulse splashed out $14 on one, and then, 'when the deal was done', worried that her mother would not approve. Her father's fortune would have allowed her to buy any of the clothes she desired, but she was well aware that in Mrs Borden's eyes, thriftiness was next to godliness and vanity a sin.

Clothes were one source of excitement, and another was vicarious romance – when the young riding master married and brought his new wife to live in rooms at the Seminary, it became 'the talk of the school'. May wrote home about such details of her school life with uninhibited spontaneity.

Her year at Rye climaxed on a triumphant note when she passed her final exams with flying colours. Her relief was immense, and she was so excited by her success that she celebrated by sending the news to her parents by telegram before immediately turning her thoughts, with equal excitement, to a forthcoming dance in New York. It was 1903 and she was aged seventeen and looking forward to the summer holiday. This was to be spent in Switzerland, France and England to extend her education through travel.

If she was anticipating dreary weather in the English capital when she wrote a short story for her school magazine entitled 'A London Fog' (her first published work), the food, when she got there, was an unpleasant surprise. She thought it was 'abominable'; huge unappetising portions and leathery meat impossible to cut, rather than the daintily served meals she enjoyed in Paris. Arriving in London, weary after the long journey from France, she and her travel companions encountered a number of other shocks. They had been 'scared to death' when a man ran after their carriage all the way from Victoria Station to Russell Square, for they had no idea that all he wanted was the job of unloading their luggage: 'We weren't acquainted with the custom and were so frightened that we all, at least Florence and myself, had hysterics whenever his face appeared at the window', she later told her parents. Besides this drama, their hat box fell from their vehicle into the middle of the street, and at the station, a horse, frightened by an engine and cavorting around, stuck its hoof through the window of their carriage sending glass flying in every direction and knocking one of the trunks off the top.

As for the 'dirty dingy' boarding house in Marylebone, where she stayed on her arrival, sleeping in an attic room reached by 'rickety stairs and about half as large as mother's boudoir closet' and with beds with 'no springs, simply rocky mountain mattresses laid across iron slats', - this was enough to make her weep. She was dismayed by the sparsely furnished bedroom, which apart from the unwelcoming bed, had only one unsteady chair, a fire and a 'sort of table with a washstand on it ... a window ledge half hidden by the bed and a few nails in the wall to hang clothes on'. She endured this for only two nights before she swapped to the 'very reasonable but infinitely better' lodgings at the Bedford Hotel.[5]

In spite of this inauspicious introduction, the capital of England was everything she had imagined. 'It's all so undeniably and absolutely London', she wrote with exuberance to her parents. 'I simply love it and the omnibuses – I never saw anything like them.' She took a long ride in one, 'sitting up on top in the front seat' and was amazed by how many things there were to see and do – 'many more interesting things than in Paris'. At the Tower of London she was very excited to stand on the exact spot where Anne Boleyn and Lady Jane Grey were beheaded. In Westminster Abbey she attended a Sunday afternoon service and listened to 'a splendid sermon'. The British Museum she found a 'bewilderingly huge and wonderful place' where she went 'simply crazy over some of the old manuscripts' and was enthralled to discover letters written by 'almost all the English kings, a description by an eye witness of Mary Queen of Scots' execution' and letters by other famous historical people which were 'almost uncanny'. As for the National Gallery, 'words and adjectives' failed to convey the wonder of it all. She enjoyed it 'a thousand times more than the Louvre ... the pictures are hung so much better and every one is a perfect jewel'.

Carried away by the sheer euphoria of adventure, she dared to change her travel plans, hiring an automobile to take her to Liverpool and hoping her parents would not view it as a very extravagant thing to do. She arrived in Lucerne in the middle of a state carnival, the town thronged with people, and was fascinated on her approach by the view of the lake, wishing she could 'spend two or three weeks floating around' from one beautiful part to another. Her parents had spent their honeymoon in Lucerne and she found it strange to think of them 'in that same beautiful spot on the mountain'. Little did she think that she would one day return there, to marry against the same romantic backdrop. During this first visit, she was taken in by a German family who lived in a simple farmhouse on the shore of the lake. Seeing their piano, she could not resist sitting down to play, causing much merriment by providing the musical accompaniment to a family singalong, entertaining them with her rendition of the German songs she had learnt as a young child. After this 'cosy homely evening', she enjoyed a blissful night's sleep, for the beds here were 'the most marvellous beds you can imagine … four-posters, about five feet from the floor and simply towering like mountains' with huge feather pillows. She felt as though she was climbing the Matterhorn to bed, and an English girl who was also staying there, hardly slept all night in 'mortal fear' of falling out.[6]

May's high spirits throughout the holiday were tempered only by bouts of homesickness. These were severe enough to cause her to worry about how she would endure being away at university. Her high marks in her final school exams had earned her a place to study English and philosophy at Vassar College, founded in 1865 and the first of its kind to offer American women an education as academically challenging as that provided by the best colleges for men. Entrance was highly selective, and students applying there in May's time were required to speak at least two foreign languages, Latin included, and to have a good knowledge of the sciences as well as the arts. Besides expecting its students to apply themselves rigorously, Vassar built its reputation on the cultivation of strong and independent-minded women with high expectations, many of whom had made names for themselves in a variety of fields: graduating at the same time as May, Alice Huyler Ramsey became the first woman to cross

America in an automobile (the 3,000 mile journey taking 41 days and using up 11 spare tyres).

May proved a diligent student, at times working to the point of exhaustion in her determination to excel. She had a strong competitive streak, demonstrated in her gruelling preparation for her part in inter-collegiate debates between the women's colleges, where she was able to sharpen her verbal skills. This early training to argue on a wide range of issues was reflected throughout her life in her strongly held opinions and uninhibited outspokenness.

She also found an outlet for her theatrical interests, becoming President of the Dramatics Society. She had long since taken an interest in the theatre, once being so bold as to skip school to see a play by George Bernard Shaw in New York, which had scandalized her mother and prompted a visit from her father to reprimand her for her dubious taste as much as for her truancy. (When some years later, she met the playwright, by way of an introduction she related this story to him which was the beginning of a long and close friendship.)

In the climate of college, which gave free reign to May's keen intelligence and natural inquisitiveness, her imagination was excited and her horizons widened. Yet a deep sense of guilt had been instilled in her by her mother, and her desire for academic self-development brought self-doubt that in pursuing this she might be forsaking the spiritual. In one of her letters home she anxiously considered the dilemma. 'Should one strive either all one's energy for perfection and development of one's mind, or should one, in fact, should I give up college as a temptation to over emphasising the intellectual ... is it right to put so many hours on intellect? Is it misspent energy, misspent time?' She contemplated leaving college, but was then greatly comforted when she heard a sermon which seemed to reconcile intellect and faith, allowing her to write 'I really want to be a scholar – to do something with my mind – and education.'[7]

If May felt she was not always living up to her mother's expectations, her father took obvious pleasure in his daughter's achievements. When he visited her at Vassar to hear her represent her college in a debate, he was immensely proud of how well she performed.

Then, at the beginning of April 1906, there came the news of her father's sudden death at the age of fifty-three. Less than a week before he died, May had shared a short holiday in Indiana with her parents. She had only been back at college for a day when he suffered a severe stroke. By the time she arrived home, he had lost consciousness and he died the following morning. The shock of bereavement was compounded by her mother's reaction, which was one of abject terror for her husband's soul, for he had not denied his agnosticism at the end. May never forgot the expression on her mother's face as she searched her own for reassurance. Her fear for William seemed an appalling injustice to him, and made it impossible for May to comfort her.

May suffered for a long time over the loss of the parent she adored and relied upon, and whom she thought of as her greatest friend. She had lost both a father and a vital ally, but he had provided a means of safeguarding her future by leaving to her in his will investments which gave her the very substantial income of ten thousand pounds a year. His large collection of paintings, including works by Rembrandt, Van Dyck and Dürer, he divided up between his wife and children, of which May received her share to the value of over $4,000. One of the first things she did with her new-found wealth was to set up, in her father's name, a scholarship fund at Vassar which provided for one student a year to travel to Europe to study economics and social conditions.

She seemed to have a particularly intense desire to make her mark on the world. Already she was experiencing an awareness of the shortness of life which had reduced her to tears on her thirteenth birthday. She had been giving much thought to the way in which she might make her existence meaningful and was torn between the desire to do charitable work and the ambition to prove herself as a writer. As spiritual enlightenment, Mrs Borden sent her a religious text with the implicit message that one must follow where God guides, to which May tactfully replied: 'I know it is true – and yet one can't be guided when one is sitting still. It's when a man is going on the run that he can be guided to right or left – a ship has to have headway – to answer to the rudder – isn't it true? May be I am on the side of energy – ambition – self-confidence – but as long as I'm willing to be guided.'[8]

She had been thinking about working in a prison, but after talking her plans through with one of her tutors, she told her mother that she had decided to spend the next five years 'writing hard and in serious preparation' so that she would know whether she had it in her 'to do a really great work that way'.

Perhaps in order to deflect Mrs Borden's anticipated objections, she made the observation that 'Christ spent 30 years in preparation'.[9]

The seriousness with which she approached her work as a writer was typical of her ambition and self-motivation. If she was going to write, it would be with the aim of producing something of significance, and in order to achieve this she could not rely on an innate talent, but would have to spend time developing the techniques of her craft. Her immediate future seemed set and full of hope when in 1907 she graduated from Vassar. But fate was to intervene and she soon found her life going in a different direction from the one she had envisaged.

2

Collision

Mary Borden had always wanted May to become a foreign missionary and this goal took on new urgency when she saw her daughter making friends among New York's bohemia and carving a way of life for herself which contributed nothing to the Glory of God or saving the heathen. Eventually, May agreed to go on a tour round the world, suitably chaperoned by friends from the Moody Church, Mr and Mrs Bausher, the plan being that they should visit various missionary settlements to which the Bordens had given money. Her brother William had made such a trip only a few years earlier.

A few months later, she travelled to Vancouver on the Canadian Pacific Railway, and from there set sail for Yokohama. To mark the event, she founded, in 1908, a hostel for Japanese women students in Tokyo. She may have undertaken the tour on her mother's terms, but she was quick to exploit the opportunity, finding a way to invest in helping women achieve an education.

It was during her time in the Far East, in March 1908, that May met Douglas Turner in Lahore, where he was serving as secretary to the local branch of the Young Men's Christian Association. His father, a Scottish clergyman, had also worked as a missionary, and Douglas had spent much of his childhood overseas. Born in 1880 in British Guiana, he had later moved with his parents to Jamaica, and then to France, before taking a degree in theology at Glasgow University. From 1903 he had been in India, where he led an ascetic existence, living in a native bazaar so as to disseminate Christian teachings among the Indian children. He was dedicated to his work and at home in his surroundings. When the writer E. M. Forster met him he was impressed by the young man's knowledge of Indian life and observed how he was 'the only Englishman' he had come across 'who seems to care for the people',[1] a remark that has been seen as anticipating Fielding in *A Passage to India*.[2] Forster was very grateful to Douglas for taking himself and his travelling companions on a tour of the city, where they saw aspects of life not usually witnessed by tourists. After spending a day in his company, following him around the streets and being introduced to the locals, Forster thought him 'quite the most charming man' he had met in India, 'most sympathetic and full of fun'.[3]

Douglas was the type of person to whom people seemed to warm, with his ready sense of humour and easy, companionable nature, and to May his sincerity and altruism had an instant appeal. Still vulnerable from the death of her father, she responded to his gentle and caring side, and, encouraged by her chaperones, she became engaged to him within a week of their first meeting. The next day she left for Bombay, and then went on to Egypt, continuing her tour with a troubled heart, for within days of parting from her newly-acquired fiancé, she began to question their compatibility. Fearing that she was making a mistake, she wanted to break off the engagement, but Mrs Bausher insisted that she should keep her word.

Five months later the couple were reunited when Douglas joined May in Switzerland, and they were married in the Town Hall at Lausanne on 28 August, attended by her mother and several other religious friends of hers.

In September, Douglas took his young wife back to Lahore, where they rented a bungalow and in spite of her inheritance, lived frugally. May wanted to integrate with the Indian community and made a point of getting to know as many native women as possible. To overcome the barriers of language, and seeing an opportunity to extend her interest in women's education, she began to study Hindustani, and became sufficiently fluent to be able to give lectures to Indian teachers, in an Indian school for women in the native quarter. She was also actively supportive of her husband's work, receiving hundreds of students and missionaries and members of the Hindu and Muslim communities in her home; during one religious conference lasting four days she had as many as fifty missionaries staying together as her guests, sleeping wherever they could find space, or in tents in the garden. A friend of hers from this time, who first met her in Lahore, thought her very courageous in the way that she 'tackled a difficult position and one that had no official place in the British India of that day.'[4]

During this time she had one trip back to America when a few months after her marriage she became pregnant, and she travelled with her husband to the holiday home her father had built in Maine. Here, in August 1909, she gave birth to Joyce. They returned with the baby to Lahore in October, moving the following spring to Gulmarg, 12,000 feet up in the mountains in Kashmir where their second child, Comfort, was born on 15 August.

That same year, in the February and March editions of the *Atlantic Monthly*, May published two short stories, both set in India and with a religious theme, for which she was proud to receive $25 dollars a piece, the first money she had earned by her own means.

In spite of all her efforts to share her husband's life, May felt isolated, cut off as she was from the companionship of like-minded people. She was unable to overcome her dislike of the evangelical form of Christianity with its fervent emotionalism, and what made her loneliness worse was that she knew that her marriage was a mistake. It could not yet be described as a disaster, and in many ways she felt she did not deserve Douglas. She could certainly find no fault at all in his behaviour towards her. He was a devoted husband and father, and willing to do whatever made her happy. But he was not her intellectual equal and his interests were far removed from hers.

For the present, the remedy seemed to lie in a wandering existence, and in February 1911, the Turners travelled to Europe, spending a month in Paris, and then crossing the Channel to England. Here they rented a furnished house in London, and another in the country at Wraysbury in Buckinghamshire. In the summer they were on the move again, this time independently. May took a house on the coast of Scotland at Lossiemouth with her daughters, while Douglas travelled to Persia as honorary secretary of the Persian Society, remaining there throughout August and September.

Over the next year, the Turner family continued their restless way of life, dividing their time between America and England, and there were trips to Scotland where Douglas introduced May to his extended family. The confines of marriage to a man with whom she had so little in common, however, and the demands of family responsibilities, were making her ill. Douglas decided she needed a rest and took her to Tours in France where his parents had rented a house for the winter of 1912.

She had at least begun working on her first full-length novel, *The Mistress of Kingdoms*, which she was to publish under the pseudonym of Bridget MacLagan. It is centred on the life of an American heiress called Barbara Witherow, who, in spite of her fanatically religious mother, studies philosophy at university, writes poetry, and on a trip to India, meets a poor missionary called Colin Trave. After a hesitant and brief courtship they marry in Europe before returning to live in India. Although struck by his goodness, she enters marriage 'with the rapture of passion denied her' and aware of 'multitudinous pitfalls'.

With the heroine's life so closely mirroring May's, it is difficult to know where to separate fact from fiction, but Barbara's exploration of her unease at marrying Colin – 'how alien to her his mystic sense of God', her fear that her own 'religious antagonism' will render her 'incapable of sharing his spirit life', and her alternating optimism and despair as she tries to come to terms with a loveless union – all this has the quality and power of spontaneous introspection. What Douglas made of it is not known, but in later years, May confessed embarrassment about drawing so much raw material from her own life story in her first novel. When her eldest daughter, Joyce, started writing at the age of seventeen, May would not, at that time, let her publish her work, giving as her reason that she might later regret it.

At the end of 1912, the Turners went back to Lahore with the intention of winding up their affairs and returning to make their home in Europe. How much agreement there was between the couple over this move is hard to say, but Douglas later attributed leaving India to a crisis in May's personal life, something she vehemently denied. In any case, in March 1913, they moved to Mayfair, renting a house in Carlyle Square. In an attempt to make Douglas feel happier in England, May rented a house for his parents in Paddington, and he found work with the poverty action group Rowntree and Tawney.

Then in April, May received news that her brother William had contracted spinal meningitis in Egypt and was fighting for his life. A distinguished scholar and linguist, William had always had an exceptionally close relationship with his mother and had grown up to fulfil her expectation that he would devote his life to missionary work. Possessing the same singleness of purpose as his sister, he had attended Princeton Seminary after graduating from Yale and by the age of twenty-six had already established himself as a leading light in the Moody Church community. En route to China where he was determined to work with Muslims, he spent time in Egypt, learning Arabic and studying the Koran. When May received the news of his illness, she left at once to be with him. Mary Borden and her youngest daughter Joyce were unaware of his condition, since they were on their way to Lebanon where they were expecting to spend the summer in the mountains with him, and efforts to reach them by wireless had failed. He was conscious enough to recognize May when she arrived at the Anglo-American Hospital in Cairo, and for the next two weeks she stayed at his side, the infection sometimes appearing to subside, only to return as severe as ever. By this time his mother and younger sister were being kept in touch by frequent telegrams as they travelled to Brindisi to catch a steamer to Port Said. Their boat arrived at five in the morning and they had started the last leg of the journey to Cairo by train when news reached them that William had died.

When they finally arrived at the hospital and said goodbye to him, he seemed in his mother's eyes to have been transformed by his suffering into the image of Christ. Since her husband's death, Mrs Borden had relied heavily on William, eventually moving with Joyce to Princeton so that they could be near him, and, with his help, opening up her home to missionaries, lay preachers and students from the seminary. She had, though, encouraged him to go to China, believing it to be his calling. At the memorial service held for him at his home church in America, the preacher said that it was the 'strangest, most mystical working of the divine providence' he had ever experienced, for the world had such need of William.[5]

Back in England, May had started to make her way as a writer. *The Mistress of Kingdoms* had been published in 1912 to encouraging reviews. *The Times* admired 'the cleverness displayed all through' and the *Evening Standard* described the work as 'subtle and brilliant'. Her second novel, *Collision*, quickly followed in 1913. Both were published by the relatively young company Duckworth, founded in 1898, under the same pseudonym of Bridget MacLagan.

Why she chose to use a pseudonym is not clear, but the most likely reason was a fear of her mother's disapproval. When Mrs Borden did read her work, she expressed regret that May did not put her efforts into something more spiritually uplifting, a criticism she eventually took to heart, writing the novel *Mary of Nazareth*, but by that time her mother was dead.

There is a passage in *The Mistress of Kingdoms* in which the narrator describes her strategy of defence, as a child, against her mother's efforts to influence her behaviour:

> Soon she had settled into a consistent habit of disobedience. She had reasoned this plan out quite simply. Her mother wanted her to be, above everything else, a Christian, and she was determined to be a beautiful, clever woman; every experience her mother desired for her was to help her to be unworldly; every experience she desired for herself was to help her to know the world; therefore, she need do nothing her mother wanted, if she could avoid it without being found out. If possible, she was to keep her mother in ignorance of her disobedience. It would be easier to follow out one's plan secretly. She must consult no one, must train herself. She had settled into the task seriously.[6]

The Mistress of Kingdoms, written two years before Virginia Woolf's first novel, *The Voyage Out*, is striking for its portrayal of an independent-minded heroine, and one who aspires to equality in her relationships with men. This theme, moreover, was being acted out through May's involvement with the suffragette movement.

Although she did not see herself as a militant, during one protest in the autumn of 1913, when hundreds of women from all over England gathered outside the Houses of Parliament, with stones concealed beneath their coats, May was chosen, as the youngest present, to become a martyr to the cause. Cheered on by the angry throng, she took a stone from her pocket and flung it at the window of the Treasury building (Lloyd George was the Chancellor of the Exchequer at the time). To her chagrin, it missed its target, and so did a second one, but in a last frantic effort to live up to the expectations of her comrades, and with two policemen nearly upon her, she threw her remaining stone. It soared over the heads of the crowd and crashed spectacularly through the glass, resulting in her victorious arrest and five days in a prison cell at Bow Street.

During her incarceration, her friends and family brought her lunch in baskets, and novels to read, which helped to pass the time, but when Douglas paid her 25-shilling fine without consulting her she was mortified because it prevented her transfer to Holloway Prison. Later, she wondered whether she would have been brave enough to survive the ordeals of force-feeding, and the harsh treatment which had caused the death of one protester.

A feminist slant to her novels was part of a general interest in politics which had been there at an early age. As a child of ten she had been informed enough to comment in a letter to her grandfather on the outcome of the recent Presidential election which went in favour of the Republican William McKinley. Her second novel, *Collision*, set in India, was more ambitious, for included in a crowded cooking pot of ideas she covers issues of empire and race and the clash between opposing cultures and ideologies, using satire to attack certain views and attitudes. The cast, both English and Indian, represent different viewpoints, with the novel divided into five parts for each of the principal characters.

It was unusual for a novel at this time to be set in India, particularly one which included Indians. The year before, Ethel Dell had published *The Way of an Eagle* which was fairly representative of the genre of romance novels which were the staple of those set in India. It could not be more different from *Collision*, which has more in common with Forster's *Passage to India*, published eleven years later in 1924 but partly based on his first visit to India during the time he met Douglas. May certainly appeared to share Forster's dislike of typical Anglo-Indian life and all it represented, not least through her juxtaposing of the atmosphere of indulgent 'slothfulness' in the homes and meeting places of the English with the oppressive heat and dust and poverty in the bazaars, where small children play next to open drains, and babies die of starvation and disease.

There is real pathos in the character of Susan Digby, whose typical Anglo-Indian life with its 'unutterably dragging' social round of tennis parties, dinners and outings to the local Gymkhana Club, is felt as a prison. Her stifling existence in India with its 'habitual, daily sameness of consistent conduct' has changed her from a wild and spirited person into someone who plays her role as the wife of an administrator of the Raj with a graceful sense of duty, but suffers continual headaches and a 'horrible nervous feeling'. The novel charts her dawning sense of her own futility in India, and the 'aching emptiness' of her existence.

The arrival of Susan's old friend on a visit from England, a femme fatale with an 'unimaginative mind and untouched heart', only makes matters worse. Imogen Daunt is a famous socialist and a suffragette, who embraces the idea of 'sex equality and free love' and who is 'possessed' by her 'mission' to liberate and educate Indians. Readers are invited to laugh at her naive liberalism, but her actions leave a trail of tragic disasters.

May's first two novels were felt to show considerable promise. But if her determination to succeed as a writer was beginning to bear fruit, not everyone was kind about her ambitions. Forster felt she was using her inheritance to buy her way into the London literary scene, and certainly her wealth allowed her to entertain in style. But she had a genuine flair for party giving, and excelled at entertaining her guests. She was often at her best when surrounded by interesting people, engaging in serious conversation and the interchange of ideas and could hold forth with formidable confidence. Although petite – she was 5 foot 2 inches – she had considerable presence. Her friend, Juliet Huxley, described her as an 'intelligent, quick and witty' woman 'who was always very knowledgeable about politics and many international problems' and whose parties 'were always remarkable'.[7]

Whereas May sparkled as a literary hostess, Douglas often felt ill at ease, and differences between the couple were becoming increasingly apparent. His prolonged absences from home, touring Persia and the Balkans through his work, only allowed the gulf between them to grow as she began associating with avant-garde artists and writers. She became a patron of the arts, and in the autumn of 1913 financed a series of plays produced by Norman McKinnel at the Vaudeville Theatre.

In December, the family crossed the Atlantic once again to spend Christmas with the Borden family in Maine, remaining there throughout January and February. By the time they sailed back to London, May was pregnant with her third child, due at the end of November. In America, she had invested in a company called Brown Spinwright, which was introducing a new patent spool for cotton mills. Douglas was appointed as an agent for the company in England, which involved negotiating for the introduction of the spool in mills around the country. However, he was no more suited to the life of a salesman than May was to that of a missionary, and after a few trips to the north of England to visit some factories, the job came to an end.

On their return to London, where May rented a house at 2 Abbey Gardens in Westminster, it was harder to ignore the disappointments of her marriage. Most likely it was through her new friends the Hueffers that she was brought into the orbit of the artist Percy Wyndham Lewis in the spring of 1914. Born in 1882, he was thirty-two when May met him, four years her senior. Undeniably good-looking, tall with black hair, moustache and large sensual eyes, he had a certain sex appeal which many women found irresistible. The previous autumn he had broken away from Roger Fry's Omega Workshop to start The Rebel Art Centre and its experimental movement Vorticism. May was impressed by his intellectual adventurousness, and although she was worried that she did not understand his work, she soon joined his long list of wealthy female patrons. When she moved in June to a small house at 33 Park Lane, she commissioned him to decorate the drawing room and to paint six panels for the walls, for which she agreed to pay him £250.

To Lewis, May had the 'attractive freshness of the New World' and of 'a classless community'.[8] He in turn gave her the excitement of romance. Clandestine meetings took place; she told him her nom de plume was Bridget MacLagan, and suggested he might like to call her Bridget. When she knew that Douglas was going away on one of his trips to the north, she wrote to Lewis, 'Next week I've three clear days. Please make them nice for me'. Lewis was happy to oblige, making not only himself available, but also his flat where she stayed the night with him. The letter she sent him afterwards reveals something of her infatuation for him. 'You make everyone else seem flat – just as your pictures makes other pictures look dull. But I am more lucid about you and why you appeal to me. It doesn't matter does it, whether I understand your technique or not as long as I adore you, not too stupidly? If I'm an artist at all it is in living. I mean in the understanding of human relationships.'[9]

In spite of worries that she might not fully appreciate his work, she was 'happy with that delicious "malaise" that comes when one is obsessed by another personality.'[10] May, though, was just one of a number of lovers Lewis collected around him without committing himself emotionally to any of them. Married women, according to one of his biographers, 'provided the thrill of deception without the fear of entanglement'.[11] Whether or not May was aware of his notoriously cavalier treatment of his various mistresses, it did not take long before she was on the receiving end of his off-hand behaviour. 'You have made me unhappy', she wrote to him frankly after he had stood her up.

You hurt me. I can't go on like this. You must be considerate and human. You must not tell me to come to John Lanes' and then get drunk and go away without seeing me. You've no idea how these little episodes interfere with the current of primitive feeling. I could love you madly and give you pleasure if you'd take just a little trouble, to be courteous. You say I'm not primitive enough and I – good God – Your voice was horrid over the phone – I love you and you must think for me, sometimes, and of me.[12]

At other times she adopted a tone more reminiscent of a mother talking to a child: 'I am wondering if you posted Mrs Ezra Pound's letter – Please look in your pockets.'[13] Impatience with his unreliability is also detectable in a letter inviting him to eat with her: 'Dinner tomorrow at exactly seven o'clock.'

At the end of June, the Turner family rented Charter Hall, in Berwickshire, for the summer months. May disliked the house intensely. It had a dispiriting effect on her, and she wrote a depressed letter to Lewis complaining about her surroundings:

The big house is of an unclear grey color – It is the middleclass Mansion. The awful and sinister mean between the castle and the hovel – It is like the coliseum – it says 'I am large and comfortable, built for breeding and my children are the backbone of the country' – I hate it, and I hate the large fat trees, smug, squat, all of a uniform green, that stand about … too self-possessed to be affected by the wind – Douglas says if I make up my mind to it, I can be happy here – But why should I? Every time I turn around it hits me. I suffer like a person whose clothes rub them raw in many places.[14]

She decided to escape back to London for a few days on her own, reserving a room at the Savoy, and asked Lewis to dine with her.

The trip to London did little to improve her spirits, and her time with Lewis was unsatisfactory. She joined him for a dinner which had been arranged for contributors to his new journal *Blast* at the Dieudonné Restaurant, where it seems that they quarrelled. Afterwards she wrote him a letter from the Savoy Hotel.

> Something ugly, unpleasant has grown up suddenly out of our intercourse. I don't say that it is in you or in me. Two odourless acids mixed, may make a bad smell – We get on each other's nerves – we are bored with each other – we offend each other. I regret this – There is no reason why it should be permanent, so long as we don't expect too much.

She was prepared to admit to being 'tactless, inconsiderate and stupid on several occasions ... This is because I am vain and spoiled but I am also fine enough to know that you are a great artist ... you are also a faulty human being and you have hurt me, many times.'[15]

However much May cared for Lewis, she was realistic enough to realize that there could be little chance of her finding lasting happiness with him, and she wisely suggested that they 'abandon this attempted intimacy and take refuge in a more gentle formality – or a more formal gentleness'.[16] This graceful withdrawal from the destructive elements of her liaison allowed her to remain on friendly terms.

When Lewis became ill with septicaemia she invited him to Charter Hall to recuperate, during which time he started working on a portrait of his hostess. If she thought less of him as a person, she still held his artistic talents in high esteem. When he sent her some designs of furniture she had asked him to do for her, she was 'struck all over again' by his genius, and she put in an order for a dozen copies of *Blast* to 'broadcast through the world'. She also planned to build a gallery at the back of her London home for his paintings, although this idea was eventually cast aside, along with the rest of her pre-war life.

3

Croix-Rouge

When May argued authoritatively that a Liberal government would never declare war, she was not completely misguided. As late as 28 July 1914, Lloyd George had told a journalist that there could be no question of his party taking part in 'any war in the first instance.'[1]

In the great outpouring of national patriotism, which defined the first few months of the war, Douglas enlisted with the London Scottish Territorial Regiment, and at the beginning of October left for France as an interpreter with the Indian troops. Although heavily pregnant, May followed him, staying for a few days to give him moral support. Back in England, she impatiently waited out the rest of her confinement, preferring to stay at her house in the country. She could not face London, telling Lewis in a letter that if she 'were feeling more energetic and looking more presentable' she would 'come up to see the pictures' but adding 'I don't believe I will just at present – you won't misunderstand my silence.'

On 29 November, her third child was delivered, named Mary after her mother and maternal grandmother. Lewis sent May a congratulatory telegram to which she replied, 'I've a very nice daughter and find myself feeling absurdly cordial to her; though she may be considered a national calamity.'[2]

With deadlock on the Western Front, it had become apparent by Christmas that the war was not going to be over as quickly as initially anticipated. Adjusting to this fact, and impatient to help the cause in some way, May, while still pregnant, had put her name down with the London Committee of the French Red Cross who were recruiting nurses from England. Presently she was summoned to meet its formidable president, Vicomtesse de la Panouse, wife of the French military attaché, who told her about a typhoid epidemic in Dunkirk and asked if she was willing to nurse typhoid patients. With no nursing experience and only a little knowledge of French, May hesitated only a moment before answering yes, and agreeing for herself and for two qualified nurses to travel with her. She later described the way in which the Vicomtesse had looked at her with 'the hint of an ironical smile touching her lips'. May thought that she had probably viewed her as a spoilt American who had more money than sense. But the need for nurses was great; the Croix-Rouge Français had been prepared for 25,000 casualties, and the sick and wounded already numbered half a million.

Before leaving England she arranged for her house in Park Lane to be used as a war centre, and she wanted to settle financial affairs with Lewis. She owed him money for the painted panels, which he had almost completed, and she had not entirely given up the idea of having her room decorated by him in the future. In the meantime, she suggested that he might like to have the pictures on exhibition somewhere as 'people ought to have a chance to see them!'[3]

At the end of January 1915, and having only ventured downstairs for the first time after the birth of Mary on New Year's Day, 'feeling rather stupid and weak in the knees' and only up to seeing people 'in a mild way', she was setting off for Belgium to work harder than she had ever had to work before.

If she regretted leaving behind her three young daughters, her need to play an active role in the war took precedence. She was not in any case a maternal person, and, like many women of her class and generation, she had always employed a nurse to take care of the children.

Whatever she had been expecting to find, her arrival across the Channel was deceptively reassuring. As she sailed into Dunkirk harbour and found it filled with ships she was impressed by its beauty and brilliance, and it was hard to take seriously the threat of the German Army less than 10 kilometres away.

From Dunkirk, she made her way by tram to the converted hospital a mile from the town, in the seaside suburb of Malo-les-Bains. A haven for the rich in its pre-war days, it was now a desolate place. Overlooking its long, sandy windswept beach lined with deserted hotels and holiday villas, was the grand façade of the casino, now fallen into disrepair but housing the makeshift hospital where May had come to work. It made an incongruous setting, the huge, tarnished chandeliers of the gaming rooms hanging above rows of dingy beds, and the grim surroundings reflected in vast gilded mirrors.

She was later to write about her experiences here in her short story, 'The Beach', in which she contrasts the crowds of people, who in peacetime used to arrive at the casino on gala nights in their smart cars, having spent the day at the races, with those who now arrived throughout the night in ambulances, from the latest battle at the front, not 'wasters' but 'wrecks', with their bodies blown to pieces: 'When they take their places at the tables, the croupiers – that is to say, the doctors – look them over. Come closer, I'll whisper it. Some of them have no faces.'[4] Patients were brought in from the dressing station behind the trenches with a label attached to their blanket giving their name, providing them with a 'ticket' to the casino: 'like a luggage label. It has your name on it in case you don't remember your name. You needn't have a face, but a ticket you must have to get into our casino.'[5]

She had been warned that conditions at the hospital were primitive, but she was dismayed by the paucity of equipment and absence of trained staff; until her arrival there had been no nurses at all. She found it heartbreaking to see how even the dying were forced to crawl from their beds to sit on open pails. With as many as forty thousand sick and wounded men in and around Dunkirk, beds were in such short supply that some men had to lie on stretchers covered with straw, or even on cardboard mattresses on the floor. May had brought with her from England urgently needed medical supplies, including strychnine and morphine which was particularly hard to obtain, but this only went a short way to meet what was needed.

In spite of the wind howling off the sea through the broken panes in the glass veranda, the 'dark smell of rotting swamp, the smell of gas gangrene' pervaded the wards and made her sick. She would have to run behind her screen to vomit and then pause to breathe the fresh sea air, before returning 'to that dim purgatory of gaunt heads, imploring eyes and clutching hands'.

But if the Vicomtesse de la Panouse expected May to return home defeated, she could not have been more mistaken. Her sense of purpose had never before been so intensely focused. In later life she acknowledged that with her work in both world wars she had found her true vocation, describing it as the place where she felt the most alive.

In the old gambling rooms May learned to clean and dress wounds, give injections and medicines, and prepare the wounded for operations. In time she became expert at all these skills, handling the fragile glass ampoules with speed and efficiency, and knowing intuitively how to respond to the needs of her patients. At the end of her daily shift she would take the tram along the beach back to her hostel in Dunkirk. In 1915 she believed, as others, that this was 'the war to end war'.[6]

Although the need for nurses and doctors had persuaded the French Army to recruit from across the channel, the Vicomtesse had warned May that the French military were not eager to introduce English nurses into their hospitals, and that part of her role was to 'break down their prejudices'. She seemed to have met her match in the unyielding and harsh authority of Mademoiselle Jacquier, the nursing officer sent to take charge of the hospital, who demonstrated her determination to undermine May's efforts to care for the patients at every opportunity.

Then, at the beginning of March, tensions were heightened when May and her English nurses deliberately disobeyed the rule which forbade them to work at night. Alarmed that two particularly ill men had been left in the care of a drunken orderly, they organized a rota to look after them, and repeated this for the following three nights. When Mademoiselle Jacquier discovered this usurpation, a huge showdown ensued, which was to have an unexpected outcome, playing into May's ambitions to make a real difference to the lives of the wounded at the front.

Although the French nursing staff had caused endless problems for her, she had found the officers 'charming', and the chief of staff for the French Eighth Army, Colonel Morier, particularly so. She confided in him the distressful inadequacy of night nursing, and her battles with her superior, impressing him with her compassion for the patients and her earnest desire to improve the quality of their provision. He suggested that she should write a letter to the French Commander in Chief, General Joseph Joffre, offering to run her own field hospital. She needed no further encouragement, writing a letter that very night, but insisting on her own terms. The hospital would be run as a military unit with May as its directrice; the French Army would be responsible for the transport, doctors, orderlies, food and ordinary hospital supplies, while she would pay a certain sum towards the installation, recruit her own nurses and have carte blanche in running the unit.

When her offer was accepted she could not believe her good fortune, writing triumphantly to her mother, 'It's the thing that every woman in England would give her eyes to get and can't get.' If she overemphasized the number of women wanting to volunteer to work in the war zone, it was certainly true that during the first year of the war political, military and social resistance to women's involvement at the front made it extremely difficult for them to take an active role. A number of other British women offered to set up and run hospital units at the front, but were forced to look elsewhere when the British authorities turned them down. The Scottish Women's Hospitals, founded by the Scottish surgeon Elsie Inglis, ran fourteen fully equipped hospitals on every Allied front, except those under British control. When Dr Inglis offered her services to the War Office she was famously dismissed and told to go home and sit still. As an Anglo-French unit under French command, with its French CO, British Directrice and mixed nationality of staff, May's field hospital, which would initially serve the 36 Corps of the French Eighth Army, was a unique formation for its time.

A mobile hospital close to the front was urgently needed. Red Cross trains took six hours to come from the trenches to Dunkirk, a desperate journey for the seriously wounded. The Vicomtesse de la Panouse, who had by now recognized May as someone with both money and ability, wrote to thank her for the invaluable contribution she would be making, with its 'inestimable benefit to the wounded soldiers of our army', but expressing concern that it would be 'too much to place on the shoulders of one person'. It was a challenge she relished, however, and her excitement and impatience to have the unit ready spurred her on as she assembled equipment, staff and transport. Colonel Morier was as good as his word, helping her in every way he could and providing transport and staff to ferry her around as she researched the different types of huts she would need to house the hospital.

To begin with, the unit was to consist of twelve long wooden portable huts, with reinforced windows to take the strain of heavy firing, which could be packed up and transported at only a few hours' notice. One of the huts was to be fitted out as an operating theatre with a glass roof and divided into separate rooms for X-rays, operating, dressing and sterilizing. Another hut would serve as kitchen and stores, where supplies would be received each day from army trains on their way to the field kitchens behind the lines. Two more huts were needed for the staff to live in, and the remaining ones were to be equipped as wards, with twenty beds in each. Nine vehicles were needed: three to carry the wounded directly from the trenches, assisting the regular French army ambulances, and the rest to carry the huts and equipment.

When May added up the cost of creating her hospital, estimating that she would need about £4,000, plus £200 a month running expenses, she instigated an urgent advertising campaign for funds, writing to the American newspapers, and calling on help from friends and family. Her letters home during this time convey her mood of elation mixed with anxiety. She told her mother that she needed 'Pots and pots of money, and endless supplies'.

One way to raise extra funds for her hospital was to give up the lease on her house in Park Lane, and to sell the furniture. With this in mind, May met Douglas in Paris in spring 1915, to discuss plans for the future. It was in any case in their interests to make their permanent home in France, where her income from American investments would not be liable for supertax. At that time the English authorities would not give children passages to France unless they were to remain in permanent residence there so, in April, May returned to England to shut up their house in Mayfair, fetch the children and bring them with their governess and nurse to live in a furnished house in Paris at 21 Bois de Boulogne.

She also had unfinished business with Lewis, of a financial nature if nothing else. Since she needed every penny for her hospital, she had to postpone the decorating project indefinitely, and the finished paintings needed to be collected and stored somewhere. Her occasional letters to him from the front dealt with the question of money owed, and a distinct coolness had crept into the correspondence. In a letter dated 16 May she wrote somewhat caustically, 'You speak of coming out to drive an ambulance. Can you drive and do you understand the mechanism of a car?'

She had given him her permission to show the pictures wherever he liked; two of these were then entered for the Vorticism Exhibition at the Doré Gallery which opened on 10 June.

Then on 23 June she received a letter from him on the thorny subject of unpaid money, albeit for services not yet rendered, prompting an indignant reply. 'Your very extraordinary letter of the 18th of June received this afternoon. I had no idea that you were capable of writing me such a letter. You must please remember that the pictures were to have been finished last September and that you yourself said that you considered that you had no right to receive the fifty pounds which was intended to be a fee for the decoration of my drawing room and the designs of furniture. It was your idea that this should not be paid but I told you that I intended to pay anyhow and in my last letter I repeated the assurance.' With her typical directness, she finished the letter with a warning: 'It's not worth your while being rude to me, you only lose a friend who might have some time been of service to you.'[7]

Nevertheless, the outstanding fifty pounds were sent off the following week. Lewis seems to have regretted his outburst for the next month he sent a letter which attempted to make peace: 'The poor artist (imaginary melodramatic figure) asked the rich woman (howls from the gallery) for the settlement of an obligation a little forcibly.'[8] No reply to this, or further letters from May to Lewis, appears to exist after this time, but she was still in his thoughts when he enquired in a letter to Ezra Pound on 23 July 1916, 'Do you ever hear of Mrs Turner?'[9]

4

Behind the Lines

In July 1915 May's efforts to establish her own unit came to fruition when l'Hôpital Chirurgical Mobile No 1 was finally set in
operation in a field in Flanders. Situated just outside the village
of Rousbrugge on the road between Dunkirk and Ypres, it was
seven miles behind the firing line. In the months preceding May's
arrival in Flanders, with most of Belgium and a large swathe of
northern France now under German occupation, the Allies had
been attempting to break through the enemy positions on the
Aubers and Vimy ridges. On 22 April, they were taken by surprise when the Germans launched a major offensive at Ypres
with the aid of chlorine gas; the first offensive using poison gas,
which inflicted a slow and horrific death by asphyxiation. In this
Second Battle of Ypres, the Germans made substantial gains,
encircling the town and taking all the high ground. Although not
completely abandoning Ypres and Belgium territory, the Allies
were forced to withdraw. They had suffered 58,000 casualties.

By the time May's hospital opened, the British were left
holding Ypres, and were in charge of the section of the line
between the town and Dunkirk, but her unit remained under
the control of the French military authorities. As a front line

MARY BORDEN

Greeting visitors to her hospital (May, in the middle, above)
With King Albert of Belguim in 1915 (below)

46

hospital it received only the most seriously wounded; in its first six months, over 800 extreme cases were treated there, with only 68 deaths, a mortality rate considered extremely low for a hospital dealing with severe surgical cases. It was a source of pride to May when later the medical inspector informed her that her hospital's 5 per cent mortality rate was the best statistic of the entire front, and its reputation in the trenches was such that the wounded, including officers, pleaded to be sent there.

The unit started out with seventeen staff – a combination of nurses, doctors and orderlies. As agreed, May recruited the nurses herself, and her standards were exacting: those whose work failed to impress were asked to leave. She took her responsibilities for her staff very seriously, and they in turn relied on her as a source of strength and someone who remained calm in any situation. Her head nurse, Miss Agnes Warner, a 'frail' woman with 'eye glasses and grey hair', was an American graduate of the New York Presbyterian Hospital and remained with the unit throughout the war. Also working as a nurse there for a time was Ellen La Motte, another American war writer.

The second winter of the war brought added misery in the trenches of the Western Front, with many of the combatants becoming ill from constant exposure to the extreme cold and wet. The ubiquitous mud became a hazard in the hospital too, carried in from the sodden fields surrounding the wooden huts on the boots of the stretcher-bearers, and turning the floor of the reception room into a sea of sludge.

Through the long winter months gales battered the flimsy huts, lifting the roofs and whistling in through the cracks. Beds had to be positioned to avoid the holes where driving rain leaked into the wards; May took to sleeping beneath a mackintosh sheet with an umbrella over her head. In particularly ferocious gales the roof of her sleeping quarters was sometimes blown completely off, and, too weary to stir, she remained huddled under her blankets until her orderlies came and put it back. At night she fell asleep to the sounds of the guns booming and grew so used to the accompaniment of shellfire that when she returned to Paris on leave, the silence at night kept her awake.

At the end of each day, she conducted her final round of the huts before joining her nurses and orderlies for the routine midnight cocoa, drunk from army regulation tin mugs as they gathered around the cluttered table in the sterilizing room. She was usually up again before dawn to repeat the rounds, watching the sky lighten upon a new morning and, beyond the gateposts of the hospital, the convoys lumbering along the road to Ypres, with the columns of men in heavy grey-blue coats, 'staggering across the mud of Flanders'.

As the war dragged on, with the lines moving neither forward nor back, there were long days of boredom and inactivity. Nevertheless, there was an endless cycle of tasks to carry out, filling hot-water bottles, sterilising equipment, scrubbing down tables, adjusting pillows, bandages and fracture pulleys, and checking the general condition of the patients. Sometimes there were visitors to look after: Albert, the King of Belgium, came once to look round the hospital, and when patients were to be awarded the Médaille Militaire or the Croix de Guerre, this would bring one of the generals.

Besides the daily routine of hospital work, May had the continuing responsibility of maintaining the unit's finances. The unit was expanding, too. In January 1916 a training hospital for surgeons was established, where recent surgical graduates, or those who needed to retrain, were sent to gain experience before being put in charge of their own field hospital, and by July 1916, the original unit had increased to eighteen huts, with two more fitted out as operating rooms. A dental department was also opened, and a new mortuary added.

By the time the unit had been in operation for a year, most of the French troops had departed from May's section of line and she felt her hospital could be more useful elsewhere. The British and French had started their joint and simultaneous offensive on a 40-mile front north and south of the Somme, and since this was where the heaviest fighting was in progress, she wrote to Colonel Morier suggesting she transfer her hospital to that region. She did not have to wait long for permission to do this, but when the director of the health service for 36 Corps heard she was intending to move her unit, he wrote to ask her to change her mind, insisting her hospital was still needed where it was for the few French troops left. Not wishing to deprive the corps of a service still valued, she proposed setting up a new unit on the Somme, under the French Sixth Army, to be run in the same way as her original one which she would still continue to finance and manage.

From her home in Paris, she wrote to the Commander in Chief of the French Sixth Army putting forward her proposition, and was profoundly disappointed when she received a reply turning her offer down with the explanation that the General in Chief had decided not to recruit any more foreigners into Zone Armée. She had been working at the front for the past fifteen months, and was authorized to do so, but now she found herself entangled in red tape, which not only put a stop to her plans to start a new hospital, but threatened to keep her out of the action altogether. She was immensely frustrated.

When she set her heart on something, her determination was tremendous and now she bombarded French military officials, including General Joffre, with letters. She renewed her offer to put up 200,000 francs to run her own unit, but if this was not acceptable, she meekly declared her willingness to work under any conditions; all she asked was for the opportunity to continue to dedicate herself to full-time nursing work in the area of greatest conflict. She included a lengthy résumé of everything she had so far contributed to the French Red Cross, referring to the praise her unit had received from the Medical Inspector of her region, and pre-empted all possible arguments against her transfer; she even resorted to a little emotional blackmail by mentioning that if the decision to bar her from working was

Cutting from the New York Times, *14 January 1917, showing May's hospital*

on account of her nationality, she had for a long time felt in her heart a Frenchwoman.

A native at heart or not, she expressed her longing to serve at the front with such passionate sincerity – her devotion and commitment to the soldiers of the French Army radiating so powerfully through the somewhat confused grammar and phrasing – that even the most reluctant of officials could not have failed to be moved. In any case, even if only to halt the highly charged emotional missives arriving on his desk, at the beginning of September, General Joffre at last granted her permission to serve the Sixth Army under General Fayolle. She was given the task of helping to install, finance and run the 2000-bed l'Hôpital d'Evacuation, 5 kilometres behind the firing line at Bray-sur-Somme, and the most important military hospital in the French Army.

One month later, on 8 October, she drove south from Flanders to the Somme through sparsely populated country, to the ruined village of Bray, beyond which a 40 kilometre stretch of traffic streamed in both directions between the large clearing station and the trenches, carrying troops and ammunition. Beside the road, she surveyed the curious vista of 'innumerable camps, armoured trains sidetracked in fields, munitions spread out under canvas, batteries of big guns waiting, regiments of cavalry', until 'suddenly, beyond the crossroads where English guns and French lorries struggle through the mud', she had her first sight of the hospital 'with its great wooden sheds spread out in a hollow', and surrounded by barren chalk hills, all vegetation laid waste by war.

Convalescent French soldiers at May's hospital watching the ducks on the pond

The Battle of the Somme had begun on a perfect summer's day on 1 July 1916, with 100,000 Allied troops taking part. By the time May started working in the region, the continual firing of shells had transformed the countryside into a landscape of utter desolation, and the death toll was running into tens of thousands. As her motor rolled in at the gate of the hospital, May took in the scene of row upon row of hurriedly built wooden huts with their peaked roofs of corrugated iron, linked by narrow boardwalks. To the right of the entrance, beneath a covered porch joining three huts, ambulances were unloading the wounded. From here, they would be checked by a staff of doctors who would divide them into three categories: the '*grands blessés*', to be operated on as soon as possible, the less urgent 'stretcher cases', and the 'sitting cases'. To May, the hospital looked like an 'American lumber town' and she recorded her impressions in a letter. 'A city of huts, and the guns beyond the hill sound like the waves of the sea, pounding – pounding – and the sky is a whirr with aeroplanes, and sometimes we are bombarded and all the time troops and more troops stream past.'

Of the 3,000,000 who fought at the Somme, one third became casualties and in her first six weeks alone, the hospital received 25,000 wounded. 'All day and often all night I am at work over dying and mutilated men' she wrote to the American magazine *Brooklyn Life*. 'There is such a tremendous inflow of wounded that I often can't sit down from 7.00 am to midnight, except for a quick lunch and dinner. Impossible to tear oneself away from the men who are crying for drink, whose blood is dripping in pools on the floor, to write letters.'[2]

The pressure of juggling her different roles was enormous. As well as often nursing round the clock, and managing the hospital, she had to keep up the momentum of her fund-raising. Although l'Hôpital d'Evacuation was well equipped in military lines, she relied on donations for many basic items such as nightshirts, bed socks, bed jackets, towels, handkerchiefs, water-pillows, air-cushions, bed-rests, hot-water bottles, large

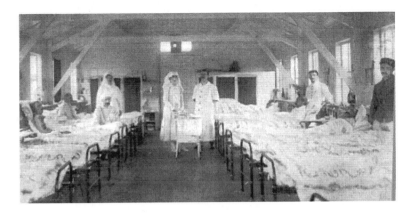

Cutting from Brooklyn Life. *May in her uniform on the left*

pillows and fracture pillows. In America, the Camden Surgical Dressings Committee, using the yacht club as their base during the summer, provided essential dressings, as well as 'comfort bags' filled with a range of goods for the soldiers, from pipes and puzzles, to soap and socks.

May had set up the Borden-Turner Hospital Fund for financial aid and gifts, enlisting the support of her mother, whose home in New York became a collection point, and tried to send regular publicity reports to the American press. Although the German sinking of the *Lusitania* in May 1915, with 108 American citizens on board, had shocked the nation, for many people living in the United States the war in Europe was remote and May's publicity campaign took considerable time and energy.

Her bulletins from the front conveyed in vivid detail the horror of war:

> The guns are pounding. An attack is announced for tonight. No one of all our staff of a hundred surgeons will go to bed. The struggle is ceaseless. An inflow of men covered with blood, men without faces, without arms, without legs, men raving in delirium, dying in your arms as you take off

their clothes, and an overflow of men operated on who go into the interior to be nursed back to strength, and another outflow of the dead – the dead.[3]

Her first hospital had been well supplied with nurses, but at l'Hôpital d'Evacuation she had only twelve. She soon realized it was impossible for so few nurses to look after the occupants of two thousand beds, and so, with the agreement of the chief doctor, Monsieur Olivier, she concentrated them into one quarter of the hospital, putting them in charge of eight hundred beds reserved for the most seriously wounded, which became known as the 'Grand Quartier'. Even then, this meant that, including May, there were only thirteen nurses to look after twenty rooms with forty beds in each, as well as the reception room and operating theatres.

It was the reception hut where she spent the most hours, and her work here is described in detail, sometimes very graphically, in her collection of war writing. At one end of the hut, she had her 'kitchen' – 'an arrangement of shelves for saucepans and syringes and needles of different sizes, and cardboard boxes full of ampoules of camphor oil and strychnine and caffeine and morphine, and large ampoules of sterilized salt and water'. Down the centre of the hut were four brick ovens on top of which large cauldrons of water were kept on the boil for hot-water bottles, a vital means of restoring bodily warmth to the frostbitten men arriving from the battlefields, some of whom had spent many hours, in the coldest winter of the century, in no man's land, lying with the dead as they waited to be picked up.

Next to the kitchen, a cubicle had been partitioned off to create space for an incubator which had been improvised by hanging electric light bulbs from a wooden frame encircling a specially made bed, where 'a man could be cooked back to life again'. At the other end of the room, behind a wooden screen, the wounded were brought from the ambulances and lifted onto a table, where the orderlies undressed them, the removal of the heavy army regulation boots revealing feet shrivelled and frozen from standing endlessly in the icy, waterlogged trenches. May overruled the military request that the uniforms should be preserved for future use, allowing the orderlies to cut through the clothes with scissors or knives when necessary to avoid inflicting extra pain. While the wounded were wrapped in blankets and hot bottles put at their feet, she would go quickly between them, giving injections of camphor oil, caffeine or morphia.

May came to respect and love in equal measure the orderlies, who were all above the age of sixty and thus too old to join up: 'Gentle, very gentle, were my old ones when they lifted a shattered limb or cut away the blood-stained coat from a bleeding side. Their gnarled peasants' hands are beautiful to me and their grizzled heads have majesty.'[4] In the wards, she was comforted by their presence and touched by the way in which their quiet

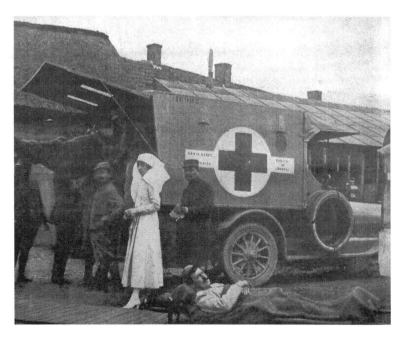

May directing the removal of wounded French soldiers to her hospital

empathy extended to her own well-being, as her memories of that time reveal:

> I look down again at that dreadful place under the flickering light of our hurricane lanterns. It is one in the morning. The door at the far end is still opening and shutting, opening and shutting – for still they are coming from the battlefield – and my old ones are going quietly and steadily about their business. I can see them from behind the wooden screen where I have a dozen fine needles on the boil. I have been on duty 36 hours and am become a sleep-walker, an automaton, and then one of my old ones puts his head round the screen and holds out both his old hands, one with a tin cup of pinard, the other with a hunk of bread. He has brought me his casse-croûte and he says in his rough voice, 'Faut manger, ma soeur.'[5]

On the busiest nights there was virtually no floor space in the reception room left uncovered, just a narrow strip in which to manoeuvre between the long rows of men lying side by side on stretchers. Sometimes the place was so crowded that there was no more room to place another stretcher, and the wounded would have to spill out into the corridor, waiting their turn. It seemed to May that her hospital represented 'the second battlefield' where all those working fought to save lives. She took on the role of receiving the wounded from the ambulances and judging which were the most urgent cases. During heavy bombardments, when a seemingly endless stream of wounded would arrive, these skills of detection could make the difference between a life saved and a life lost:

> I had to decide for myself. There was no one to tell me. If I made any mistakes, some would die on their stretchers on the floor under my eyes who need not have died. I didn't worry. I didn't think. I was too busy, too absorbed in what I was doing. I had to judge from what was written on their

tickets and from the way they looked and the way they felt to my hand. My hand could tell of itself one kind of cold from another. They were all half-frozen when they arrived, but the chill of their icy flesh wasn't the same as the cold inside them when life was almost ebbed away. My hands could instantly tell the difference between the cold of the harsh bitter night and the stealthy cold of death.[6]

All night the battle to save lives would continue:

It was my business to create a counter-wave of life, to create the flow against the ebb. It was like a tug of war with the tide. The ebb of life was cold. When life was ebbing the man was cold; when it began to flow back, he grew warm. It was all, you see, like a dream. The dying men on the floor were drowned men cast up on the beach, and there was the ebb of life pouring away over them, sucking them away, an invisible tide; and my old orderlies, like old sea-salts out of a lifeboat, were working to save them. I had to watch if they were slipping, being dragged away. If a man were slipping quickly, being sucked down rapidly, I sent runners to the operating rooms.[7]

All her senses were alert to the task of watching over the men, while everything else she dealt with 'automatically':

I go from one man to another jabbing the sharp needles into their sides, rubbing their skins with iodine, and each time I pick my way back across their bodies to fetch a fresh needle I scan the surface of the floor where the men are spread like a carpet, for signs, for my special secret signals of death.[8]

Her alertness to the needs of her patients was instinctive, but she was aware of her growing reputation for saving lives. When she was told to expect a mortality rate of 30 per cent at Bray-sur-Somme she was determined to reduce this figure; she managed with her team to come close to halving it, and the hospital was commended for the best service in the sector. Yet the irony of nursing the men back to health, only to return them to the front, did not escape her:

> Just as you send your clothes to the laundry and mend them when they come back, so we send our men to the trenches and mend them when they come back again. You send your socks and your shirts again and again to the laundry, and you sew up the tears and clip the ravelled edges again and again just as many times as they will stand it. And then you throw them away. And we send our men to the war again and again, just as long as they will stand it; just until they are dead, and then we throw them into the ground.[9]

In retrospect, May found it hard to imagine how she had endured the relentless horror of her work:

> Looking back, I do not understand that woman – myself – standing in that confused goods yard filled with bundles of broken human flesh. The place by one o'clock in the morning was a shambles. The air was thick with steaming sweat, with the effluvia of mud, dirt, blood. The men lay in their stiff uniforms that were caked with mud and dried blood, their great boots on their feet; stained bandages showing where a trouser leg or a sleeve had been cut away.[10]

She developed coping mechanisms, later describing a process of disassociation:

> I think that woman, myself, must have been in a trance, or under some horrid spell. Her feet are lumps of fire, her face is clammy, her apron is splashed with blood; but she moves ceaselessly about with bright burning eyes and handles the dreadful wreckage of men as if in a dream.[11]

If she was able to go through the motions of her work with a necessary degree of detachment, she did not become hardened to death and suffering, and the humility of the dying never failed to move her:

> I did not count the number who died as I knelt beside their stretchers. Great strong broken men who apologised in whispers for the trouble they gave in dying; slender boys whom I held in my arms while they cried for their mothers and who mistook me for some anxious woman I would never see; old patient humble men ... who went quietly, so modestly; the French poilus of 1914–18.[12]

An image of women, and particularly nurses, exploited by the French and English War Offices for propaganda purposes, was that of saintly martyrdom, but although her work was traumatic and distressing, she later wrote of it giving her 'a sense of great power, exhilaration and excitement'. She was after all in a position of authority and influence and playing an active part, rather than waiting helplessly at home for an end to the conflict. As it had for many women, the war allowed her a freedom which she had not known before, and although she felt an underlying sense of guilt about her long absences from her children, she believed she had a more important role to play in running her hospital.

In her autobiographical 1930s novel, *Sarah Gay*, in which the protagonist is a nurse working in a hospital near Soissons during the First World War, May speaks for herself and her heroine as she reflects on the conflict between work and the domestic sphere:

> She was no more unnatural than most mothers at that time ... the maternal instinct was deflected, during the years 1914–18, from children to men. It was all a question of danger and helplessness. Sarah felt toward her wounded men as she would have felt formerly toward her children had they been

ill. She had become not unnatural but more natural, simple, concentrated and ruthless. The ideas imposed upon her by her community weren't effective now that the community was disintegrated. She no longer thought as she was supposed to think. She thought in her own way, instinctively going for what she wanted, and she had got what she wanted out of war, work that gave her a sense of being at last fully and gloriously alive.[13]

How much the Turner girls missed their mother is difficult to say, but May could ensure some continuity in their lives through their being overseen in her absence by Mrs Harrison, who had been her trusted companion since 1912, and before that, for many years, had been employed by Mary Borden. When May was able to return to her family in Paris during periods of leave, it often meant a difficult adjustment. She was happy to see her children but at the same time, it was hard to switch her thoughts away from her work and to give them her full attention. Nevertheless, the change of scene was needed, even if the city had been transformed by war. Many of the larger hotels and shops had turned part of their premises into hospitals, and even rooms in private homes were converted into wards, so that one might discover a famous duchess in a hospital blouse attending patients in the elegant surroundings of her Louis Quinze salon.[14] Madame Vassilieff, a Russian immigrant, had started up a canteen in Montparnasse, famous for its paintings by Chagall hanging on the walls, and worn furniture and odds and ends collected from flea markets. The place was frequented by famous figures of the day, as well as poverty-stricken artists who went there to keep warm because the Germans had control of many of the coal mines and Paris was feeling the effects of restriction. Gertrude Stein, however, who was sometimes a guest at 21 Bois de Boulogne, recalled how the Borden-Turners' home was heated when most people had no coal, and how very pleasant it was going to dinner there and being warm. Stein liked

Douglas, but she seemed to be more reserved about May in her reminiscences of her visits to her home. 'Chicagoans spend so much energy losing Chicago that often it is difficult to know what they are', she wrote, before adding, 'Mary Borden was very Chicago.'[15]

In fact, May's years of travel had left her with a feeling of dispossession and rootlessness and she would often describe herself as like a wanderer or an exile. Since she was married she had lived in a constant succession of houses, and had begun to weary of the lack of continuity to her life. She started to look for a more permanent home for her family in Paris, and in January 1917 she fell in love with a house on the Left Bank, at 13 rue Monsieur, which she described as 'rather absurd' in its appearance, and reminding her of a Normandy manor. The entrance was approached through a tunnel which opened up into a courtyard. Inside the front door, an imposing staircase led to a suite of rooms that in turn led to a garden, with other gardens beyond. It needed work doing to it, but she knew at once it was right, and it filled her with excitement to imagine living there. She took out a lease on the house for nine years, the longest term she could get, at a rental of 18,000 francs per annum.

At the beginning of 1917, when l'Hôpital d'Evacuation was taken over by the British, May was asked if she would stay on, but her loyalties were to the French soldiers, and she could not contemplate remaining under a different army. Her medical team had transferred to the Champagne district where a field hospital was under construction at Villers-sur-Condon, between Soissons and Rheims, in preparation for a major spring offensive on a 40-kilometre front on the River Aisne. She heard a rumour that the job of managing the new field hospital had been allocated to someone else, a Frenchwoman, and to add insult to injury, that a General Ragueneau had vetoed May's appointment because he felt that she lacked the necessary aptitudes to organize her nurses during a period of great activity.

She received this news with considerable indignation.

Addressing the matter head on, she wrote to General Raguneau to set the record straight, describing at length the good record of her hospital and the achievements of her nursing staff. Further letters were fired off to the French War Office and other relevant military officials whom May hoped might argue on her behalf.

Whether or not there was ever any real objection to her moving to Villers-sur-Condon, the delay in her transfer was more likely due to the machinations of military protocol, about which she seems to have been a little hazy, judging from the somewhat perplexed letter she received from a Colonel Duvon, Le Chef d' État-Major of the First Army. As he pointed out, with a wry apology for entering into such dry administrative explanations, however much he wanted her in his sector, they could not arrange their affairs simply by common agreement without the involvement of the commander-in-chief, who alone had the authority to make the decision where to send her. In any case, by March May had joined her medical team in the role of director in time for the start of the campaign.

5

Love Letters from the Front

In spite of the demands of her hospital work, her fund-raising, family commitments and battles with officialdom, she had still found time to finish her third novel, *The Romantic Woman*, published at the end of 1916 by Constable. Although it opens in 1915, war, as the narrator and protagonist Joan Fairfax explains, is 'really not in the story at all', but serves as a backdrop to the meditations, in middle age, of a now wiser protagonist as she sheds light on the tangled relationships between herself, her husband, and two other married couples, whose effect upon each other leads to a tragic climax.

Joan is an American heiress, a romanticist with an overheated imagination. She marries an heir to an English dukedom, only to be overwhelmed by the differences between the Old World of Europe and the New of America; these are blamed in part for her misreading of her husband's character, whereby shallowness is romantically perceived as enigmatic English reserve, and outward polish mistaken for a fine intellect. She is seduced by her husband's good looks and the 'exquisite diction of the well-educated Englishman' who is 'merely one of his class, the complete and meaningless output of a very finished system'.

May also used a more complex structure than she had for her first two novels. Breaking away from the convention of a linear narrative, the story is told through a series of backwards and forwards time shifts; as an early precursor to the experimental modernist techniques which became common among the writers of the 1920s, May used the time jumps to build suspense through the device of half-revelation, both of plot and of psychological insight. As well as the clash between different worlds, many of her other fascinations are present in the themes of the novel: the outsider in society, self-deception, people trapped by conventions in stultifying lives and marriages, the power of parents to mould their children to an image of their own making. Nearly all the characters have been damaged by the codes of behaviour of the particular world into which they have been born, and the narrator is equally critical of the American dream of success, with its showy consumerism and 'lust of possessions', as she is of the traditions of the upper English class. There are also some sharp satirical descriptions of Chicago 'society' and its New World pretensions:

> Society, that small nucleus of snobs, which has evolved itself somehow out of the prairie, Society has to justify its existence daily. Without traditions, or titles, or world-old names, without landed estates, or hereditary noses, or state decorations, without any of that stability of a group revolving about and deriving its life from a royal palace, it is obliged to fall back upon clothes for its insignia.[1]

May was also producing poetry and short prose pieces which flowed directly from her experiences of war with an often shockingly brutal vividness of descriptive detail. Unusually for a female war poet, she wrote about trench warfare, the machinery of war, the ravaged and surreal landscape. She described the newly introduced tanks, first used on the battlefields of the Somme, and the mud, which inflicted such abject misery during the Third Battle of Ypres, is the subject of an entire poem. Extending her experimentations with form, her poems dispense with formal metre and rhyme and her lines are unusually long, whereas her prose vignettes incorporate elements of poetry, such as alliteration and repetition.

Forster, when he read some of her work in the *English Review*, was baffled, writing about it to his friend Malcolm: 'Stuff curiously disposed in metrical lengths. Quite three pages of the prose ran into the rhythm of Hiawatha. I cannot make out what she is up to, but then never could. Some sort of effect is evidently intended.' As an afterthought he added, 'I have often since the war broke out thought of her party at that coniferous grange.'[2]

It was not just war, however, which inspired May to write verse. In April 1917, she composed a love poem, telling the person for whom it was written, 'it is a long time since anyone drew poetry out of me – It's partly the war – but mostly you.' The recipient of this poem was a dashingly handsome and courageous young officer, Captain Edward Louis Spears. Their paths had first crossed in 1916 during the battle at Bray-sur-Somme, when Spears had appeared at May's hospital, accompanied by his Alsatian dog, searching for a lost British company. He had been struck by the appearance of a small woman, in a mud-splattered and bloodstained apron who opened the door to him, and later brought him a cup of tea, and he had been astonished and intrigued to find women so near the front. Although only a brief encounter, it left a lasting impression on both of them, and May would later say that, for her, it was love at first sight. They met again briefly in January 1917, when he gave her advice about her work at the time she was preparing to leave l'Hôpital d'Evacuation, and again when she was based behind the Chemin des Dames during the Nivelle offensive. By April they were exchanging almost daily letters, and meeting as often as possible.

Louis Spears was a born and bred Frenchman with Anglo-

Irish roots. His paternal grandfather was Alexander Spiers, a well-known figure in France who had left England as a young man to settle in the French capital where he taught English at various prestigious institutions. He spoke seven languages, and later became an examiner at the Sorbonne, an *inspecteur général de l'université*, and achieved distinction with the publication of an English–French and French–English dictionary. His son, Charles, married Melicent Hack, related to the Aylmer family at Donadea in County Kildare. Louis's maternal grandmother, Lucy Hack, was brought up in Ireland as a strict Protestant but after her marriage, she travelled to Europe with her husband who worked as an engineer on the railways. Melicent, their only child, was raised in Sicily where life was dangerous and rough and it was habitual for her father to keep a pistol on the table at mealtimes in case of an attack. How this affected Louis's mother is uncertain, but her great beauty, and her talents as an artist and musician, hid an instability which led to the breakdown of her marriage, not helped by Charles's philandering.

Louis was born on 8 August 1886, in an affluent district of Paris near the Bois de Boulogne. He spoke English as fluently as he did French – though he never learned to pronounce his r's which meant that in spite of his family legacy, snooty English people always identified him as French. His parents separated shortly after the birth of his sister, Kathleen, an acrimonious estrangement which left him with little contact with his father. Melicent offered no compensation for this, openly favouring her daughter and showing vindictiveness towards her son. He had a solitary upbringing with much of his childhood spent travelling abroad and in France itself, mostly with his doting grandmother, Lucy, who became the primary figure in his life in the absence of his parents. He was a frail child, and due to ill health he was taken during the winters to his grandmother's villa in Menton for the warmer climate of the Mediterranean where he was taught by a series of tutors. Although he lacked a good education, he had a fierce intelligence and the desire to learn, developing a love of

Edward Louis Spears

literature and reciting poetry by heart. His happiest memories were of holidays in Ireland at the Aylmer estate and castle of Donadea, and to Voutenay, a medieval chateau in Burgundy where he had cousins through his great-aunt's marriage into the Rafinesque family.

Lacking both a father figure and exposure to a peer group as a child, Louis always felt an outsider, not helped when he joined the British army, where his foreign accent and education set him apart, earning him the nickname in his mess of Monsieur Beaucaire, after a Frenchman in a play. A deep-rooted insecurity made relationships difficult for him, and he often experienced long periods of loneliness and self-doubt.

Warding off unhappiness with hard work, and driven by ambition, he had risen quickly through the army ranks. When the usefulness of his French upbringing and ability with languages was brought to the attention of the War Office's intelligence department, he was appointed as liaison officer between the French and British forces. Although this job brought fulfilment, and important new friendships, including a lifelong one with Winston Churchill, it also led some to view him with suspicion and he was aware that he was now classed with the staff officers who were despised for their relatively safe and easy life. His affair with an older woman called Jessie Gordon was showing signs of strain due to their long periods apart during the war.

Then into his life came May, radiating charm and warmth, and captivating him with her adventurous and courageous spirit. She was able to draw him out, understanding his insecurities and vulnerabilities. She called him by his nickname Beaucaire, 'B' for short, using it as a term of endearment, and encouraged and supported him in his work, even if she felt unable to help him as much as she wanted to. 'If it were not war – I could help – I mean if it were politics or something of that sort', she told him, 'but dear B – I believe in you and in your mind – you are so very young – you have so much before you – Be glad of your difficulties – that only measures up to your opportunities. If you had none it would not be worthwhile.'[3]

She fulfilled a longing in him to be wanted and admired, and besides this she had all the attractions of beauty, intelligence and wealth. She in turn found with Louis an intimacy and passion which had always been missing in her marriage to Douglas. She was greatly attracted by his 'swift and daring mind' and his mercurial energy. He made her 'feel alive again' and she found herself succumbing to all the afflictions of high passion; gazing at his photograph, counting the days until they could be together, and waiting impatiently for his letters which she would then read again and again: 'I run to my room sometimes – shut myself in – take out your letter of yesterday – read it – handle it.' If the post did not bring a letter from Louis, she was cast down. Each night, before going to sleep, she wrote to him by the light of a candle in her hospital hut. She felt in a curious state of mind, she told him, because although the future was dark and uncertain, and disaster lurked there, she was happy because she loved him.[4]

Yet however much she longed to be with Louis, she was unable to rush off to him whenever he wanted her to, and he was quick to feel rejected. Aware that her work was becoming a source of tension between them, she tackled the subject in a letter. 'Dearest of course I am coming back to you' she reassured him.

This photograph is reputed to capture an early meeting between May and Louis who is standing with his back to the camera far right

> I have an idea … that you have an idea that I am staying away
> because I do not want to be near you, so very much – Is that
> true? If so, it's a very 'bete' idea – & I don't think you would
> really like me to give up working – If I clothed myself in
> idleness, lay in a perfumed bath half the day and anointed my
> toes with sweet smelling oil – would you find more pleasure
> in me? I wonder – It is true that I am spoiling my looks.
> That is stupid – I regret that – but after all you want me to
> be myself don't you B – and that self is an active creature.[5]

It irked her too that Louis did not always appear to take her
seriously enough, particularly when she wanted to discuss
politics or engage in intellectual debate. She protested against
his habit of 'laughing and kissing' her in the middle of what she
was saying, 'particularly when it's sensible', and took recourse to
writing him a letter, so he was unable to interrupt:

> Caresses are delicious but they are no more interesting than
> a celestial brand of 'fine champagne' in themselves – A word
> – from your soul to mine – A word from the distilled essence
> of your thought to mine, thrills me more than a kiss – B –
> and if our minds were not in tune, I wouldn't want to kiss
> you at all – Perhaps you've never known a woman quite like
> me B – but there you are – you must hold my mind, by
> understanding – & respecting it – otherwise you'll bore me –
> But you won't lose me B – nor I you.[6]

Louis may have felt threatened by May's need to work, but he
was also understandably concerned for her safety and wellbeing.
During the Nivelle offensive on the Aisne, her hospital was
partially destroyed by shellfire, and she and her team were
stretched to their limits. From the first day of action, on 16
April 1917, hopes of an early victory without too much loss of
life had been quickly quashed. The German defensive positions
had been well prepared and the plan to break through them in
one swift advance proved disastrous. In the days that followed,

shortages of ammunition, the superiority of German air power, and the ill-fated deployment of the French tanks, which were obliterated before they had a chance to breach the German defences, combined to impede progress, and the advance fell far short of expectation. Small gains were made at the expense of many deaths and French Army medical services struggled to cope, virtually collapsing under the strain. By the time the campaign ended on 9 May, the number of French casualties had reached 167,000.

Once the French offensive in the region was at an end, May felt the best course was to return to her original unit, still based in Belgium and now in the most exposed position it had been in so far, repeatedly coming under attack. She took a no-nonsense approach to this. 'Being under fire really means nothing, for one soon learns how to avoid being hit', she said in an interview at the time, but the bombardments, she found 'really terrifying, when you hear houses being crushed all about you, and you never know but that at any moment you, too, may be crushed'.[7] On 5 June, her hospital came under a particularly heavy bombardment, causing extensive damage to the buildings. Several orderlies were wounded, as well as a patient, and one of the nurses, who, walking between the huts that night, was struck by a shell and so badly injured that her foot had to be amputated. The next day the bombardment was followed up with a gas attack.

By now May's contribution to the war effort was earning her honours. In March she had been cited in French Army Orders for the commitment, courage and steadfastness she had shown on the Somme during a particularly severe bombardment, and immediately afterwards she was awarded the Croix de Guerre, becoming the first of only two American women to receive the medal. Then on 18 June, she wrote to tell Louis about 'something rather wonderful' which had happened that day. General Pétain, now commander-in-chief, had visited the hospital and after touring all the wards to speak to the patients, he had out of the blue presented her with a palm for her Croix de Guerre, the highest class of the award, and was told by his aide that she ran *'l'Hôpital le plus chic sur tout le front'*.

She was taken by surprise, and described to Louis the moment when Pétain had pinned the medal to her dress as they stood in the field together in front of the tents and surrounded by officers and generals. Later on in the day though, her initial pride and excitement gave way to feelings of guilt and disappointment that other deserving women in her hospital had not been rewarded for their bravery and dedication. 'Why should everything come to me?' she asked Louis. 'It's not fair.'[8]

He thought otherwise, however, and pressed for her to be awarded the Légion d'honneur, which she pleaded with him she did not want, arguing that she had been given quite enough already. Nevertheless, in August this was to come to her too, presented again by the commander-in-chief.

A few days after Pétain's visit in June, May had to be rushed to a hospital in Dunkirk for emergency surgery. There is an element of secrecy surrounding this, but the outcome was the end of a pregnancy. She and Louis had already talked of their mutual desire to have a baby together when their future was settled, and they hoped for a boy, whom they wanted to call Michael. But their future was far from settled and a pregnancy would only add to the complications, and cause far greater distress to Douglas and her family.

Whatever the sequence of events, she was seriously unwell when she was taken to hospital on a stretcher, and complications necessitated her undergoing two operations. Her anguish was accentuated by her longing for Louis who could not be with her, and the fact that their relationship must be kept hidden. When she was strong enough to put pen to paper, she wrote to him of her ordeal. 'When I awoke from the anaesthetic – in that long bare hut – I wanted to ask for you, but I remembered in time – It was very hard again the second time they operated, not letting your name come to my lips when I was so weak and delirious – They tell me now that it was touch & go – for two days - but I wasn't meant to die.'[9]

What reason for her ill health Douglas was given is not known, but he came to see her, treating her with kindness and affection, and even if guiltily longing for Louis, she was grateful to him and comforted by his presence.

When she was recovered enough to be discharged from hospital, she was taken back to her unit and carried into her room on a stretcher, just as she had left it a week earlier. Confined to her bed, and still feeling very tired and weak, she immediately had to throw herself into the organization of her medical team in preparation for the Haig offensive to take control of the Belgian coast. For once she had no appetite to be part of the action, her reserves of energy too depleted to deal with the workload. Yet there was no possibility of opting out. 'I cannot get free from it – & it is as if I were a dead person running it', she told Louis.[10] Dealing with such administrative matters was at least a distraction. When she was left alone to convalesce, she spent 'hour after hour thinking and longing for B' as all around shells fell from the long-range guns. She was cheered when the doctors told her she could go to Paris the following week if she could have a carriage to lie down in. Douglas wanted to take her away with the children to the seaside to recuperate, but she was desperate to see Louis first and planning how they would spend their time together revived her spirits.

She had booked a room at the opulent Hôtel Crillon where she could rest when she first arrived. Afterwards they would go to his new penthouse flat at the Trocadero, with its views of the left bank of the Seine and the woods beyond. He had acquired it from a Belgian prince who had spared no expense in its decor, having all its interior walls hand-painted. A steep circular staircase leading up to it from the floor below was painted to look like a birdcage and the master bedroom like a villa at Pompeii. On the roof was a tiny artificial lake in which Louis kept some water tortoises which proved to be a liability as they kept jumping off the roof and narrowly missing the heads of those passing in the street below. This rooftop flat was to be their first shared home and she was looking forward to arranging the final touches.

Thoughts of homemaking with Louis, though, were mixed with worries about 'how and when and where' she could break the news of their relationship to Douglas. 'How to hurt him the least – I don't know – I suppose it is futile to hope to save him any of the horror', she wrote to Louis. 'I wonder if you realize, what a tremendous and invincible thing my love for you is, to carry me so far – to make me take this step – Do you Do you?'[11]

The burden of deception weighed heavily upon her on holiday with Douglas and the girls at St Laurent-sur-Mer. Tillie, the children's nanny, greeted her 'as of old' and she had an irresistible longing to confide in her but must have known that to give in to it would bring no lasting comfort. Preoccupied and isolated by her own misery, she believed her silence was explained by her being very tired. Her daughters – Mary, now aged two and a half, Comfort, aged six, and Joyce, nearly eight, were affectionate company. In a letter to Louis, May described how, sitting at the bottom of the garden where she was staying, she had 'looked up at the little house on the hillside' to see 'two small white flying figures come running down, arms outstretched – "mummy – mummy"'. She had taken them into her arms in a 'curious dreamy anguish. Then Mary Borden tumbled out from somewhere, like a ripe peach tumbling off a tree.' The thought of failing them filled her with despair, yet she could not envisage a future without Louis.

At the end of her convalescence she returned to Flanders, 'the same grey dreary country', to prepare for the launch of the campaign.[12] She had hardly arrived back before she was called upon by the French War Office to deal with an emergency situation, taking charge of withdrawing 400 French children from a district at the northern front bombarded by German mustard gas, used for the first time. The job was made more difficult by the fact that many of the children, including babies, were without their parents as their fathers were in the trenches and their mothers working in the harvest fields. She thought of her own children, at home in Paris, and wished she could see them. When Tillie sent her a ravishing photograph of them it made her heart ache. She remembered how Mary had rushed into her arms with such 'utterly absurd dignity'. And 'yet', she told Louis, 'I still dream about Michael the prince of joy'.

May's hospital during the Haig offensive was attached to the French First Army under General Anthoine, which was involved in the opening of the Third Battle of Ypres on 31 July 1917 and given the role of guarding the British northern flank across the Yser Canal after it had been taken from the Germans on 27 July. Throughout the first two weeks of August the rain was incessant, falling day after day and creating a quagmire in which the notorious battle was fought. The appalling conditions caused by the wettest autumn in many years were exacerbated by heavy shelling which had destroyed drainage canals in the area.

May's letters to Louis during this time reveal sweeping swings in mood. At first she was fairly cheerful as she tried to make her living quarters more welcoming, scrubbing floors, painting the walls of her hut, putting up curtains and even landscaping the surroundings with tubs of geraniums and trees in pots 'to give this whole ugly show – style'. Her trunk and bed had gone missing in the move, although her pillows had turned up, and the wind and rain still blew into her hut, but these were minor irritations and she did not want Louis to worry about her, telling him that although she had had no time out of the hospital since arriving, she was in good health because all the 'tramping around in the mud ... and the wind and the rain' made her ravenous.

It was not long though before the strain of her work began to show: 'I am tired. My feet ache – My knees ache underneath – My back aches – I wish you were here – you would rest me – I am all aches.' The physical discomfort was only a small part of it. 'I am becoming obsessed again by the obscenity of the war', she told Louis. 'The wounded that have come in today, are beyond all descriptions – It is strange that we are able to save any - I am on night duty tonight – you will say I ought not to do it – but the morale is not all that it might be and I want to be an example to the women that weep and wail.'[13]

Writing late at night, she spoke of the mutilated men who continued 'to come in and die'. She was particularly moved by the death of a twenty-year-old. Afraid and quite conscious to the very end, he could not bear to be left alone. At midnight he had whispered for the priest to be called. May brought an orderly, Guerin, who was also a priest, to his bedside, where she watched him do a 'wonderful thing'. He put 'all his strength, all his faith, all his tenderness at the disposal of that boy – and he reached across the chasm – and got to him – Guerin, by the force of his own will, changed for that wretched terrified child, the character and quality of death – it was as if he quite simply, lifted him up and carried him across the river.'[14]

Before writing this letter she had been down at the little hospital cemetery where she found the rows of crosses in the twilight pitiful. She told Louis of her plans to put a monument there in marble.

> I have begun to have that drive, so common to so many, to place in this swift and dreadful current of life, something that will last a little while. Soon, we will all be gone from here and no one will remember and no one will know how the men died ... I suppose the 'font' of ambition is the desire not to be forgotten – I would like to write poems for you that will make you the subject of thought and dreams, years after we are gone – Abelard & Eloise have never been forgotten – Dante's Beatrice is still alive – Why not my lover,

who will be remembered for his services to his country, why should he not be known too, because of me?[15]

The need to translate her experiences into writing was fuelling her creative output, although she regretted not having more time for composition. 'I'm beginning a sort of poem', she told Louis on 10 August, sending him the opening lines of what was to become 'Unidentified', and which she would later include in her collection of First World War writing.[16] Three other recent pieces on the theme of war were published in the August volume of the *English Review*; these, along with a collection of other war poems and prose pieces, she had sent to a literary agent in London under the title *The Forbidden Zone* and she had since heard back that Collins publishers were buying it. The frankness of her writing was too much for the military censors, however, who feared its negative effect upon the morale of the soldiers, and insisted that certain passages be removed. A French translation received a similar response. May would not condone suppression of the truth and decided not to publish the work under these conditions.

But a shared love of poetry had been a bond between May and Louis from the start and she continued to write poems for him. One of these reveals the way in which her experiences of war seemed to taint everything:

No, No! There is some sinister mistake –
You cannot love me now – I am no more
A thing to touch, a pleasant thing to take
Into one's arms. How can a man adore
A woman with – black blood upon her face,
A cap of horror on her pallid head,
Warriors of madness in the sunken place
Of eyes; hands dripping with the living dead.
Go lover close your proud untainted brow –
Go quickly – Leave me to the hungry lust

Of monstrous pain – I am his mistress now –
These are the frantic beds of his delight –
Here I succumb to him, anew, each night.

But her relationship with Louis sustained her, bringing her 'the
very special and profound joy that one finds in a thing that one
loves and knows well', as she put it in a letter to him celebrating
the ease that existed between them:

> Recognition is one of the elemental pleasures – Isn't it? To
> refind and recognize – things one likes – people one loves –
> places one cares about – is the real comfort don't you think
> so. New things are pleasant – Surprises may be delightful
> – but the deep deep comfort of perfect knowledge – of
> accustomed – ness – isn't it the greatest joy in the world. For
> this is a bog world and a lonely world and it is surrounded
> by eternal darkness, and the most wonderful thing one can
> hope for is to find a companion – who will stay close beside
> us – close enough to keep us brave and warm our hearts ... I
> remember so well the day I arrived in Paris from Dunkirk and
> how we lay down silently side by side, in each other's arms,
> mouth to mouth. All the relief. The exquisite recognition of
> our bodies. That finding each other again. So it will always
> be, my darling. Will it not?[17]

But Louis despaired of the difficulties ahead of them in finding
a solution to their future. She did her best to soothe him, but his
pessimism distressed and alarmed her. 'Your letter of Tuesday
troubles me – I want to get into a car and go to you tonight.' But
it was quite impossible for her to get away:

> The wounded are pouring in – I have only a moment before
> dinner and must go back to work after – Dear – I'm afraid
> that you will not understand why I do not come to you, at
> once – Surely you do understand – you love me because I am

myself – I can't leave my post here for any but a desperate reason – for a few days more – We are in the midst of a battle. The hospital is working well – I hold it all in hand – I can't let go.[18]

Louis was also under immense pressure in his work, and at times he too held a terrifying weight of responsibility in his hands. Since the failure of the Nivelle offensive, disillusion within the French Army had led to unrest and indiscipline within some units. To begin with, the French had tried to conceal the extent of the disorder from the British military and diplomatic representatives in Paris. Only when the trouble reached crisis point at the beginning of June 1917 did Pétain alert Haig. Louis was instructed to go to the front to assess the situation and then to report his findings to the war cabinet in London. When he was interviewed a few days later at Downing Street by the chairman of the War Policy Cabinet Committee, Lloyd George, Louis was aware of a fear in some quarters that the Prime Minister was tempted to make peace with the Germans. Lloyd George asked him whether he could give his word of honour that the French army would recover. Although he was unable to give his word, he said with conviction that he was prepared to stake his life on there being a recovery. The enormity of the position he had been placed in made him feel faint.

It was hardly surprising that May and Louis' time together, so longed for, could easily be spoilt under the weight of too much expectation, and because both were tired and anxious. Paris jarred with her, seeming 'a feverish and irrational place' and she did not like the fact that they were spending so much time apart, with other people not known to one another. He accused her of behaving jealously, a criticism she indignantly refuted: 'I'm not that type.' She pointed out the compromises she was prepared to make for him. 'If it were not for you, I should stay on in the war zone until the end – I feel more decent running round in the mud in rubber boots – than buying bath salts and crêpe de Chine nighties.'[19]

If not the jealous type, May certainly would have been disturbed had she known that when Louis was on a trip to London in August with the French war cabinet, he had visited his old flame Jessie Gordon, a meeting which was to have explosive repercussions. In September, Douglas gave May an anonymous letter he had received, which read, 'It may interest you to know that your wife is the mistress of Col Louis Spiers. Ask her about the enclosed erotic outburst given to him, written on Hôtel de Crillon paper and dated July 13th.'[20]

Louis had carelessly left in Jessie's flat a poem May had written for him, and when Jessie came across it, she had been stirred enough by jealousy to send a copy of it to Douglas. He told May that he did not believe it was genuine, although she suspected he thought otherwise, but since he asked no questions, she was saved from revealing the truth.

Her confidence in Louis, however, was shaken to the core. She was stunned by his indiscretion, and, struggling to make sense of the anonymous note and its implications, she wrote him a distraught letter. Louis tried to play it down as the vengeance of an abandoned woman, but May felt betrayed and violated. In her already fragile state of mind it took a supreme effort to keep going and, probably due to emotional anguish, she spent a day in bed with pains, observing how very washed out and tired she looked, a ghost of her former self.[21] Although the letter affair continued to haunt her, it was a tribute to her generosity of heart that she was able to make allowances for Jessie's actions. 'I feel so dreadfully – being the cause of such suffering to another woman … is it revenge she wanted, it may be that her chief revenge will be to have made it more difficult for you to make me laugh – ?'[22]

In fact, Jessie's meddling achieved the effect opposite to the one she might have wanted, pushing May to accept the need to tell Douglas herself as soon as possible, and to seek a divorce so that she was free to marry Louis. For his part, he still seemed to harbour doubts about her intentions. If she appeared reticent to him, it was simply emotional paralysis about taking the next step, and his insecurity, engendered by fear that she would never leave Douglas, was wearing her down. 'You ask me if I am keeping my side of the bargain', she wrote,

> Did you mean to ask whether I had modified my relations with, i.e. gone back to Douglas? – That you know is impossible – if you should die tonight, I should remain as I am and until I followed you would lie in no other arms ... But since I tell you everything – I must tell you that I am terrified of hurting him by telling him – I am ill, because – of being separated from you and because the fear of hurting him – It is anguish to me.[23]

She appealed to him to be patient. Soon she would be returning to him, and never before had she looked forward to seeing him with 'a feeling of absolute need and of such profound conviction' that they belonged to each other. But she was still ill with fatigue and emotional strain, and warned Louis, 'I shall just want to rest – rest – scarcely speak – just be with you and rest.'[24]

By the next morning, however, she had revived enough to write joyously to him, 'Such a glorious day – Cold – brilliant – An Americans day – A day to spend racing across the prairie and to have supper round a camp fire under the stars – and sleep rolled up in blankets out under the sky.' Her earlier fatigue and low spirits seemed to have dissipated:

> What fun it is to be in love in the very centre of the whirlpool of the world as you and I are – you're there, at the heart of the struggle & I'm with you – and if there's one thing I care for more than others, it's just that, the feeling that one's in it, that one's at the hub of the universe where things are spinning fastest – It's not the same as being at the top – It's got very little to do with – success, tho' I suppose it means

incidentally that one's succeeded – it's just the sensation of having one's hand on the pulse and of feeling it throb, falter, flicker, leap again – and that's what you do ... I enjoy the feeling of your immense nervous power.[25]

Although her work had sometimes created tensions between them, her experiences at the front meant that unlike many couples who encountered the dividing influence of war, they had a shared knowledge of its reality. They knew and understood its full horrors – but war had brought them together, and against its backdrop the exhilaration of their love affair was intensified.

Earlier in September May had heard that a play she had written some time before might be put on in London. The actress Violet Vanbrugh, the eldest of three sisters who all had successful careers in the theatre, had read it, and she and her manager were interested in staging it if May was prepared to make some minor changes. Now she had received another letter and it seemed very likely that the play would go ahead, but she would have to meet the manager to discuss the changes. This would involve a trip to England.

6

The Trauma of Parting

In early October, May travelled to London and took a suite at the Carlton Hotel in Pall Mall. She could no longer put off asking Douglas for a divorce and she had sent him a letter asking him to meet her. Buoyed up by her relief at finally having made the decision, she was in good spirits as she parted from Louis at Boulogne with a last long kiss goodbye on the terrace of the hotel where she had been staying. Arriving in the capital in the middle of an air raid, she sat down to a hearty meal, later writing to Louis, 'I've such a wonderful dinner inside me that I can't bother about bombs.' She was unable to use the telephone to speak to him because 'the exchange has taken to the cellar'.[1] Next morning she had a meeting with her agent and Violet Vanbrugh's manager to discuss her play. It was hard to turn her mind to the world of the stage, talking about the cast and which theatre to use. She spent the afternoon rewriting the first act and was optimistic that the contract would be signed. Not wanting to see anyone, for the next few days she hardly left her hotel, having her meals sent up to her and working as hard as she could.

Douglas sent a wire to say he could not come for another five days, and he was not sure whether leave would be granted.

Even then, she continued to work flat out on the new version of the play, and with the end in sight she was looking forward to getting it typed up and sent off for Violet to read. She had become rather bored with it but could 'see that it might be a success'. Although she was 'very much incognito' in London, she had one obligatory outing to the Red Cross at the invitation of Madame de la Panouse, who made a big fuss of her, making her feel like their 'little prize package'.

It was the evening of Saturday 7 October 1917 when the moment May had been waiting for finally arrived and Douglas came to her hotel. She had already sent him a letter that morning to try to prepare him for the news that she wanted a divorce. 'I wanted you to come to London so that I could talk to you of something that is heavy on my heart. I want to tell you the truth, as bravely as I can. I have never lied to you and never pretended – You know how it has been with us – you know – since the day we were married – there has been something – a want – Now I have found out what it all means and is.' She had been going back over their life together, 'which you have dignified & made fine; by being so true – but I see no way out, except by telling you the truth now'.[2]

It was a letter written with great sorrow. 'The die is cast – The blow is dealt that man whom I profoundly respect – and who has been true to me from the day he first saw me', she wrote to Louis the same day. 'May I be able to give you enough of the joy and of the meaning of life – to justify what I've done – I destroy one life – in order to create another – our life B – we must make it fine.'

When May came face to face with Douglas, she was in a turmoil of emotion, but she somehow managed to compose herself enough to sit through dinner with him. Afterwards they went upstairs to her sitting room, where they sat down beside each other in silence. Now that the moment to tell him had finally come, she was suddenly overwhelmed and broke down in uncontrollable tears, shaking all over. She was in such an agitated state that she could not speak and so instead handed him a copy of the letter she had sent him. He could not comprehend its meaning and asked her to explain, gently encouraging her to talk to him. At last she forced herself to get the truth out, telling him of her love for Louis. He sat quite still as he listened to her. When she had finished he still seemed unable to take it all in. He asked her what she wanted to do about it. 'Set me free', she answered. The atmosphere was 'very strange and quiet' as they talked about what should be done. Douglas agreed to file for divorce without naming a third party, on the condition that they wait until after the war because 'he could never live it down in the army' and could not bear people's sympathy. This nearly broke her up for a moment, but she insisted that she did not want to wait at all.

His other condition was that he should have full custody of the children, and because he believed that it would be better for the girls to have one parent 'who was completely theirs', rather than dividing their time between two, he proposed beginning a new life with them in which he would try to compensate for the loss of their mother. When she asked him if this meant that he would take them completely away from her he replied that he would. Yet he could not believe that she would be happy taking this step and losing everything – her family, her reputation. She would be 'going into the world of divorced women', and he would be one of the 'few who would think kindly' of her.[3]

May passed a fitful sleepless night before meeting Douglas the next morning. They had intended to discuss the separation further but he arrived in a distraught state and told her that he was in no fit condition to talk and would not stay. 'He touched me profoundly', she wrote to Louis. 'If only I could have had some other relationship with him – but marriage. It is all, unspeakably sad.' In spite of his conditions, she felt Douglas had been 'phenomenally unselfish'. His only motives are 'my happiness and the children's welfare – he puts himself out of it', she later told Louis.[4]

The talking continued that evening when Douglas returned to the hotel. The finality of a divorce was still hard for him to accept, and again he expressed his desire to wait until after the war, giving as his main reason his inability to look after the children while he was in the army. May responded that to take care of the children for another year or more, 'with the knowledge always present' that she would lose them afterwards, 'would be an unbearable agony'. The idea of it made her start to shiver and shake, but she went on talking, trying hard to make him understand her feelings, and being more open with him than ever. She explained how she had never been his emotionally, and this had caused her to feel 'an unreal being'.

During her talk to him, she was aware of speaking as she might have talked to her father, and it filled her with gratitude that even at this point in their relationship he was comforting and supporting her. She believed him when he told her that 'the worst thing in the world to him' was her being unhappy, and later he did relent and give her at least temporary care of the children. But however hard they were trying to end their marriage decently, neither could bear to give up custody of the children, and this became the cause of a bitter battle which ended up destroying what love and compassion they now shared for each other.

A few days later May returned to Paris. Douglas had accepted, at least verbally, a divorce and she was anxious that the legal proceedings should start as soon as possible. Yet her mood was still volatile. The strain of the break-up of her marriage, and all the months of nursing at the front, had taken their toll; she was physically and mentally exhausted. In need of peace and rest, which could not be easily found at rue Monsieur with major renovations taking place, she moved to the Hôtel Crillon to recuperate. She was still feeling weak and highly strung, when she received a letter from Douglas in which he appeared to have changed his mind about the divorce, hoping there was a chance that her feelings for Louis were no more than a passing infatuation. She was beside herself with distress and wrote a desperate letter, imploring him to keep to what they had decided, and insisting that she was set on marriage to Louis.

Douglas was alarmed by the tone of her letter and went to visit her at the Crillon, where they discussed the divorce further. After he had gone she wrote to him again, anxious to convey her gratitude for his perfect loyalty to her, which 'sets a high standard',[5] but he had to understand that there was no chance of reconciliation. She wanted her relationship with Louis kept secret until the divorce was finalized, and she told Douglas that she had therefore instructed her friends to say only that they had separated. It was particularly important to her that her mother should not hear anything about it. Knowing that she would strongly disapprove and no doubt bring her influence to bear, May was anxious that Douglas kept news of the divorce from her mother until it had been irrevocably settled.

Seeing there was no way he could change her mind, Douglas at last consented to divorce proceedings being set in motion, and on 18 December 1917, May presented a petition to the Civil Tribunal in Paris for dissolution of her marriage, and for the custody and control of the children to be awarded to her.

Her health though was still cause for concern. When she was given a chest X ray, the sight of it caused Louis to faint. She was diagnosed with an infection of the left lung, thought to have been picked up while she was nursing patients with gangrene, and was instructed to have a month of complete bedrest. To pass the time, she started a journal, kept jointly with Louis, in which she recorded the progress of the war. In their new home, with Louis taking care of her, she felt better and stronger each day. They celebrated their first Christmas together quietly on their own, with the girls away with Douglas.

At the end of January she left Paris to continue her period of rest by the sea at St Jean de Luz. The divorce hearing had taken place in Paris on 8 January, and, full of romantic optimism about a future with Louis, she wrote to him, 'Our marriage is going to be one of those perfect poems that will make people wonder.' It would be another eight weeks before the divorce became absolute, however, and by French law an interval of ten months had to pass before she could remarry. Neither she nor Louis could bear to wait that long, and they were hoping to find a possible solution. The marriage could take place in England, but Louis was too busy with his work to travel there, raising the idea that the ceremony could possibly be held at the British Consulate in Paris, which was under British jurisdiction.

In the meantime, May and Douglas were communicating through letters, making arrangements for dividing up their belongings and addressing the contentious issue of what should happen to the children. She had begun to feel, as Douglas had in the beginning, that it would be disastrous for the children to be divided between them. One reason for feeling this was because she wanted Louis to be a part of their lives and she felt that they would resent him unless they were able to develop a relationship with him uninterrupted. The only solution seemed for Douglas to take them away or leaving them entirely to her.

It was hardly surprising that, presented with such a stark choice, Douglas said he would take his daughters away, even though he had no means of looking after them, while he was still in the army. May seems either not to have expected this answer, perhaps because of his circumstances, or not to have thought through the consequences enough to realize that she was incapable of accepting such an outcome.

Another meeting between Douglas and May was arranged where it was decided that she would have custody of their daughters until the end of the war. She assured him that this would only be a trial situation, and if the girls were unhappy, she would hand over their guardianship to him. She realized she had caused Douglas added pain over the children, and appreciated now that they needed both their parents, but hoped that they would come to accept that the separation was inevitable, 'very sad, but not ugly in any way'.

As for most of their possessions they had shared, she cared nothing at all. He could take what he wanted from their homes in London and the country, although there were a few things of sentimental value which she expressed her wish to keep, 'the etchings, the big tiffany lamp, the drawing room rug, my books and my best china and Dresden finger bowls'. She was grateful to him for being so fair, and wished he could be happy as she was.

At St Jean de Luz, spending her days alone, speaking to no one, she had time for quiet reflection, and it seemed to be doing her good. But then on 3 February, Louis received a telegram from her asking him to come as soon as possible. He caught a train that night and was frightened to arrive at the station to find she was not there to meet him. He found her in bed, recovering from a miscarriage. It had been a frightening and painful experience, but by the time he arrived, he found her 'looking much better than in Paris' and feeling considerably gayer 'owing to relief at not being sick'. She had had no idea that she was pregnant but the doctor told her the foetus was three months. Taking in this news she felt it explained her immense fatigue and the various pains which she had attributed to symptoms of her chest infection. She was instructed not to move for a fortnight, and for the next few days Louis stayed at her bedside.

In spite of the happy time they spent together, Louis was anxious about her physical and mental health. She suffered from constant headaches, a symptom of the strain she was still under, and both of them were on edge, quick to overreact and blow things up out of proportion. Their see-sawing emotions seemed to be delicately balanced between awful despondency and perfect happiness, easily tipped downward by the slightest setback which seemed to threaten their relationship. Louis' insecurity was often the source of their quarrels. He was upset to know that May was still receiving letters from Douglas. In response, she wrote Louis a letter expressing her despair at his lack of faith in her which she told him would drive her from him:

> B. can't you see that this nervousness of yours, this lack of confidence – will kill me – if it goes on. You say you are disappointed that I don't look well ... for our marriage – wouldn't you help me to get well by saving me this sort of torment and pain? ... I am doing my best to get well – Do you think it is not a disappointment to me to be weak and ill? What will become of us, if this goes on? You will loose [*sic*] me ... before our life is half fullfilled [*sic*] ... all this makes me feel that your love is a tyrant – your tyrant.[6]

Then on 3 March, Louis caught a train to St Jean de Luz, and in a repetition of his earlier visit, May was not at the station to meet him. After walking to her hotel through deep snow, he discovered that she had left the night before for Paris, neither of them having received the wires they had sent each other. Louis was horrified at the thought of May travelling in her weakened state. He took the night train back to Paris, where May was waiting for him at the station, fearful that he would be angry with her.

Although tired from her journey, May was well enough to resume writing in her journal the following day. The news was not good. On 21 March 1918 the Germans had launched their first offensive of the spring on the Western Front, relentlessly pushing back the Allied lines with their heavy and sustained bombardment, while also stepping up their attacks on Paris. On 8 March over 90 bombs had dropped on the city during an air raid, followed up by four separate bombardments using a new weapon, 'the Paris Gun', which could be fired from a distance of up to 132 kilometres. May's journal entry on 23 March records the first day of the bombardment from three emplacements at Crépy, 74 miles away, noting that although the Germans were trying to reduce the morale of the city's inhabitants by the onslaught, it was having a different effect because 'the Parisians so interested in the gun that they are not paying any attention to the battle'.

In Paris, out of all the doom and gloom of war news came word from the British Consul that Louis and May could be married there once the divorce papers were through. The ceremony finally took place on 30 March to the sound of the Paris Gun. As May got ready, she heard a shell fall close by; debris landed on the roof, and she took shelter in the bath, lying flat and hoping that no splinters would disfigure her if the house was hit. Her brother John had come over from New York to give her away, and the British Ambassador in Paris, Lord Bertie, and the American ambassador were witnesses. She had managed to keep her divorce a secret from her mother, and Douglas claimed to have found out that it was finalized only when he read of her marriage in the English newspapers.

At this stage, no one could imagine that in four months' time, on 29 September, Ludendorff would be forced to call for an armistice. In spite of the initial success of the German offensives, they had been at the cost of huge casualties. A depleted and exhausted army, combined with the arrival of American troops to back up Allied forces, allowed them to counter-attack, and put pressure upon the Germans which they could not resist. On 11 November the armistice was finally signed in a railway carriage in a siding in the forest of Compiègne in Northern France.

Louis and May were in the very heart of the victory celebrations, joining Pétain for the parade in Strasbourg on 25 November to salute the return of Alsace and Lorraine, which Germany had annexed in 1871. Four days later, on 29 November, they were invited by Lord Derby to dine at the embassy in Paris with King George V. She was supremely happy as she looked ahead to a world without war, with a partner with whom she wanted to 'share everything, including name, house, friends and bed and breakfast'.[7] In the complex, clever but vulnerable Louis she had found a soulmate.

7

Trouble on the Horizon

The joy of being together in their first months of marriage was matched by the enchantment Louis and May felt for their house on rue Monsieur. They had already spent ten thousand pounds on structural repairs and redecorating, and now they filled it with books, paintings and furniture. May loved to browse through the second-hand book stalls on the *quais* and hunting for objects of interest to add to their growing collection. One of their most memorable finds was a plaster copy of Houdon's bust of Voltaire, bought in Tours for a few francs after it had languished in the cellar of a convent for many years; it was thought by the nuns to be the head of a saint and when they discovered it was 'the heretic' they threw it out. May stood it on a marble column at the top of the stairs, and when in time it moved to England with them, it would remind her of their first home together on the Left Bank: the library lined with old volumes picked up on the *quais*, the panelled drawing room, the stairs leading down to the garden where a nightingale would sing each summer, and how at night she would wake to hear the nuns chanting in the convent near by. Rue Monsieur was more than just a home to them; it came to represent a place of special significance, and long after they gave up permanent residence there, it was somewhere to which they would retreat for its restorative powers.

It also proved the perfect setting for entertaining. Keeping open house during the Peace Conference, May once again threw herself into the role of society hostess, giving lavish receptions, dinners and musical evenings. She revelled in the opportunity to bring together statesmen, soldiers, artists and writers, including T. E. Lawrence, Winston Churchill, Maynard Keynes, Lloyd George, Paul Valéry, Henri Bernstein and the poet Jean Cocteau. The writer Lady Millicent Hawes spoke of how May and Louis' hospitality reminded people of the old great days of the salon, while May would recall how their home seemed 'full of colour and music and laughter'.[1]

Although her inheritance enabled her to indulge her enjoyment for party giving, she did not spend her money without concern for spiralling costs, noting in the journal she was still keeping that the price of living was fearful, and that although cake shops were open again, 'by way of reform the limit of prices in Restaurants has been removed', but at least 'butter is allowed'. [2]Although she was still very wealthy, her war work, and rue Monsieur, had eaten into a sizeable chunk of her capital, but she was in her element as a hostess, and she felt tremendously lucky and privileged to be experiencing the extraordinary atmosphere in Paris during the Peace Conference.'[3]

In the polyglot gatherings around the table at rue Monsieur, where many of the finer points of the treaties were discussed and thrashed out by delegates, May often sat silently in a corner of the room, shrinking into the background to observe the heated debates, drawing her own conclusions and making mental character studies of individuals and nations. The Americans had taken over the Crillon, and a large part of the Place de la Concorde, and May followed with interest the relationship between the country of her birth and her two adopted homes. 'Some people think America & England are the closest allies', she reported. 'Others think France and England – it is certain that Wilson got on very well in London.' When she had the chance to see President Wilson in the flesh, at the Hôtel de Ville, however, she was not at all enamoured, finding his smile 'quite disturbing – glassy — & fixed'.[4]

The last entry of May's journal is dated 15 April 1919, in which she describes having lunch with Mrs Wilson, and a reception in the evening for the Polish prime minister, Paderewski. Sitting next to his wife during dinner, she mentioned that the last time she had seen her famous pianist husband was in New York's Carnegie Hall. 'An expression of great sadness came over her face – she clutched my hand and gasped, "My dear child – what a different world." '[5]

The signing of the Paris Peace Treaty on 29 June was the cause of much public jubilation. There was music and dancing in the streets, café bars remained open late into the night overflowing with people celebrating, and a military parade along the Champs-Élysées was enthusiastically cheered on by flag-waving crowds who lined the boulevards. May, however, noted the disillusionment felt by many and venturing into new literary territory, she used her observations of the Peace Conference to write a spoof entitled *The Diary of Sir Peter Pottle, Serious Snob, being a Faithful Rendering of Paris Gossip during the Peace Conference.* When she told Lord Derby of her plan to write a novel about the Peace Conference, in which fictional characters would mix with real figures like Lloyd George and Clemenceau, however, he pleaded with her not to publish it and she never did.[6]

Although May looked back on these days as the happiest of her life, some detected signs of inner turmoil. Lord Derby felt he had never seen a woman so nervous, having noticed how she trembled all through a dinner she was hosting. The truth was, that although she had looked forward to a peaceful existence with Louis once the war was over, their lives were still fraught with worries, not least being the agonising question of custody of the children, which had never been resolved.

May had not shown a natural affinity with motherhood when her daughters were small. Her involvement with the day-to-day care of her children was even more remote during the war, but once she gave up her hospital work at the end of 1917, she had seemed to take more easily to parenting, enjoying the experience of family life with a partner she adored. At the end of the war, she had told Douglas that she considered it best for the girls that they remain with her, but with no restrictions on him seeing them as much as he wanted.

Although he seemed to accept this decision at the time, he must have been brooding on it, for at the beginning of 1919, he threatened to go to the English courts for custody of the children and, if this failed, he would try the French courts, and as publicly as possible. May remained outwardly calm, and did her best to persuade him to change his mind, arguing that she did not believe any court in the world would take three daughters away from their mother. After several more letters back and forth, the situation appeared to have been defused, with Douglas agreeing not to carry out his threat.

Another source of anxiety was Louis' work. Since Winston Churchill's appointment as secretary of state for war, Louis had become, in effect, 'his man' in Paris, although in Whitehall and in the French capital he was viewed as his spy.[7] Louis had impressed Churchill with his acute grasp of the threat posed by Bolshevism, and his hard work in promoting Allied armed intervention against the Bolsheviks, in which they both strongly believed. Encouraged by Churchill's praise of him, given both publicly and in private, Louis set his sights on the post of military attaché in Paris. This roused his enemies to line up against him, with accusations of unscrupulous behaviour. Louis fought back, but the ensuing row further undermined his reputation at the War Office, where Field Marshal Sir Henry Wilson, already an enemy, now called for his dismissal.

All this put him under huge strain. He suffered fainting fits and at the end of October was diagnosed with nervous depression and advised to take a long rest. In the end he decided to resign, not without great bitterness. In a letter May sent to Churchill, drafted by Louis, she referred to his adversaries who 'have done better than they knew. Their persecutions have borne fruit. Thanks to you – he has pulled thro', but he's a sick man now … it's been a horrid six months – but it's over now.'[8] May had suffered on her husband's behalf as she watched his enemies turn on him, and her own physical health was poor. Early in 1920 she became ill with an infection, thought to be a recurrence of the one she had had at the end of 1917, and went to stay in Fontainebleau to convalesce.

Away from Louis, she thought a great deal about their relationship. They had been married almost two years and she cared for him more than ever, but she worried that she did not always show him enough affection. It did not help that they were more often apart than together, a pattern that was set to continue. In August, while he remained in London, May took her daughters to Deauville, accompanied by Louis' widowed sister Kathleen and her young child Béatrix. May thought her niece impertinent, but her heart went out to Kathleen, whose face she described as worn and lined from worrying about her straitened circumstances.

Now in the early stages of pregnancy, May felt out of sorts and she missed Louis terribly. 'How little time we've had alone together since we've been married – almost none', she wrote to him from Deauville. 'We must go alone to London this winter and have three quiet months – by ourselves waiting for Michael – that will be delicious. We'll just sit by the fire in the evenings & read and talk and be quite peaceful and alone and if it's foggy outside we'll be all the cosier – I shall adore it.'[9] In the meantime, she found little to amuse her in the French seaside resort, disliking everything about her surroundings, and the people she tolerated even less, complaining to Louis of a lunch she had endured with 'a lot of talk about what was chic – & who was "elegant" – I was bored to death and felt I couldn't stick Deauville more than a week.'[10] She scarcely had the application to work on her latest novel for distraction, managing only an hour a day at most. She hatched a plan to drive to Venice and, aware that Louis might try to prevent her because of concerns for her health, she wrote to persuade him of the benefits of going by car, rather than travelling by train; she wanted to see all the marvellous countryside on the way and if she got tired she would stop and rest at the Italian lakes.

As it turned out, Louis' work commitments continued to keep them apart. Having resigned from the War Office in June, he had been carving out a new career in Eastern European trade, and was made a director of the British Corporation of Mine and Steamship Owners in Russia.[11] In the autumn of 1920, his work took him to London and Eastern Europe, while May remained in Paris where she forced herself to work on her novel, motivated only by the need to get it finished before the baby was born. It was with relief that she could finally report to Louis that she was making progress with the culminating chapters, with only three more to go. 'Then I shall work it over from the beginning but that is not so much of a strain.' But as her pregnancy progressed, she confided in Louis with a degree of alarm, that her writing had changed. This fear was part of a more general insecurity that seemed to be assailing her. She was feeling big and uncomfortable, and concerns about looking odd made her less inclined to eat out and be social. On her own, her thoughts were morbid and her nights fitful, interrupted by recurring nightmares in which Louis was unspeakably cruel to her. The changes a new baby would bring were also on her mind. 'I'm somewhat troubled', she told Louis, 'by the idea that when Michael has arrived you will no longer be so angelic to me – you must think about this.'[12]

***

But a far greater crisis was looming. After his demobilisation from the army in 1920, Douglas had found a job in London working for the League of Nations Union. He needed somewhere for his daughters to stay when they came to see him and his friend Hugh Gretton – a fellow and tutor at Keble College, and the nephew of the Dean of Canterbury – provided a solution by inviting him to share Radcliffe Observatory House which he lived in with his wife in Oxford. The Grettons also had a country home, and when the girls came during the summer, they stayed there with Douglas. After this visit, he sent a letter to May asserting his paternal rights and requesting that his daughters return to live in England. He proposed that Comfort and Joyce attend a boarding school in Headington, while Mary remain with him at the Grettons where she could go to the local kindergarten.

May had no intention of agreeing to the children being sent to live so far from her, especially when Mary was only five years old. She argued that it would not be in their best interests to board before the age of thirteen, no matter how good the reputation of the school, and besides, she saw no reason to move them from their French school where they were day scholars, an education supplemented by tutors for various lessons at home. Then Mrs Gretton entered the fray, putting pressure upon May to change her mind, an interference that could only inflame the situation. She seemed to have formed a particularly close attachment to Mary, and during the autumn wrote several times to ask that May allow her to stay in Oxford for part of the winter. May's unease over this was accentuated when she discovered from her other daughters that Mrs Gretton had asked them to call her 'Mamie'.

So far, May had managed to avert a head-on collision with Douglas, but his continuing unhappiness about the status quo had been gathering momentum. For a start, he did not approve of the way his daughters were being raised. Conventional Parisian society shunned the rue Monsieur because Louis and May had married after a divorce, and this fact confirmed his worries about the life his children were leading. He felt that it was too cosmopolitan and that they were not being given a religious upbringing or receiving enough discipline, instead being allowed to stay up late and mix with people of questionable morals. These included May's friend, Millicent Hawes, who had been divorced twice and had several affairs during her unhappy first marriage to the Duke of Sutherland – none of which was likely to commend her to Douglas.

In a renewed attempt to regain influence over the girls, he wrote to May at the beginning of November to say he wished to have them to stay on alternate weekends, as well as all the school holidays. In addition, he wanted Mary to remain with him for several months after Christmas. When May flatly refused to consent to this proposal, Douglas wrote again, threatening legal action if she did not relent. She retaliated by instructing her own solicitors in Paris to deal with future correspondence regarding the matter. In spite of this serious development, when Douglas travelled to Paris at the end of November, he and May overcame their differences in order to celebrate Mary's sixth birthday together at rue Monsieur. Under the impression that Douglas understood and accepted her feelings over the care of the children, and since she planned to take up temporary residence in London for the birth of the baby, she let him take them back to England for Christmas as had been originally agreed.

On 28 December, with the children's nurse and governess, she travelled to England where she had taken a lease on a house at 11 Portman Square. The girls were expected back on 4 January, but when she arrived in London she found a letter from Douglas's solicitors informing her that he had applied for full charge and custody of his daughters and that he would not be returning them to her. The very next day, May took a train and taxi to the Radcliffe Observatory House in the grounds of the college, accompanied by Mademoiselle Fischer, the children's governess. The door was opened by a maid, who, when asked by May, confirmed that Mrs Gretton lived there, and that Douglas was at home. They were then ushered into the drawing room where a few moments later Mrs Gretton appeared. They managed to exchange a civil greeting but May's request to see the children seemed to flummox her and she left to get Douglas. He soon entered the room, putting out his hand in greeting, a gesture May ignored. She was finished with any pretence of friendship; from now she was waging war. Although she was in a highly wrought state, she had her wits about her enough to know that everything that passed between her and Douglas could be used as evidence in court, and she later recorded, in all their grim detail, the events which took place that afternoon.

Her insistence on seeing the children was met with prevarication by Douglas who argued that she had no need to when it was not long since she saw them last. 'I wish to see them to tell them the truth, that they are being kept away from me against my will and that I may never see them again', was her stark reply. Douglas wanted the girls to remain in ignorance of what was going on, a suppression that May found unbearably cruel. She gave him an ultimatum – she would not leave until she had told the girls that she did not consent to being separated from them and would 'wait here till I see them or until you put me out of the house by force'. She had brought a suitcase with her and was prepared to wait until nightfall if necessary, and then go to a hotel and return the next day. Faced with such a prospect, Douglas tried to evict her from his premises, prompting a defiant exchange that showed how low relations had sunk between them:

'You cannot wait here, this is my house.'
'Then I will wait in a taxi at the door.'
'You cannot wait at the door. These are my grounds.'
'Then I will wait outside the lodge gate in the street'.[13]

In the end the stand-off was resolved only after several hours when Douglas called a solicitor, who ordered May to leave the house.

A dramatic climax to all this came as she drove away in the taxi and saw her youngest daughter walking towards the gates of the lodge, her hand held by a gentleman she had never seen before. Putting her head out of the window she called out to her daughter 'Bébé Mary Borden'. At the sound of her voice the girl turned to her mother, but her companion, who was Mr Gretton, started to run, pulling her after him. Asking the driver to stop the taxi, May tried to catch up with them, but being heavily pregnant she was unable to run fast enough, and in her effort to do so she tripped and almost fell, then watched with despair as they disappeared behind the doors of the house she had just left.

To add insult to injury, Mrs Gretton gave May a letter from Comfort written that day which revealed that Douglas had arranged for the two older girls to go to a boarding school, and that he had given them the impression that this was with the agreement of their mother. To discover the whereabouts of the school, she was forced to engage the services of a private detective agency and then to pass letters to them. Meanwhile, Douglas hired someone to carry out surveillance to prevent May taking the girls back. She later learned that at the time of her visit to the Grettons, Joyce had been unwell and that neither she nor Comfort had been told she was there.

Quite what the girls were told at this stage about their enforced separation from their mother is not entirely clear, but family folklore tells how Joyce and Comfort threw a letter from their bedroom window at the Observatory House saying they were being held prisoner, and pleading to be rescued. Douglas, though, was prepared to allow May to see them only on the condition that they had no contact with Louis, an impossible request as far as she was concerned. Where he had acquiesced in the past to her wishes, he was now as determined as she was to keep the children, with the result that a bitter custody battle ensued, with both parents trying to undermine each other's character in their affidavits and calling on their supporters to write references on their behalf.

Douglas attacked May's suitability as a parent, citing the negative 'influences and excitements' of her house, and pointing out that the girls had been very reluctant to return to Paris to live after the summer holidays, and had complained of having practically no companions of their own age there. The French artist Paul Maze, who had been a liaison officer with the British army, wrote a statement in which he referred to stories which had circulated in France during the war about May's fast way of life and indiscreet relationship with Louis. In this line of attack, Douglas had a trump card, and one that was particularly painful for May. When, in April 1918, Mary Borden had learned of her daughter's marriage to Louis, she had written to Douglas, expressing the view that he should keep the children, a letter he was now able to produce. 'How can they be brought up as they should as things are now?' she had asked at the time. The Grettons, and the novelist John Buchan, endorsed Mary Borden's view, referring to the happy relationship they had observed between Douglas and his daughters, and praising him as a father.

For her part, May accused him of cowardly behaviour in the war, in contrast to Louis who had been wounded four times, and highlighted the fact that he had lived off her fortune. She said that Mrs Gretton was scheming to steal the girls away from her, and to take her place as their mother, while Mademoiselle Fischer gave a statement saying that the children did not like Mrs Gretton, and how much they missed May. Millicent Hawes described the happy home-life she witnessed at rue Monsieur, although her character reference was possibly undermined by the fact that Douglas in his affidavit cited her as someone of disreputable influence. Her claim that all the most interesting people of the day flocked to rue Monsieur probably did not hold much sway with his side either.

When it came to recalling the details of their marriage, both parties were guilty of being economical with the truth, bending facts to suit their case, which resulted in denials and counter affidavits. In the meantime, until a decision was reached by the courts, Mary was allowed to return to live with her mother, while Joyce and Comfort were sent as weekly boarders to Headington School, and May was prevented from seeing them until they were finally allowed to visit her at the end of January.

On 2 March 1921, she gave birth to the son, named Michael, she and Louis had dreamed about for so long, but the outcome of the custody battle hung over them, marring the happiness of the occasion. It was a difficult delivery in which she nearly died, and it was several days before Louis felt her to be out of danger. Whether rightly or wrongly, she attributed the birthing problems to the strain she was under, this becoming one more thing she held against Douglas. Now Michael's well-being gave her anxious state of mind another focus, and it particularly distressed her that she was too weak to nurse him. The first-time father, however, displayed a down-to-earth approach to his new role. When called from his dinner to May's bedside to find her in tears because she could hear her son crying, he told her firmly that there was nothing whatever the matter with him: 'he was annoyed with being washed and said so'.

One potentially encouraging piece of news came in a cable from May's mother who wanted to make amends for supporting Douglas, something she now bitterly regretted, according to her son John. Although in ill health, she intended to come to England to see how she could help in the custody case, which was becoming increasingly unpleasant, with Douglas still raising objections to Joyce and Comfort visiting their mother when Louis was there.

On 22 March, May was lifted out of bed for the first time since Michael's birth, and for the next few days she shut herself away with her lawyer, working on a counter affidavit, a physically and emotionally exhausting task. Four days later, after another morning with her solicitor, she, Louis and Mary drove to a hotel in Crowborough for a brief respite. Although they did nothing but 'loaf and sleep', worries over the custody battle were ever present, with Louis recording in his diary that they had not heard from Comfort or Joyce for a week. He suspected that they were being 'got at by Turner' who 'thinks he can do anything with impunity since the last hearing went all in his favour'.[14] When at the end of the month the affidavit was at last completed, relief was replaced by the worry that they had been too violent towards Douglas and thereby played into his hands. May was a powerful adversary, but he knew how to attack back with equally wounding ammunition, and five days after she had submitted her affidavit, Louis recorded in his diary that Douglas had filed two new and nasty ones.

Accusing her of making melodramatic appeals to the children's emotions, he claimed that they felt unable to speak to her of the happy times they had with him and the Grettons. He described how after staying with her for a weekend in February they had appeared in a very excited and nervous condition, and how when he returned them to their boarding school the next day, Joyce had been 'wistfully affectionate but strangely silent and subdued', and Comfort would do nothing but cling to him and weep, all of which he interpreted as further evidence of the emotional pressure May was putting them under. He also wrote that the girls were being bombarded by letters from May, and that Comfort had complained in irritation that it was 'perfectly awful the number of letters she had to write' in return.

It was true that, prevented from seeing her daughters, May was frequently writing to them, as well as sending food parcels with treats of exotic fruit and cake, enough for the whole school to enjoy. These were received with displeasure by the headteacher who had to put a stop to them, an intervention to which May did not take kindly. From the point of view of her daughters, it was another awkward situation with which to deal, and they displayed a high degree of sensitivity and tact in painful and difficult circumstances. In a letter responding to her mother's unhappiness at not seeing them for so long, Joyce showed commendable maturity for a twelve-year-old: 'Do not be sad, it is only five weeks to the Easter holidays and then we will see you and the Baby and have a nice time together. Of course it seems a long time but I expect if you are cheerful it will pass quicker than you expect.'[15] Comfort sent a short poem she had composed in an attempt to help her mother remain positive:

> There's a silver lining to the dark clouds shining
> So turn your dark clouds inside out
> Till the girls come home.

Although they wrote of their homesickness, and how much they missed their mother, they seemed to have settled reasonably well, quickly becoming involved in extracurricular activities; Joyce was so busy that in a letter to her aunt she wrote of wringing her hands 'at the amount there is to think about & do', words reminiscent of her mother's letters from school at much the same age in which she revealed the burden of living up to her own high expectations. Comfort took a less serious approach, showing her excitement at taking the part of a boy in a play and relishing the opportunity this gave her to have her hair bobbed for the sake of authenticity.

The preliminary hearing, on 5 April, began ominously for May. The judge said that she had to choose between Louis and the children, and he cast doubt on the legality of her second marriage. Then her solicitor argued her side of the case and the judge did a 'volte-face' and asked Douglas to withdraw his objections to Louis and, for the sake of the children, to compromise. Although this was something of a relief, it meant that nothing had been resolved, since all the affidavits were withdrawn and a new set of proposals had to be prepared.

Straight after the hearing, May met her mother who, with her daughter Joyce, had just arrived in England. In spite of her declaration that she had come to help her daughter, May suspected her of different motives, and was distressed by the thought that she had only come to find out the details of the break-up between herself and Douglas rather than out of affection. Such fears could not have been eased by the knowledge that her mother was also having meetings with Douglas, whom she described to May as 'a fine religious fellow', whereas her daughter's behaviour continued to disappoint her. During their meeting alone together, she expressed her disapproval of May writing some of her more 'outré' novels.

To May, it seemed her mother could hold significant sway in the custody battle, but if Mary saw herself as providing an important role as an intermediary between the warring factions, it was not at all clear to May and Louis whether she would ultimately help or hinder their case. The relationship between mother and daughter wavered between highs and lows. Where one day Mary appeared to give her complete support, so much so that when May suggested a new proposal of divided custody, her mother argued against this, saying it would be bad for the children, and they should apply for sole custody. The next day her mother's attitude seemed less cordial, sending May into despair and creating new tensions between them. Her sister Joyce stepped in to smooth things over, reassuring May that her mother's mind was made up, and that she only wanted explanations, and warning her not to plead with Mary.

In the middle of all the negotiations and meetings over custody, Michael's christening took place on 11 April at St Martin-in-the-Fields, in which Winston Churchill stood as godfather. A few days later, on 15 April, Comfort and Joyce were allowed to visit their mother, and the entire family left town to stay at Ightham Mote, a fourteenth-century moated manor house in Sevenoaks.

May and Louis found little to cheer them there. The house was uncomfortable, and snowy weather and bitter cold kept them confined indoors. They passed time poring over records of the manor, said to be haunted by the ghost of Dorothy Selby who, according to legend, was locked up in the tower by supporters of Guy Fawkes after she betrayed him in a letter. The prospect of a ghostly apparition may have excited Louis, who believed in the occult, but May felt tired and nervy, 'the house heavy on her hands', and relations between herself and her mother reached a particularly low ebb.

The children were also showing signs of strain. Both were distraught at leaving their mother when they returned to Oxford at the beginning of May, weeping and clinging to her as she handed them over. A few days later, Louis received a distressed letter from Comfort, who, thinking her mother was in France, begged him to pass on a message to her that she wanted to be taken home to them. She sounded so upset that he was afraid she might do something desperate, and Joyce was concerned enough about her to write to her aunt saying that Comfort was too homesick to go to school. Then, unbeknown to May or Louis, Comfort turned to another source for help, writing to the judge who had presided over the last hearing, expressing her unhappiness at being kept from her mother. Having read the letter, he summoned her father to his chambers. Douglas took an unrelenting line, arguing that it was clearly bad for the girls to see May, and quoting the view of the headteacher of their school, who, he claimed, had advised that they should not see their mother for three months in accordance with school rules. May's response was to make an immediate application for sole custody.

Douglas had also strained the patience of Mary by insisting that he would not accept the idea of his youngest daughter living permanently with May, or of Comfort and Joyce leaving their school. Faced with this implacability, she wrote a statement saying the children should remain with her daughter. Douglas called a meeting with her and Joyce in which he threatened to use evidence he had not wanted to file before, to which they replied that May had more too. As the conflict escalated, Comfort, having taken things into her own hands and found a sympathetic, if neutral ear, wrote again to the judge, asking to see him. He promptly arranged another hearing for 11 May, where he interviewed the three girls, their mother, Mary and Mrs Gretton. When the children were asked what they would prefer, Mary told the judge she wanted to divide her time between both parents, whereas Joyce said she had too many people to consider and suggested she stay at boarding school, which she preferred, seeing her mother at weekends. Such apparent frankness greatly disappointed Louis, who thought her disloyal and devious. It did not go against them, though, for when May attended the court hearing early the next morning, she was awarded temporary custody, with the condition that Mary should visit her father when her sisters were not there. Now there was nothing more to be done other than to wait for the final decision at the end of the year.

It was not easy to shake off the atmosphere of worry as May and Louis tried to get on with their lives, and they found English life lacking compared to Paris where they had more friends. The Churchills were among the few to visit them at Ightham Mote where May captivated Churchill with her stories about her hospital.

Distractions in the way of company helped to lift the attacks of despondency, but when May was away in Paris, Louis was quite panic stricken, bringing home to him how much he relied upon her. He reread her letters from St Jean de Luz, which made him weep. 'Life is so hard', he wrote in his diary. To May, he said that they should 'give more time to being happy together'.[16] Then it was his turn to go away, to Prague, leaving her behind in an English heatwave where she was laid low with food poisoning, and Louis returned to find her in a nervy and exhausted state, in need of a thorough rest. Swapping Ightham Mote for a house in Rye, they tried to enjoy a family holiday, braving the beach to swim in the sea in spite of howling winds.

Ignoring the vagaries of British summer weather was one thing, but the unhappiness of the girls was a serious cause for alarm. Reluctant to visit their father as arranged, Comfort became so distressed on the way to his house, 'showing the whites of her eyes', that Louis feared she might collapse. Joyce wanted him to prevent them going, but the visit had already been postponed once and May did not want to do anything which might jeopardize their chances of being awarded custody.

As she and Louis prepared to leave for a six-week holiday in Venice, leaving Michael in the care of his nurse, they received a miserable letter from Comfort describing the pressure her father was putting her under and begging for help. May cancelled her seat on the train to Paris, insisting Louis went on without her, but when she realized that her legal team were all away and nothing could be done, she relented and with some reluctance left the country. May missed the children constantly, was inconsolably miserable and frequently tearful, and her heavy smoking, of which Louis disapproved, led to them quarrelling. It was only when they stopped at rue Monsieur on their return journey that she was finally able to relax. Misgivings about her absence from her family were compounded when she saw how much her son had changed, and both parents were shocked enough to agree that they would not separate from him for so long again.

May had managed to finish the book she had been working on during her pregnancy, and in August 1921 it was finally published in America, by Alfred A. Knopf, under the name Mary Borden and entitled *The Tortoise*. The story centres on the heroine, Helen, who is married to a wealthy Englishman high up in the affairs of the state, but who has fallen in love with a womanising French officer. She is on the verge of leaving her husband, a shy and awkward man, when war breaks out. Working as a military nurse, Helen comes to realize how much she loves her husband and that her feelings for the French officer were superficial and illusory, blinding her to the true values of life. The opening scenes take place in Helen's English country house and in the French officer's ancestral home in Paris, moving in the middle section to an evacuation hospital, where, in a rather contrived piece of plotting, both men end up in a critical condition. After becoming separated, and fearing that she has lost him for ever, Helen and her husband are finally reunited for a happy ending.

May's fears that her writing had changed when she was working on *The Tortoise* were not entirely imaginary, for her fraught frame of mind during the period of its creation seems to have worked its way onto the page, infusing the novel with an excess of dramatic tension that pushes it over the edge into melodrama. A review in the *New York Times* was scathing, feeling that the anguish of her characters had been prolonged for so long that the reader's sympathy was exhausted. It was never published in England.

As 1921 drew to a close, she appeared in court to hear she had been awarded full custody of the children. Her relationship with Douglas, however, was irrevocably destroyed.

With Joyce and Comfort visiting their father for Christmas, May and Louis went to Paris to recover from the stresses that had plagued them all year in the sanctuary of rue Monsieur. 'Thank God this year ends better than it began', wrote Louis in his diary. 'We could not have stood the strain, as it is we have both been profoundly affected – our nerves have been strained so that they will ever carry the marks and our characters have been changed.'[17]

He had made an important decision about his future, deciding to stand as the National Liberal parliamentary candidate at Loughborough: shortly before leaving for Paris he had spoken to the full executive committee and won their unanimous backing.

May with her much-adored son Michael in 1922– one of a series of publicity shots for The Sketch *which appeared with the title 'a chevalier of the Legion of Honour with her baby'.*

8

A Welcome from the Windy City

In Paris May was able to put the past behind her and recover her good spirits. Louis, though, was less easily cheered. He was depressed to discover how much things had changed, and to find that it was impossible to recapture the magic of the old days now that he no longer held the position in Paris that he had once enjoyed. When they gave a dinner and ball at rue Monsieur, it did not live up to his memories of parties they used to have; there seemed less of a crowd and he noted the absence of embassy members. Even a clown cabaret organized by May fell flat – although she felt the party had gone well. All the same, when his time in the capital was cut short by news that in England a February election was in the air, he was as sorry as ever to have to leave. When he spoke to May a few days later he was relieved to hear her sounding happy, but somewhat taken aback that she had gone to a fancy dress ball on her own dressed as Mistinguette, the Parisian music hall artist famed for her exotic costumes.

She was soon called back to England to support Louis after the death of his grandmother, Lucy Hack, the one constant and loving presence throughout his life. May's idea of covering the coffin with lilies, Lucy's favourite flower, was one that he appreciated, sure that he would always remember the way their fragrance had filled the church. He may have been less grateful to May when she accompanied him to Loughborough where he had to address a meeting. She did not hold back from telling him that he had gone into far too much detail and had been unconvincing. His next speech went better, although he was so nervous that his hands trembled as he read from his notes.

May did not always welcome criticism when it was directed her way. Michael's nurse, Sarah Lubbock, was dismissed for giving the impression that parents were an unnecessary nuisance. She could not, however, be faulted for the admirable attention she had given her charge and on the evening of her departure, the infant was inconsolable, and May was unable to get him to sleep. Sarah was replaced by the indispensable and much loved Nurse Lamb, whose steady and calming influence exerted itself over the family for the next five years. She became a figure of security, not only for Michael, but increasingly for May and Louis, revealing a sound and intuitive understanding of human psychology as she guided them through his boyhood, often averting conflict between parents and child with her quiet authority and wisdom.

Michael, known by all as Peti (pronounced 'Pe-ti'), short for 'Le Petit', was adored by his siblings and parents. Louis' pleasure in him was immense, and he devotedly recorded his development in what grew to be three volumes of scrapbooks. His son released in him an unconditional love which had been absent from his own relationship with his parents, but it did not escape his notice that his son demonstrated his affection for his mother by screaming with joy whenever she appeared, whereas his own presence evoked no comment at all.

Another presence was also slowly but surely infiltrating their life during this time, with quite a different effect from that of Nurse Lamb's. At the end of 1918, Louis had taken on a secretary,

Nancy Maurice, the daughter of a colleague, and granddaughter of the social reformer Frederick Denison Maurice. She quickly proved herself to be extremely efficient and dedicated, and became, as time went on, not only invaluable to him, but a rival to May. Fourteen years younger than May, she was tall and slim, well educated, and possessed a sharp mind when it came to organizing Louis' work. Although lacking May's physical attractiveness, social ease and vitality, Nancy had determination and persistence, and she used both these traits to win her place in Louis' life, earning his affection with her devotion and loyalty. Her growing importance is rather eerily traced in the progression from an early photograph in which she appears as a solitary, tiny speck, standing in the distant background of the garden of a holiday house the family had taken one summer, to her position in the foreground of later snapshots, where her penetrating stare seems to boldly assert her right to be alongside May and Louis.

The autumn was dominated by the election campaign in which gossip about May's divorce threatened to undermine Louis' chances of success. The family made contingency plans for the future, even playing with the idea of moving to America and buying a ranch. As it turned out, he was elected unopposed; the Labour candidate was prevented from standing after he arrived two minutes late for nomination time, and the Conservatives honoured an agreement not to put up a candidate against him. Straight after this win, Churchill, who was recovering from appendicitis, asked Louis to campaign on his behalf in Dundee, a duty he duly undertook, staying for two and a half weeks, and taking Nancy with him.

Although preoccupied with family life and the need to play her part as the wife of a politician, May had by no means given up her literary ambitions, and for the previos two years she had been struggling with her latest book. In August 1923, tired and under the weather, she travelled on her own for a much-needed rest in Venice. Here she was introduced to Noël Coward, the beginning of a life-long friendship. He found her enchanting, describing her as 'a small attractive woman with deep sleepy eyes and a rather nervous smile'. She told him that she had just completed a novel called *Jane Our Stranger* and not knowing her background, he visualized 'a light, slightly "jejune" little book written to pass the time, and dealing, probably amateurishly, with the adventures of some winsome housemaid'.[1]

As it turned out, this, her fifth novel, brought her the success she had set her sights upon as a student at Vassar, catapulting her into the best-seller lists and making the literary establishment sit up sharp with excitement at the appearance of an exciting new writer. Glowing reviews compared her writing to that of Charlotte Brontë, Joseph Conrad, Henry James and Edith Wharton, the first three at least all being authors whose work she particularly admired.

In writing *The Romantic Woman*, May had stirred up a hostile reaction from American society people who did not take kindly to her sardonic portrayal of them. (Her equally acute observations about the English class system seemed to provoke no comment.) In *Jane Our Stranger*, set mainly in Paris, before, during and after the First World War, it is French social culture and the exclusive world of the aristocracy which come under the magnifying glass. The heroine, Jane Carpenter, is an American heiress, but unlike her predecessors in May's earlier novels, she has never known the luxuries of wealth, having been abandoned by her mother as a child, and handed over to the care of her puritanical aunt, where, in a world of stern and simple values, she has learned to be God-fearing and virtuous. Although earnest, she possesses a passionate and impulsive nature, and is prone to accidents, as well as violent outbursts, which earn her a reputation as a 'savage', whom other children should avoid. But the freedom of the open country, where she climbs trees and accompanies her aunt, a respected ornithologist, on energetic walks, provides her with a healthy physical outlet for all that is untamed in her

May and Louis pose for a magazine photograph at their Lutyens-designed house in Little College Street

nature, and with her statuesque frame and ugly face, there is something quite magnificent about her.

Jane's sheltered childhood in a small town in the American Midwest is abruptly brought to an end when her socially ambitious mother arrives on the scene and sweeps her off to Paris, where she schemes to marry her off to the head of one of the old families of the Faubourg Saint-Germain, the impoverished Philibert, Marquis de Joigny, a man of outrageously degenerate and decadent tastes and in need of limitless funds. Jane, in all her innocence, is unsuspecting of her mother's plans, happy just to be a part of her life at last, and Philibert, her opposite in every way, has to work hard to win her hand, but in the end her own romantic idealism leaves her vulnerable to his patient and coldly cynical courtship. Once she has agreed to marry him, she is pulled into an alien and impregnable world, where she will always be the outsider, and where her American ways are as baffling to her adopted relations as their customs are to her.

The story of her doomed marriage is narrated by Philibert's brother, Blaise, a passive observer of her painful initiation into the artifice and double standards of his family, and her own transformation as she learns from them the art of concealing one set of feelings and conveying another. On the surface, she complies with her husband's attempts to mould her into a sophisticated woman of the world, eventually becoming *'une grande dame'*, but inside she is uncompromising in her Puritan ideals. For the sake of her daughter, she reconciles herself to her loveless marriage, finding some comfort with Blaise's bohemian friends, while Philibert works his way through her fortune, building a huge palace to fill with treasures and indulging his obsessions without restraint, including his passion for the malevolent and destructive Bianca. In the end, when Jane sees that she has lost her daughter to her husband's world, she retreats to her childhood home in America to end her days.

When *Jane Our Stranger* was published in the United States in October 1923 by Alfred A Knopf, it was greeted enthusiastically by the critics, but fell relatively flat with the public. Then four months later it was launched in England by William Heinemann and became an almost overnight sensation. Its success was helped along by the air of mystery surrounding its author. Few had heard of the young American heiress who appeared to have intimate knowledge of Parisian society and had captured it with such penetrating precision. In the French capital it gave the gossips something to talk about, as Philibert bore an uncanny resemblance to the Marquis de Castellane, married to an American heiress, who used her fortune to build a palace in the French capital. May denied all such connections but they did no harm to the reputation of her novel, which went through six reprints within its first year.

Capitalising on the success of their new author, Heinemann reissued *The Romantic Woman*, which received fresh appreciation and further accolades for May. Arthur Waugh, writing in the *Telegraph*, described her as 'one of the most vivid and engrossing figures that have dazzled the book world for many years past'.[2] She did not lose her head in all the excitement and firmly refused permission for her first novel to be republished, because, having reread it, she thought it 'very bad', and far too autobiographical. From this time on, she disowned both her first two novels, confessing in later interviews that she was so ashamed of them that she would never disclose the name under which they had been published. She felt *Jane Our Stranger* marked a milestone on the road of her profession precisely because she had developed her imaginative powers, no longer needing to rely for subjectmatter on her intimate world, and creating a heroine unlike anyone she knew.

She was of course delighted to receive such a rapturous reception, but she found it faintly disconcerting that *Jane Our Stranger* had become a 'commercial commodity', as if she had 'invented some new kind of soap or toothpaste'.

> Books have a way of behaving like obstreperous offspring, of disowning their parents, of taking the bit in their teeth and bolting; and authors have a way – those that I know – of taking violent dislikes to their books once they have been taken over by the public. One has a lingering affection for a book of one's own that is a failure; I don't know why; but it is so.[3]

Taking back a degree of authorial ownership, she gave her critical attention to a self-review of her novel for the *Daily Sketch*. 'Why should authors not review their own books', she argued, since 'they should know what they were after in the writing of them, and they ought to know, after reading the reviews of the critics,

The successful author

where they have failed. Is the book, as it formed itself in the head of the author, the same book that reached the public? Is it something better or worse or different from what he thought it was?'[4]

Rejecting popular consensus, she made it known that she had not intended Jane to be 'a sermon from the pulpit', or wanted people to see its theme as 'the good old moral one of virtue rewarded in the end', because this, as far as she was concerned, was not the case, and her heroine got nothing out of being 'a virtuous prude'.[5]

Jane Our Stranger had thrust May into the limelight, and she knew how to play up to it par excellence, seeming perfectly at ease with the attention. George Bernard Shaw observed her transformation from his first meeting with her before the war when she was 'an innocent, dowdy, somewhat dull little American', into 'a brilliant, witty and wicked French woman',[6] and with Louis beside her, they made a glamorous young couple, with the promise of a brilliant future ahead of them. They were now living in what was frequently referred to as one of the finest houses in London, built by Lutyens, at 8 Little College Street, just behind Westminster Abbey and within earshot of Big Ben. With its grand entrance hall, resplendent with pillars and a marble staircase, and a dining room with a steel floor, it was both elegant and stylish, and to this they added their impressive collection of French and Italian furniture and old paintings.

But not everything was perfect on the domestic front. Douglas was still unhappy about the way his daughters were being raised and at the end of 1923 he renewed his attempt to gain custody. May's racy novels, with their depictions of bohemia, free love and infidelity, were seen among his friends and supporters as shameful evidence of her unsuitability as a parent, and more letters were written in praise of the secure and happy environment he provided for the girls when they were with him. This was not to be disputed, for he was a devoted father, but the children were once again caught in the crossfire of accusations, bitter ill feeling and rivalry between the parents they loved. Mary was particularly vulnerable because she had developed a closer relationship with Mrs Gretton, with whom she sometimes stayed without her father, an attachment that would always be viewed with suspicion by May.

Although Douglas failed in his attempt to win the children back, disagreements with May over their upbringing periodically flared up into more heated disputes, and when this happened, judicial intervention was once again seen as the only way forward.

There were other worries too. May and Louis were spending less and less time together with the different demands of their careers, and this was causing tensions in their marriage. His work obligations were unremitting and so often took priority over everything else. When they were due to spend a week together in spring 1924, at the last minute he had to cancel the arrangement, inducing May to lose all patience. 'I am furious about Vienna', she wrote to him. 'I am much more important – you have a rendezvous with me and ought not to throw me over ... you must have a rest – All this working at high pressure is hopeless.'[7] But weighed down by work worries, Louis could speak of little else when they were together and May felt oppressed by the often overcast atmosphere at home. He seemed to her a changed man from the one she had married, and she was frequently hurt by his fits of bad temper and increasing remoteness. But she, too, was preoccupied with her own career. Sometimes she simply did not have the time, or energy, or even the inclination, to support him in the way he wanted. She had started work on another novel, and after an intensive day of writing, needed to unwind by going out. As Louis was so often tied up with his parliamentary work or his other business concerns, she often went out without him, which became another source of friction.

With her marriage going through a rough patch, May began to pine for her American roots. She had not been home since Christmas 1913, long enough for her to begin to wonder where home really was. Like the narrator in *The Romantic Woman*, who reflects that 'the American lot had grown accustomed to think of me as one of the English. I perceived that I existed nowhere, and belonged to nobody', May claimed that sometimes, even in the middle of a party and surrounded by people, she could suddenly be 'overwhelmed by a feeling of loneliness, a sense of being lost, of belonging nowhere, of being a woman without a country'.[8] When the columnist A. P. Herbert visited her in Little College Street to interview her about 'that much discussed book *Jane Our Stranger* ... you may dislike it, or you may rave about it; but you cannot ignore it',[9] he dismissed her claim that she felt homesick for the Midwest, believing that her heart resided in Westminster. He was perhaps being frivolous, but even if she exaggerated her sense of being an exile, her homesickness was genuine and profound. 'It disturbs not only the surface of one's life, but attacks like an undercurrent its very foundations', was how she described its effects. 'Sometimes when that feeling overtakes me, I doubt my own identity and wonder who I am. I must be bored I say, not really homesick. But on second thought, I, who have suffered much from that malady, know that homesickness is a real illness that saps ones vitality.'[10]

It was this frame of mind that she attributed to her growing dependence on a couple called Rome, and the fact that she found herself particularly drawn to the husband, Claude, who, on some level, reminded her of her father. He reciprocated, only with the complication that he fell in love with her. He told her how unhappy he was, and that if only he could marry her, his life would be different. Her feelings towards him were confused. She was sorry for him, and his friendship was comforting, but not long after he had declared his feelings for her, she set sail for America – a trip which would show everything in a different light.

Boarding the liner with Peti and Nurse Lamb at the beginning of August 1924, May had much to be excited about. Louis was to join her in Camden, Maine, and in her joy at going home for the first time in ten years, she had planned a long list of things they would see and do together. She wanted to show him the Grand Canyon and drive into Canada; they would go camping, catch fish for their supper and fall asleep at night beneath the stars. Her brother John put a slight dampener on this daydream, advising against camping in August because of 'no shooting, poor fishing and lots of mosquitoes', but in her heightened state of feeling as she started her journey across the water, everything seemed to be imbued with an aura of romance and tranquillity. Even the cement works 'looked in the twilight like green palaces', and the moonlit sky serene. The estuary of the Thames made her think of Joseph Conrad. 'I would not have been so keenly aware of the beauty if he had not written of it', she told Louis later in a letter. 'That is one of the functions of art – to renew the heart.'

She and Louis had parted on a loving note at Liverpool Street Station and she had been filled with remorse at not supporting him enough. She knew she had not been easy to live with, often showing her exasperation with him and saying things in anger that she later bitterly regretted. She had asked him to forgive her, and believed that having made up, they were closer than ever. Now, away from him again, she felt incomplete and empty. 'It is strange how one grows into another person – We are now, Siamese twins', she wrote to him. 'I've been a selfish brute. But next winter we'll concentrate on you for a change. It's about time we did.'[11]

Her euphoric appreciation of art and beauty soon ran out of steam under the tedium of the nine-day crossing and being cooped up with her fellow passengers. Her only real pleasure was being with Peti, although, bored and restless, she made friends 'in a dull way' with a group of polo players travelling with her, but before long was complaining about them to Louis. 'A more stupid lot of men than these Polo people I have never met – They've not got an atom of brain between them – & are all suffering apparently from the most awful small-head.'

Furthermore, 'the salutary experience of being treated with utter indifference' by them, had shown her that she was a very 'uninteresting middle-aged woman' without her husband. 'No one on board has ever apparently heard of me before – I do not exist.'[12]

On her arrival in New York, though, she was treated as a celebrity and given the tributes of respect as both a successful writer, and the wife of an English politician. Soaking up the attention, she met reporters in her suite at West 58th Street where she confidently aired a breadth of views, feeling particularly well versed in the subject of the relationship between England and America. She chided the American people for misunderstanding the attitude of the English toward them, arguing that their nation was now recognized 'as the coming world power' and that the two countries shared the same ideals, and should aim to unite in a common world policy. She expressed her belief in total disarmament and in the work of the League of Nations, slipping in the fact that her husband was at that very moment in Geneva as a British delegate at a League of Nations conference on disarmament. She did not miss the chance to have a dig at the British Prime Minister, Ramsay MacDonald, and the Labour Party, criticising them for not being socialist enough, and arguing that the party had done nothing to relieve distress among the unemployed.

If it was quite unusual for a woman of that time to speak in public about world politics, she was equally happy to discuss the latest fashions or give her opinion on matters of child-rearing. She was fiercely assertive in her desire to express herself as she saw fit, confidently claiming this as her right without regard to assumptions about what was male preserve or otherwise, or of causing offence to her homeland by unfavourable comparisons. In an interview with the *New York Times*, she was critical of America for lagging behind England in its respect of individual freedom and treatment of women. She had praise for women authors in England who she felt were producing better writing than the men, and she condemned the moral crusade in America which censored so much. Sticking her neck out even further, she turned to the differences between English and American husbands, speaking up for the former, who, in her experience, treated their wives as companions, rather than dolls. Although she admired American wives for their lack of narrow-mindedness, she thought the lives of English women more normal for they did everything that men did. Her comments about relationships between the sexes were picked up by newspapers all over America and in England.

But for all her observations on marriage, she was about to discover that her own was in crisis. Louis had found evidence of Claude Rome's infatuation with her, and this had thrown him into a turmoil of jealousy and suspicion. When May heard that he was in America on business but did not intend to join her, she was devastated. She wrote him a six-sided letter in which she knew she was fighting to save her marriage and her whole world from falling apart – to say nothing of the humiliation which a public rift would cause. How was she to account for his absence when she had talked of nothing but his coming and people were expecting them everywhere? Did he not realize what the consequences would be if he stayed away? 'My family – my connections – are important people in this country', she told him, and if there was any suggestion of a rupture between them 'a scandal would swamp the country'. More than that, were her brother John to suspect, he would have nothing more to do with them and would wash his hands of their affairs. She insisted that nothing had happened between her and Claude, 'in the accepted worldly sense'. She had told Louis that she liked him, but she could not be frank because his 'nervous jealousy frightened' her, he was 'suspicious of so much'. His possessiveness exasperated her when she had to give an account of her every action and when she had given him proof of her love in so many ways.

She reminded him of how unhappy she was in London, and how often she had told him that she felt she did not belong anywhere, and of her constant longing to return to her country. She had not realized 'how deep it was and how it rendered life a strain' until she was back on American soil and felt suddenly 'an immense sense of *"bien être"*' that she had not known since she left home. She realized now that her friendship with Claude was a mistake. She was a person who 'lives much in the imagination', she told Louis, and what had held her sympathy was a resemblance to the man she had revered as a child. In America, she had found the real presence of her father and now saw how deluded she had been.

In a last desperate plea, she appealed to him not to desert her after all they had suffered to be together. She had been 'through Hell' to marry him. 'Why should I have gone thru' all that – if it was not forever? No two people could be so strongly bound together', she told him, and she had never loved him with such overwhelming tenderness as when she last left him at Liverpool Street Station. 'You looked into my face & saw the truth there – you should still believe it.'[13]

Whatever his feelings when he read this long and emotional letter, Louis could no more face life without May than she could without him, and he was persuaded to relent and make up with her. His wounded pride was not easily placated, however, and he wanted revenge. Insisting that she sever her friendship with Claude, he drafted a letter for her to send him in which his fury is palpable. 'My husband forbids you his house – with this decision I entirely agree, it is a matter of surprise to myself that I can have lacked in frankness to the one and only man I have ever or ever will care for – I cannot conceal from you that the idea of seeing you would be absolutely repugnant to me now … The only result of attempting to see me would be your getting kicked down stairs.'

***

Reconciled and together in America, the couple embarked on a hectic round of social engagements in Chicago, which showed Louis that May had not been exaggerating the preparations that had gone into his visit, or the position the Borden family held there. Wined and dined by high society and May's old debutante friends, the couple created a stir wherever they went, and everyone seemed anxious to have their share of them. 'Few visitors from London have received such a welcome in the Windy Metropolis', ran a newspaper article which finished by attributing May's particular popularity to her 'love of fun and her talent for saying amusing things'.[14] Their every movement was commented upon in the Chicago papers, including their highly awkward absence, due to a mix-up in their schedule, from a special dinner party held in their honour by her brother John and his wife. As one newspaper referred to the faux pas, 'like Banquo's ghostly presence at the feast, the spirits of General and Mrs Edward Louis Spears were all that was vouchsafed to do honour to the dinner'.

Into this hectic socialising they managed to fit a trip by themselves to the Pacific Coast, and they were about to set off for the Borden plantation, Glenwild, when Louis was summoned home for the general election. Adding an air of Hollywood glamour to the proceedings, after their ship docked at Southampton, they chartered an aeroplane to fly them to Loughborough where they dropped campaign leaflets from the air before coming in to land. Whatever the constituents made of this tactic, it failed to win Louis his seat. The Conservative candidate was elected.

9

An Extraordinarily Stirring Story

As Louis suffered political defeat, May enjoyed another success with her next novel, *Three Pilgrims and a Tinker*, published in
England by Heinemann in October 1924. The heroine, Marion
Dawnay, is Jane's opposite, a free spirit in the mould of Imogen
in *Collision*, and someone who behaves 'as if the whole of life
were a game'. Set in the English Midlands, where Marion is reluctantly taken to live by her third husband Jim – a very different
world from the cosmopolitan and bohemian existence to which
she is used – the novel explores the autobiographical theme of a
marriage drifting apart, making space for an interloper.

In a social world that revolves around the hunting set, Marion
feels isolated and lonely. With Jim increasingly remote and
silent, and so often absent from the home that he seems to have
forgotten her existence, she turns for comfort to the secretive
Captain Waring, a man who has been plagued by bad luck. At
first she is filled with pity for him, and even repelled by his aura
of unhappiness and cynicism, but then finds herself strangely
and irresistibly attracted to him, craving the peacefulness and the
'complete lovely sense of well-being' she feels in his company.
Jim is aware that he is losing his wife, but unlike Louis over the

Claude Rome affair, he remains passive. He has never found words easy, and his inarticulacy has been accentuated by his loss of self-esteem since gambling away his money and losing his job. He keeps up the façade of being someone he is not, even though he fears that Marion has discovered the truth about him, that he is weak, shy and lonely, like all the other men he knows, but who pretend to be otherwise in the belief that their women won't love them unless they are strong and ruthless.

Marion's four children – three daughters (the Pilgrims) by her earlier marriages, and the baby son (the Tinker) she shares with Jim, are deliberately modelled on May's own children, aged fifteen, fourteen, ten and three, and the title of the novel is a wry acknowledgement of the itinerant life the girls had led. She consulted them on aspects of the story, and gave their fictional counterparts a central role in the novel, with events often seen through their eyes. Much as they are portrayed with affection, however, the novel does not endorse a vision of easy maternal fulfilment. Marion often feels suffocated by the responsibilities of motherhood, but in a climactic denouement in which she and Jim are reconciled through their children, she comes to value their happiness and stability above her own need for freedom which she has always prized.

Of all the autobiographical elements in the novel, the most striking is Marion's love for her baby son which she feels with an intensity akin to being in love. In the final paragraph, Marion, aged thirty-six, as May was when she started to work on the book, meditates with regret on the swift passing of years, and feels the 'fierce longing to live furiously while there is yet time', or to be able to go back and have it all over again. In particular, she mourns the passing of her son's babyhood, and the inevitability of a separation from him over which she cannot have control. As she holds him in her arms she thinks, 'we'd like to be like this always … but we can't Tim … in just another minute you'll be a man and I will have lost you'.[1]

* * *

Although in every sense a lesser novel than *Jane Our Stranger*, for many of the critics *Three Pilgrims and a Tinker* confirmed May's talents as a writer and made her one of the most successful contemporary novelists in England and America. In London the book quickly entered the best-seller lists in company with Galsworthy's *The White Monkey* and Margaret Kennedy's *The Constant Nymph*, and was praised for its uncanny insights into human character, motives and thoughts, which a writer on the *Evening Standard* felt amounted to 'a kind of genius'. A review in the *Daily Graphic* described it as the best novel on the subject of hunting that had ever been written, and the *Sunday Times* thought it an 'extraordinarily stirring story'. In America it was reprinted before it went onto the book stands, with one reviewer being so effusive as to describe May as a 'prophet'. Shortly after its publication she was in Paris where she wrote ecstatically to Louis, 'people are all buying & talking about The Pilgrims'.[2] But she was sensitive to the contrast in their present fortunes, and was careful to reassure Louis of how much he meant to her. 'I had the same little thrill & shiver in my heart at the station today that I had in 1918 – when you met me coming from the front', she wrote to him. 'You are such an attractive man, B! And you've shown such strength of character over this election business – I admire you for it ... Darling – I adore you – you were never so absorbing to me as now.'[3]

At the end of the year, four months after they had been summoned home from America, they set sail once more across the Atlantic to spend the festive season with May's family. It was a joyful homecoming as their ship steamed into New York harbour on Christmas Eve. Her mother, now living in a newly built East River apartment, had organized a big welcome party for them, and all the trimmings of a traditional Christmas. Joyce lived in the penthouse above, which from its terrace surrounding it on all sides gave a spectacular view of the city. She had bought both floors as a duplex apartment but wisely insisted the architects remove the inside stairway between the two in order to keep her autonomy.

Although closer to her mother than May, Joyce had felt even greater pressures to conform. Aged seven when her father died, she had taken the full brunt of her mother's grief which had pushed her ever more deeply into religious intensity. By her own account, Joyce grew up behind an encircling wall of forbiddance, and as a consequence of not being allowed to dance, play cards or go to the theatre, had very few friends as a child. Her dependency on her mother was acute, to the point that any separation, even going to her cousins around the corner or to school, resulted in her being physically sick, so that for several years she had to be educated at home. The death of her brother William, to whom she was the closest in age and friendship, was such a painful shock that afterwards she remained ill for some time. Like May, though, she discovered inner resources to cope, a 'hard seed of potential independence' which kept her from giving in to her mother's desire for her to become a missionary, to which, from sheer exhaustion, she nearly succumbed.

Instead, she found her own salvation through singing and drama classes when she enrolled at Barnard College in New York City, which set her upon a stage career. There could have been nothing that would alarm her mother more than for Joyce to become a professional singer and actress, but she had a genuine talent, and followed her heart with a rebellious determination. She had learned how to deal with her mother, who apart from her religious extremes, she described as a 'perfectly normal woman of great charm and intelligence and with a latent sense of humour that would, at times, bubble up to the surface in spite of herself'.[4]

If it was alarming enough for Mary Borden to have her youngest daughter follow a seemingly dissolute career on the stage, and as if her elder daughter had not transgressed enough already,

May began the New Year preparing for an adaptation of *Jane Our Stranger* to be shown on Broadway in the autumn. She was also working on a new novel, *Jericho Sands*, and by August of that year was racing to get the proofs sent off before she left for two months in New York to oversee rehearsals of her play. Katherine Stewart was cast as the Duchess of Lorraine, and May's friend, Elsie de Wolfe, was called in to help with the set design.

On the opening night, a glittering audience of the socially and intellectually elite took their seats, and afterwards enjoyed a supper party at the Lido Venice; the next day the papers reported enthusiastically on this social event of the week, but the reviews could not have been much more damning, with almost universal agreement that the novel had not translated to the stage. May passed a very subdued morning reading notices in which she saw herself torn to shreds and described as a society amateur. Whether or not the play would have recovered from such a slating, due to the double booking of the theatre the run lasted for only four performances. Never one to dwell for long on a setback, however, she put on a brave face and declared the experience had done her good. She felt she had learned a great deal about producing for the theatre and was sure that *Jericho Sands* would dramatize well. She returned to England to find a parcel of copies hot from the press waiting for her in London, and in the meantime she had already started planning her next book.

In *Jericho Sands* May returned to the theme of religion, and this time made it pivotal to the story, dramatising the damage caused by an extreme interpretation of the Puritan creed with a love interest of repressed sexuality and set against a background of English country life and ancestral traditions. The heroine, Priscilla, has spent her childhood mediating between her mother, an evangelist, who has let herself go to the 'dangerous extremes of mysticism', and her worldly father, who dies an unbeliever. As a result of these divided loyalties, she becomes increasingly silent and reserved, and then, at the first opportunity, falls into marriage with a titled vicar called Simon, a fanatical Puritan in bitter conflict with the world, passing from her mother's influence to another equally oppressive. It is a hopeless mismatch, recalling the irreconcilable differences between Priscilla's parents and the author's own.

The story revolves around the breakdown of their marriage as Simon struggles against his passion for his wife and his fear of a vengeful God. After a miscarriage, Priscilla is warned not to risk becoming pregnant again, and Simon, seeing this as divine punishment, becomes celibate, and adopts an increasingly mystic existence. Yet he is tortured by jealousy and suspicion over his wife's friendship with Crab Willing, heir to one of the largest estates in England, from which the novel takes its title. Eventually he drives her into Crab's hands and she runs away with Crab to New Mexico, and then experiences a brief period

The family together at Bisham Abbey in 1926. Michael on his mother's lap, far left, Joyce, May, Louis, Comfort and Mary far right.

of happiness before she dies in childbirth.

Although rather let down by its melodramatic ending, it is a more serious novel than *Three Pilgrims* and, like *Jane Our Stranger*, strong on atmosphere. It is also the most complex in form and structure May had attempted. Playing with modernist preoccupations with truth, representation and the nature of reality, the novel takes the form of a confessional journal belonging to Simon in which he has written about his marriage to Priscilla, and which has subsequently fallen into the hands of her godfather who adds to it his own version of events and censors the parts of the manuscript which he thinks should not be made public. *Jericho Sands* received high praise from critics in America, with a more mixed reception in England, but by then she was already on to her next project.

Hardly pausing for breath after her debacle on Broadway, May began to think of staging *Jane Our Stranger* in London. Where others might have been put off by the slating it had received, she saw it as an incentive to do better next time. What was needed for this self-improvement, she decided, were lessons from the Italian novelist and playwright Luigi Pirandello, who during the inter-war years was at his most prolific, and at his invitation she travelled to Rome to observe his methods of theatrical production. Back in London, she joined forces with a number of others to set up the Forum Theatre Guild, a non-profit organization modelled on the New York Theatre Guild. Runs were to be limited to eight weeks, and *Jane Our Stranger* was one of the plays selected for the inaugural season at the Royalty Theatre.

At the same time, she had turned her hand to short-story writing, a form she had attempted in the past but found too restrictive. Now, in November 1926, she published a collection of ten entitled *Four O'Clock and Other Stories*. These not only reveal the influence of her time in Rome with Pirandello and his fascination with the themes of illusion and reality and the nature of identity, but he is directly referred to in one story, in which a drama of his is put on in London, giving rise to a curious case of double identity.

Ironically, May's interest in the problems of identity took an unexpected turn when one of her stories, *The Verdict*, about the survivor of a suicide pact who is charged with murder, resulted in a writ being brought against her because she had used the name of a living person. In this real-life case of mistaken identity, the plaintiff, from a socially prominent family, demanded she withdraw all copies of the book, which May and her publishers refused to do, agreeing only to change the name in the American edition and in future reprints. The writ led to a trial in 1927 and caused quite a stir. She refuted the charge of libel but, unfortunate coincidences aside, the story was inspired by a

May publicising her collection of short stories in 1926

real case she had followed some years earlier about a survivor of a suicide pact. *The Verdict* was a deliberate piece of political propaganda designed to promote Louis' attempt to introduce a bill to abolish the murder charge in such circumstances.

After his election defeat, Louis had explored a number of possible career options, none of which had come to fruition, leaving him deeply frustrated and restless. In April 1925 he had joined the Conservative Party, following the lead of Winston Churchill, who by this time was Chancellor of the Exchequer in Baldwin's government. Since then Louis had been looking for a seat, and his chance finally came in 1927 when he prepared to stand in a by-election at the mining constituency of Bosworth, in the Midlands. May went with him to help canvass support, and proposed that Mary, aged twelve, come with them for the summer term, a plan which provoked a new row with Douglas.

Now happily married to another American writer, Margaret Wilson, he remained close to his daughters, but his views on their upbringing were as much in conflict with May's as they always had been since their divorce. He disapproved of the disruption to Mary's education if she went with May, and also suspected that she had been bribed into wanting to go with promises of having her own pony and other such treats. As the antagonists were unable to agree, the argument had to be settled in court, where the judge enraged Douglas by dismissing the importance of an education for girls at all, and arguing that it was far better for his daughters not to go to university to become bluestockings, and far better for Mary to be removed from the stuffy London air for a spell in the country. Douglas had also felt unhappy about May's wish to send Joyce to a boarding school in Florence, but again the judge overruled him because Joyce expressed her desire to go.

Although Douglas did not prevent Mary from going to the Midlands, he insisted that she not be involved in any electioneering work, a role her mother dutifully took on, canvassing with vigour and giving speeches, which did not go down well with everyone. When she accompanied Louis to Coalville where he was to give a speech, she infuriated the Parliamentary and Financial Secretary to the Admiralty, Cuthbert Headlam, whose own address was interrupted half way through so that she could speak for twenty minutes in what he described as 'an outrageous American accent'.[5] Having been allowed to finish his turn, he left in disgust. May was not without some compunction herself. 'What rubbish I talked in my effort to win votes', she said later. She was in fact a witty, confident and self-possessed speaker, though she had to learn to deal with public hectoring from hostile Labour supporters which at times could be alarmingly ferocious.

Visiting mines in the Coalville district, she descended hundreds of feet below ground to chat to the miners as they worked, although she admitted to hating the violent feeling which seized her as the cage started its descent. Whatever the impression she made on constituents, however, the outcome of the election was another defeat for Louis, with the seat taken by the Liberal candidate.

May with Comfort (left) and Joyce (right) at home in Little College Street.

10

The Forbidden Zone

May once described the experience of writing a book as like having 'an attack of typhoid fever with headaches and fits of depression.' If this was the case, it was a torment she put herself through with masochistic regularity. Such was her extraordinary output that at the same time as the reviews were still coming out for *Four O'Clock*, and while she carried out the usual round of interviews to promote it, she was staying up half the night to finish a first draft of her next book *Flamingo*.

She rarely seemed to suffer from writer's block or from a lack of ideas, and often had another novel brewing while she worked on her present one, first waiting until it was mapped out in her head before making a start. She always felt restless until she began a new book, and once she knew what she wanted to write, she worked in a burst of frenzied creativity, but she redrafted her novels many times before she was satisfied with them, and claimed that at this stage of the process she felt miserable when she was working and miserable when she was not. Although her desire to write was compulsive, she was extremely disciplined and she saw it as a matter not of inspiration but of mental industry.

With her usual redrafting, almost another year passed before *Flamingo* was published in October 1927, and it became one of her most successful novels. Moving the stage to New York, she evokes the 'gigantic magnetic power of the city's energy' in a 'boisterous, bumptious, incredibly aspiring, tumultuous age'.[1] The principal character, Peter Campbell, is one of the most gifted architects in America, a highly strung and imaginative man who has an idea of creating a skyline of beautiful towers rising a thousand feet into the sky, a 'single unified plan' encompassing the whole of Manhattan Island, more 'wonderful than Thebes or Babylon'.

Peter has been in love with a woman he met as a child in Cornwall. Over the next thirty-four years he has caught glimpses of her three times. She has haunted his unconscious to the extent that he has designed and decorated an almost mirror image of her house in England after he has dreamed about it. Their paths finally cross again when she accompanies her husband to New York when he comes to talk to the President about war debts. Frederika is the long-suffering wife of Victor Joyce, a British member of parliament, a 'pompous bore', overbearing and selfish, and only interested in his work. She would have liked to have been cared for 'a little more' by her husband, 'but it was absurd to blame Victor for being more absorbed in England than in his wife. It was that concentration of his that she admired, and who was she, to rival the British Empire in a man's mind. Truly she must have a high opinion of herself.'[2]

The enigmatic Frederika, who 'somehow stands for a whole procession of women, to represent something strong, enduring and obstinate',[3] is a typical Borden heroine, but like her early predecessor Susan Digby in *Collision*, she has repressed her true nature to fit in with the life expected of her. She is a woman of 'quick intelligence', who has a fascination for the sciences, and would like to study mechanics at college, an idea regarded as both silly and unsuitable by her husband and society, which believes that 'a taste for tinkering with machinery and an interest in atmosphere or the theory of radioactivity was almost a deformity in a woman'.[4] In the world she has grown up in, women's 'brains were not worth bothering about'[5] and cut off from all her interests she becomes increasingly withdrawn.

This aspect of the novel has echoes of *The Yellow Wallpaper* by another American writer, Charlotte Perkins, in which the narrator, recovering from depression, is forced by her physician husband to give up all intellectual pursuits, and remain confined to a room as a rest cure, where she descends into madness. Although not as extreme, *Flamingo* captures the psychic effects of repression as Frederika's spirit is slowly crushed, and any self-confidence she has is gradually eroded by her husband's attempts to control all aspects of her life: 'One couldn't live with a man like Victor and not be flattened out, that was all. If you got in his way you were rolled out flat and there was an end of it. She had tried, so she knew.'[6] Worn down by him, she is finally 'too tired to struggle anymore',[7] and the 'passivity which she had cultivated as her one safety, hers and Victor's, had now sunk into her bones and become a deep ingrained instinctive thing'.[8] 'She had not been really very well lately. Nerves probably. She had quite absurd fits of depression, difficult to deal with and very tiring.'[9]

Peter Campbell is married to a butterfly wife whose life revolves around New York society which he despises, and from which he escapes whenever possible to the sweaty jazz clubs and his friendships with the black musicians. His mother has also sacrificed her life for her husband and children, subordinating all her own desires and interests to theirs.

Besides the bitter portrait of wasted female potential, *Flamingo* is a novel of ideas and thematic contrasts – such as that between the brash New World of America and backward-looking, 'old, polished and worldly wise England'.[10] The *New York Times* thought it the best novel ever written about New York although L. P. Hartley writing in the *Saturday Review* felt there was a suggestion of hysteria simmering throughout. The

Times thought it was a notable achievement, a view shared by Cyril Connolly who wrote a glowing review in the *New Statesman*. After this endorsement of her work, he struck up a friendship with May and was no less taken with her than he was by her novel, later describing her as a 'woman of exquisite elegance and chic, simple, cordial, ironic'.[11] She introduced him to her eldest daughter, Joyce, who became one of his closest friends.

May's campaign for equal rights and opportunities for women remained a feature of her novels. On a more personal level, *Flamingo* reflects something of her own frustrations in trying to pursue a career that she took very seriously, against the demands of an extremely full family life and all the responsibilities of domesticity, as well as supporting her husband's career, even if it compromised her own, for however much she liked to push the boundaries, there was still a clear division of labour in her own home. With Comfort and Mary attending St Paul's Girls' School, in West London, as day scholars, and Peti still a small child, it was a typically busy and lively household, with all the perils of the pram-in-the-hallway syndrome cited by Cyril Connolly as the enemy of the artist. As May later wrote, Louis, as the man of the house, had the sanctum of the study on the ground floor. She tried to write several hours each day, mostly working at a folding table in her bedroom, to the sounds of small feet stamping about overhead. If it was not possible to be at her desk, May wrote wherever she could hold a pen to paper (whether in bed or the back of a taxi) and if forced to put these down, she maintained the flow in her head composing dialogue even while fulfilling her duties at some social function, although she did once forget to turn up to her own house party at Ascot because she was engrossed in her work. In a letter to her aunt, Joyce affectionately refers to her mother sitting on a sofa where she is scribbling away at her latest novel, so absorbed that she hears not a word that is said to her. The middle of the night gave her the needed peace and quiet for writing, when, after a busy day, she relied on copious cups of coffee to keep her awake, after which she liked to unwind by reading Edgar Wallace.

When the author Elizabeth Russell observed her writing conditions, she was appalled, and May believed that her friend's sense of anger on her behalf was the inspiration for her book *Vera*, later saying that this 'bitter story of a fatuous egotistical husband had more than a little to do with her wish to save me from the fate of a normally occupied wife and mother'.[12] Elizabeth was certainly concerned enough to offer her house to May when she was away to allow her the solitude she needed to finish a novel. May accepted with gratitude, but when a few months later Elizabeth advised her to cut loose from home commitments altogether to concentrate on her writing, she could not bring herself to sacrifice her family for it, or for that matter, anything else.

She loved and needed variety in life. She was a vigorous social campaigner, sat on various boards, and was involved with fund raising for different charities. She wrote regularly for newspapers and journals on both sides of the Atlantic, using these forums to promote her various causes, in particular, poverty action, women's rights, penal reform and the care of juvenile criminals. Divorce law reform was a particular bugbear, and she frequently attacked the British government for not doing more to alleviate unnecessary suffering by making it possible for two people to divorce simply on the grounds that they both wanted to. Besides political speeches, she was often asked to give lectures and to address meetings on a wide range of subjects, and it became a fairly frequent observation in newspaper articles that she had so many different roles it was hard to know how she fitted everything in. Only Lady Astor was seen to live her life as energetically. In contradiction to her hectic way of life and extraordinary energy, interviewers frequently commented upon the impression she gave of composure, with her calm and repose and languorous movements accentuated by her slow speech.

As for her regular holidays and trips abroad, May, who had

always been an intrepid traveller and loved adventure, saw travel writing as a niche worth exploiting; included in her various pieces were a series she wrote for the *Evening Standard* when in 1924 she toured Spain, a country which in those times was untrammelled by tourists. Any experience had earning potential but the desire to share and communicate through writing was second nature to her.

Later May would say that she regretted that she had allowed herself to be too easily distracted from her writing, by events both big and small, and that had she lived less and done less, she might have written better books; but she recognized that becoming a hermit could have been counter-productive, drying up the creative process. She needed to engage actively with the world for inspiration, rather than shutting herself away from it.

In *Flamingo* Frederika is expected to be her husband's most faithful political supporter and for twenty years has been kept in bondage to 'a view of life and a political creed that irritated and bored her'.[13] This is a sentiment echoed in later novels, but May remained faithful to her promise to support Louis with his parliamentary work, and juggled this and other roles with a degree of organization which came naturally to her. She was of course reliant on help in running the house and looking after the children, and it was a particularly sad day for all when, in April 1927, Nurse Lamb left. Louis wrote in his diary that he felt Peti had lost his best friend, and nothing would quite be the same again. 'That supreme sense of safety and care nurse gave him will no longer be his, nor will we have that sense of security again ourselves.'[14] Her absence was all the more acutely felt because Peti was unwell at the time. 'His mother is frantic with anxiety', Louis wrote. Not without good cause, for Peti was of delicate constitution. During the summer of 1928, he developed an alarmingly high fever and severe headaches. Louis was on holiday in a rented villa near Villefranche in the south of France, where May kept him informed about his son's condition.

Finally able to report that Peti was over the crisis, she admitted how terribly anxious she had been. 'For me the world looks quite different now – it was black and dreadful all those days last week.' The doctors diagnosed a very low immunity to infections and recommended that he should live in the countryside for at least a year.

The worry over for the time being, May joined Louis in France who was there with Nancy Maurice and a house full of guests. Joyce, now returned from Italy, was there with Cyril Connolly, who amused himself by drawing up a list of attributes by which to assess those present with marks out of ten. He gave May 4 for charm and sex appeal, and 6 for intelligence, virtue and guts. Nancy scored 0 for the first two, 3, 8, and 6 for the last three. Only Bernard Shaw scored lower, coming last in each category.[15]

Before she left for France, May had sent Charley Evans, the managing director at Heinemann, the first chapters of the novel she was working on, about which she was having doubts. It was ambitious in scope, encompassing a Darwinian account of life on earth, from the beginning of time to the twentieth century, and using the cosmos as a backdrop to highlight the helplessness of humans in the grip of natural forces, and against which modern-day civilization is seen in decay and atrophy. In this cautionary tale of human recklessness and folly, the species is presented as 'one of Nature's most unfortunate and abortive experiments, destined to join the enormous extinct company of biological failures'.

In the closer frame, the setting is England, at the time of the General Strike, where the cast of characters is divided between the wealthy and the poor. People are perceived as their animal ancestors, allowing the author to satirize certain Mayfair types, whose indolent and superficial lives are contrasted with the poverty and hardship experienced by the colliers and their families. Included are descriptions of the working conditions underground, informed by May's contact with the mining community at Bosworth. It is another multi-stranded novel, meshing contemplation on the future of the human race, with the political, scientific, philosophical, mythological and occult, a project on a grand scale and difficult to pull off. Evans was enthusiastic and encouraged her to keep going with the book, which, he told her, had 'more fundamental brain-work to the page than the whole output of many successful novelists'. He did not think that the unusualness of her method would disturb any intelligent reader, though 'heaven knows what your public, and the reviews are going to think', he added, 'it will flutter a good many dovecotes'.[16]

Research for the novel took her to London Zoo and to Scotland, where she stayed with Professor Thomson of Aberdeen University to discover more about Erypos and Darwinian theory. The book took her the best part of a year to complete and when *Jehovah's Day* was published in the late autumn of 1928, the reviewers admired her originality and daring, and declared it provocative, challenging and powerful, even if not all liked the result; Cyril Connolly thought she should stick to the cosmopolitan world of her previous novels. Described by one reviewer as 'the queerest novel of the year', it was certainly a feat of the imagination, although her insights on the destruction of the planet because of human greed and profligate use of natural resources show once again how forward-looking a thinker she was.

She had put a huge effort into the writing of *Jehovah's Day*, working on it in a state of extreme nervous apprehension and retreating to a bungalow on the south-east coast of Kent in order to wrestle with it, taking only Peti and his nurse for company, and existing on a heavy caffeine diet. She was reminded of Balzac, who when writing *La Vie Prodigieuse* had locked himself up with his manuscript for forty-eight hours and by the second dawn the room resembled a battlefield. When she had got to the end of her own self-imprisonment, it was back to another exhausting round of political activity.

In June 1929 Louis stood for parliament at Carlisle in a campaign dominated by class conflict. Once again May was tireless in supporting her husband, canvassing all day long and sometimes making three or four speeches a night, often against rowdy heckling and boos from socialist supporters – a contrast to her usual reception as guest speaker at literary events where she was treated with admiration and awe as one of the most prominent writers of the day.

After another draining campaign, in which the socialist candidate was elected, they were glad to get away for a family holiday aboard Louis' yacht, *The Bittern*. All the Borden children had inherited their father William's love of sailing; John built a 140-foot schooner which he christened the *Northern Light*, and with his wife Courtney, took on an expedition to the Arctic in 1927. May and Louis settled for something less adventurous, taking *The Bittern* across to France and the Channel Islands, inviting various friends to join them. One of their guests was A. P. Herbert who wrote a series of articles for *Punch*, describing in comic tone life aboard the ship with its 'crew of six, electric light and every modern convenience', including the innovation of a gas-fuelled ice-maker which proved to be a dismal failure when it leaked its contents, sending the paraffin stove into flames and filling the saloon with black smoke.

May's earnings from her books were not enough to sustain the standard of life to which she was accustomed, but she wrote out of a need to keep challenging herself, and to maintain an identity beyond domesticity and her duties as a wife. These reasons for writing gave way to a much more pressing motivation when in 1929 the American stock market went into free fall. May's brother, John, who had always managed her financial interests, saw his fortune wiped out and, like many others, tried to save his situation by raising more money for investments. He asked May for a loan from her capital of $125,000, optimistic that the downward trend would reverse and all would be well, and she was determined to see him through the difficult time.

Although in recent years she and Louis had had to curb their expenses, including letting go of their beloved rue Monsieur, this loan to her brother, and the Wall Street Crash, threatened their financial security in a new and alarming way, and May's literary earnings now became a vital source of income. Her sister Joyce survived the crash unscathed due to her pragmatism in the months before, ignoring the excited advice of friends to speculate, and consequently held on to her share of their father's fortune. Unlike her mother and sister, she also declined to lend her brother money, rightly anticipating that it would disappear into a bottomless pit, although she helped him out by buying *Northern Light*. Not long after she took her husband, the Croatian violinist, Zlatko Baloković, on a world concert tour, at the same time fulfilling her dream of an ocean voyage.

With money worries pressing, it was no doubt partly with her eye on the book market that May chose this time to pull out the manuscript *The Forbidden Zone* and prepare it for publication, observing that the time appeared right for the public to hear the truth about the war. She believed *All Quiet on the Western Front*, first published in January 1929, had helped other writers to tell the truth and to 'strip the glamour from modern warfare', and the fact that Erich Maria Remarque's book was in such demand was, she said, 'the most encouraging thing in the book world for a long time'.[17] She made substantial changes to the manuscript she had prepared in 1917, rewriting and amalgamating some of the prose pieces and omitting others altogether, including a lengthy prologue that took the form of a poem, and adapting the preface with the effect of making it less raw; like other writers who published their war memoirs after a long interlude, the passage of time enabled her to adopt a greater degree of emotional detachment, although the directness of her accounts of suffering, chaos and brutality retained all their original power.

She also left out the sonnets which she had written for Louis, and a vignette in the form of a dialogue between an officer and his lover meeting in secret which juxtaposes sexual passion with the violence of war. In their place, she included the poems she had published in the *English Review*, and to her collection of sketches and poems written between 1914 and 1918 she added five short stories.

The Forbidden Zone had a mixed critical reception. On the one hand there was praise for its remarkable sense of detachment, while others found it too highly wrought. What earned it further comment was the fact that it was written by a woman, and one who had first-hand experience of life at the front. Oliver Way in the *Graphic* said he would like to see it sold by the hundred million such was its importance. But others thought differently. Published at the same time as *The Forbidden Zone* was a rush of books about the war, including Hemingway's *A Farewell to Arms*, prompting a storm of protest in the media about the shameful lack of taste demonstrated by the publication of frank war memoirs, which in turn set off a public debate about whether or not they should be read. Having encountered suppression of her work in 1917 in France, America and England, May was disgusted by the uproar, and by the fact that people still felt that the truth should be stifled. To her it was nothing less than immoral that the awfulness of war should be minimized by writers to protect the sensibilities of some – a view she made very clear in various newspaper and magazine articles, including one in the *Sphere*, in which she referred to war as the 'new taboo'.[18]

Louis had also turned his hand to writing, giving his account of the opening stages of the war in his book *Liaison 1914*, published in September 1930. It sold well, earning him a reputation as an authority on the Great War and raising his profile as he prepared to stand in Carlisle at the next general election. At the same time, May published *A Woman with White Eyes*, which received a less rapturous reception than her husband's book. It was another experimental novel in which the story is told in a series of memory flashbacks, and some reviews expressed the feeling that its intricate plot and stylistic innovations had resulted in a confusing novel, detracting from its power. The *New York Evening Post* thought it a 'brilliant and subtle piece of writing', but that the author had been carried away by her 'confidence in her own skills and virtuosity', giving in too often to the temptation to 'mystify and excite her readers', at the expense of the 'homely virtues of clarity and simplicity'. The *New York Times* agreed, but had praise for the skill and originality that had gone into its creation, and felt that even if it puzzled readers at times, it would not fail to interest them.

At the end of October May sailed to America in the *Britannic* for the launch there of *A Woman with White Eyes*, kicking off with a party given by her publishers, Doubleday. In New York she took part in a public debate about manners with Ford Madox Ford who was quoted in the papers as greeting her with the words, 'It is just five-thousand, nine hundred and forty-eight days since I last saw you', to which she replied dryly, 'You have a good memory.'

In Chicago, the chance to hear her speak at the Arts Club on the subject of literary London attracted such a large crowd that one hundred people had to be turned away. Her reflections on London's inner literary guild were candid. She enlightened the crowd on the differences between the two dominant literary circles, Chelsea and Bloomsbury, admitting to finding the latter rather intimidating. It was elitist, she told her rapt audience, and outsiders were rarely taken in. She certainly did not belong, and did not want to, for it was 'too wild and woolly' in its mood, and anyway, she was 'anathema' to Bloomsbury. 'When they found I had published a book a year for ten years, they didn't know what to make of it', she continued. Virginia Woolf, though, she considered the greatest living artist in English fiction.

She finished her book tour in America with a visit to an oil field near the Canadian border where John had sunk several wells, one of which he told her was yielding over five-hundred barrels a day. Believing that better financial times were just around the corner, May set sail for England in a cheerful mood. Once her boat had docked on 11 December, she was plunged back into campaigning for Louis, travelling immediately to Carlisle to give a speech at a big political meeting.

Michael with his constant companion

11

Family Matters

On the home front, the older children were growing up and developing independent lives. Brought up in a household steeped in literature and politics, where they were exposed to lively conversation about the arts, current affairs and philosophical ideas, they were well informed and articulate, winning scholarships and academic prizes. May had always encouraged them to speak several languages, one of her reasons being that she believed this was essential for a good understanding of literature (although when Joyce wanted to read Proust, she advised her not to, telling her he would give her 'mental indigestion') and all the children were fluent in at least two.

Joyce had a formidable intellect, passing top in her matriculation, and in her first term at Somerville College, Oxford, where she read Modern Greats, she earned a reputation as someone very outspoken and extremely gifted. She spoke fluent French, German and Italian and taught herself Russian by reading a Bible in that language with the English version beside her. She wrote poetry in French and English. She possessed May's imaginative gifts, but with a raw sensitivity that often made life unbearably painful for her and could throw her into deep fits of despair. Her erudition was matched by an unusually mature wisdom. When Comfort went to Oxford to study agriculture and became unofficially engaged to a young man whom May felt to be unsuitable, Joyce wrote a letter in which she counselled her mother against trying to break up the affair, and guided her with perceptive insights about how best to deal with the situation in order that it come to a natural end.

Temperamentally, Comfort was cheerfully open and self-assured, with an uncomplicated attitude to life, and seemed to be on a more even keel than either of her sisters, for Mary, too, showed signs of instability and had to leave her boarding school at West Malvern for a term due to acute anxiety. May had often given her views on child-rearing in magazines and newspaper articles. In theory she argued the importance of allowing children their freedom and letting them make their own decisions, but in practice she exercised a powerful influence and was possibly never fully aware of the impact of her forceful character upon them.

With Peti she was particularly over-protective – a tendency intensified by his physical frailty. When in May 1930, he left home for West Downs, a boarding school in Winchester, his parents were inconsolable. After seeing him off on the train, Louis unburdened himself (ungrammatically) in his diary: 'The misery of his mother and I is not for this book but it seems unendurable.'[1] Their distress was heightened by a homesick letter from Peti who was finding his new surroundings 'perfectly beastly'. They responded immediately with a telegram to the headmaster, Mr Tindell, the first of many anxious enquiries he was to receive from them over the coming months. Fortunately he seemed to know how to dispense the same kind but firm good sense as Nurse Lamb, empathising and reassuring in equal measure. But their concern was such that even these assurances were not enough to prevent them from visiting Peti at the weekend, and this action only served to unsettle them all.

He appeared distant and ill at ease with his parents and,

in his father's opinion, less glad of their presence than many of the other boys with theirs. Louis' sense of rejection was compounded when he visited his son's dormitory and observed that the photograph he had given him of himself had been put out of sight. After they left him, they felt engulfed in intolerable unhappiness. 'We are like two v lonely people drifting in a v small boat towards the twilight', Louis recorded. 'We miss Nannie terribly too', he added, later writing to tell her about their distressing visit to see Peti, including the fact that her photograph had pride of place. 'Don't worry about your photo being behind the others', she wrote back, before explaining, with her usual diplomacy, that the only reason her picture was favoured, was because it showed her holding Peti's beloved dog Dud.

Although stricken with worry and grief, May and Louis encouraged Peti to stick it out at school, albeit with the promise that if he really could not settle, they would take him away. This did not turn out to be necessary, but both parents were distressed by the change in his attitude towards them. This did not improve on subsequent visits, during which he seemed 'devoid of affection' and 'extremely reserved'. May's view was that he was unhappy without realizing it, and that he worried too much, something his father felt he had inherited from himself. Joyce thought he was too highly strung, and the headmaster described him as an extremely sensitive boy and feared this would make life difficult for him. Indeed, he was of a very tender disposition and having always been doted on by his parents and older siblings, teasing from other boys came as a brutal shock. After a visit from his beloved Nurse Lamb, one of the boys called her 'common', and his response was extreme in its hurt and indignation – poured out in a barely legible two-page letter to his parents – some of it written under his blanket to avoid the jeers from the other boys in the dormitory. He incited more teasing when he knelt by his bed to pray.

His letters show how very attached he was to his family, and how vulnerable in their absence. Louis, though, felt he could detect a fundamental change for the worse in his son's character as a result of his introduction to boarding school, and wrote him a letter chiding him for his spoilt behaviour. It was a relief for all when the summer holidays arrived and Peti reverted to his old affectionate self.

Although the news from America with the continuing depression was very bleak, finances were not so tight as to prevent May from giving Louis as a birthday present the charter of a small boat, a 12-ton Thorneycroft yacht, and on 22 August 1931, they set off in it for a family cruise along the French coast. At first all went well as they stopped to picnic on beaches, or for meals at little restaurants, albeit with a strict eye to economy; they fished, cooked bouillabaisse, swam and read and lazed in the sun. Then a series of calamities ruined the idyll. First May started a fire with a spirit lamp she was using to cook supper; then a mistral marooned them without supplies for several days, and finally Louis fell overboard, injuring his arm, forcing them to abandon ship and decamp to a hotel where he could receive treatment twice a day.

May had waited twelve years to publish her war experiences in *The Forbidden Zone*, and she followed this up with *Sarah Gay* (published as *Mary Defiance* in America), a fictional account of these times. Although there are descriptions of life at the front, the real focus of the novel is the eponymous heroine's love for a young captain. Like May, Sarah is married with daughters, and when she chooses to leave her husband, she sacrifices the children too. It is a novel about moral choices, but the camouflage of fiction allowed May to explore a different outcome. When one of Sarah's daughters becomes ill, she returns to England to care for her. Tormented by guilt, she gives up her lover to stay with her family. In the end, though, May was unable to resist a happy ending, killing off the first husband, a plot progression which enabled the lovers to be reunited with clear consciences.

Noël Coward told May that he thought that the confessional nature of *Sarah Gay* made it her best novel to date, but when it was published at the beginning of October 1931, she was distressed by the generally unenthusiastic reviews. Rebecca West wrote in the *Daily Telegraph* that the book had left her with a feeling of emptiness because its study of human beings was too simplified. Her literary judgement clearly mattered to May, for she was particularly upset by her words – not least, one can assume, because it was the opposite effect she strived for in her psychological character studies.

Writing from Carlisle, where Louis was standing as a National Conservative in the general election, she expressed her disappointment to Charley Evans, who did his best to bolster her spirits, recommending her not to worry about the reviews. 'Nearly all these critics are novelists manqués and Rebecca, who has always seemed to me to be an extremely complicated person, is probably entirely incapable of understanding what you were getting at in this book.'[2] The public, he assured her, were not taking much notice of the critics and a total of 6,500 copies had been sold since its publication, and it was already being reprinted.

Nevertheless, with an increasingly urgent need to raise money, May was unable to dismiss the critics quite as sanguinely. Scanning the newspapers each day, she was more alarmed when there seemed no mention of *Sarah Gay* at all. 'I don't want to let this book die on our hands without an effort', she told Charley on her return from the north of England at the end of October. Although she was slightly encouraged that it was among the six books most asked for at *The Times* Book Club that month, she was unhappy with her publishers for not creating enough interest in it. She had taken an active role in promoting the novel herself, enlisting the help of Gordon Selfridge, who had promised to give the book a prominent window display in his London department store and invited her to join his list of famous people by inscribing her name upon his window.[3] But laid up in bed for a week after her time in the north, she continued to fret about sales. 'It does really seem to me as if most other publishers did much more advertising than Heinemann',[4] she complained to Charley. She was impressed by Victor Gollancz, who she thought 'the brightest lad' in the field, and whom she knew had increased Naomi Royde-Smith's sales 'in a startling way since he became her publisher'. Charley was more concerned that she was wearing herself out. 'I was afraid you would have a reaction to all that work in Carlisle',[5] he wrote on hearing that she had returned unwell. It had all been worthwhile, though, for Louis won his parliamentary seat.

In spite of sales from *Liaison* helping to swell the family income, more economies had to be made, and May and Louis sold the lease on Little College Street, moving to a less expensive and far smaller house in John Street, Mayfair. All the same, life with less money was hard and in the continuing financial depression, John prevailed upon May for more of her securities, until, in July 1932, he asked for her last remaining reserves, which were her share of the Glenwild estate.

As well as her books, she wrote prolifically for journals and newspapers on both sides of the Atlantic, remaining an interested observer of cultural differences, although, according to her old friend, Ford Madox, she seemed to have become a little less outspoken in her criticisms when she was on home soil. When he was invited to take part in the world debate with her in New York on her visit in 1930, he landed the task of defending the American woman, but was deprived of his chance to be a knight in shining armour. 'It was rather a bum show really', he wrote later, 'because when Mary got there she refused flatly to attack her compatriots. It was of course one thing to be bitchy from the safe distance of Westminster but another to do it here in the middle of her family. So it was rather a funeral for the world's reporters.'[6]

***

May's next project was to join a group of celebrated women writers, including Rebecca West, Gertrude Stein and Storm Jameson, to contribute to a collection of semi-humorous, tongue-in-cheek essays about men for a book entitled *Man Proud Man*, published by Hamish Hamilton in April 1932. Using the story of Samson and Delilah to frame a discussion on the shifting balance of power between men and women through the ages, May argues in her essay that 'man the master' is an illusion that has been 'fostered assiduously both by the women of the world who know it to be so and by the men who suspect fearfully that it may be'.[7]

Many of her points are those that she had dramatized in her novels, and written about in journalistic form, but the collective force of these women's essays came as a shock to some people. Vita Sackville-West did not see why anyone should feel insulted, since in her opinion the tone of the essays was of 'compassionate sympathy for men for having had their noses put out of joint in recent years by the sudden energy of women'; and certainly some critics took it in good spirit, finding it hard to take umbrage when the writing was so 'delightfully witty, so shrewdly observed and so entirely good humoured'. A response from J. B. Priestley, and another from Aldous Huxley, taking up two pages in the *Spectator*, were less benign, and one male reviewer was evidently so injured that he resorted to lashing out with the misguided claim that most of the essay writers were spinsters and therefore still in a 'virgin state' and thus lacking proof for their arguments.

With the need for another quick money-earner, May returned to non-fiction for her next project, a book on the topic of matrimony, on which she had plenty to say. It was nevertheless a venture that soon wore thin. 'I'm on the last chapter of my domestic pot boiler and am sick of the very thought of marriage', she confessed to Noël Coward.[8] *The Technique of Marriage*, published in January 1933, was controversial in its attitudes to divorce (should be made easier) and marriage (should be made harder) and sex. When May's mother learned about it, she was so upset by its contents that she bought up every copy she could find, instructing her friends in the Church to do the same, and burned the lot.

One can understand why she took offence. Marriage, May argues, is not necessary for a sex life, for 'the demands of sex can be satisfied quite well without it and outside it, and are'. She chastises the Church for its inconsistency in its pronouncement on marriage, and blasts the 'barbarism' of the Christian ceremony with its idea of male possession, describing the white veil as 'an ancient relic', which has survived to make the woman's 'purity seem infinitely mysterious and precious'. In all, her book takes the view that 'married life is not a natural life',[9] although her objective in writing it was to 'persuade the mass of normal men and women in the world who marry people they are fond of, to be sensible about marriage, to keep a sense of humour and a sense of proportion in this difficult relationship'.[10] The idealism with which May had approached her union with Louis had given way to a more pragmatic acceptance of its reality, but also the belief that although 'passion fades ... happiness can last'.[11]

In *The Technique of Marriage* there are snippets of information about May's life, including some family portraits which give a taste of the Borden household. There is an endearing glimpse of Joyce as a young adult, described by May as a free spirit, unbounded by the mores of convention, highly creative and spontaneous, who, whenever she visited, descended upon the house like a whirlwind, creating chaos all around her. She invariably arrived hungry, having forgotten, or not been bothered, to eat a square meal for several days, with her hair in wild disorder, clothes 'smeared with paint', her 'shoes down at heel' and 'holes in her stockings', and affectionately throwing her arms around her mother and dropping bundles of objects onto the floor. 'It doesn't occur to her to pick things up', wrote

May. 'She doesn't notice; neither do I when she is talking, she is too enchanting to listen to.' In her description of finding Joyce in their library, absorbed in writing an essay, there is benevolent resignation at her working habits: 'She is sitting on the floor waving a dripping fountain-pen above my pretty Chinese rug, with a burning cigarette propped up in front of her on a matchbox. There are half a dozen ashtrays in the room; one is on the low table within reach of her hand, but she has used none of them; the strewn papers round her are covered with ash and cigarette ends.'[12] May saw her daughter as a brilliant and gifted bohemian whose behaviour she had learned to accept. 'She can't help being like that. If I tried to make her different I would fail, and I would do her harm. I don't want to harm her, put her in a conventional straitjacket. She is an artist, she has a spark of the divine fire; I must not put it out.'[13]

Joyce had wisely counselled her mother not to put pressure on Comfort to break off her courtship with her Oxford suitor in case it had the opposite effect – an approach which allowed her time to come to this decision herself. She had graduated from agricultural college with ambitions to become a writer, but in the meantime found work as a typist in the London office of Heinemann, where at a garden party given by the company, she met the publisher Rupert Hart-Davis. He had seen her sitting alone under a tree, and had gone over to her thinking she might be Daphne du Maurier but was nonetheless delighted by his mistake as he stayed chatting to her. The mutual attraction was immediate, but Rupert had his work cut out in seeing off a serious rival for her affections before they finally wed at the end of November 1933.[14]

When May was forty-six she began to talk about a new novel she was planning which, she told Charley Evans, was quite different from anything she had ever done before and which, as far as she knew, no-one else had attempted. She claimed that the seeds of the idea had come to her during her world tour, before her first marriage, when she journeyed through Palestine on horseback, camping along the way. One evening at Galilee, as she walked beside the moonlit water, it suddenly occurred to her that she was standing in the very spot where two thousand years before, a man who had changed the world had stood, and that in spite of her religious upbringing, she knew very little about his life. All that she had been taught about Jesus of Nazareth had failed to make him seem real, a man of history. No one had explained to her how, at a moment 'when his nation was seething with unrest, he had set out to save the people only to find all the forces of the world, religious, political and economic allied against him'.

At that stage of her life she had not felt brave enough to attempt the task of writing about the life of Jesus, and as time passed, the idea slipped from her consciousness. Twenty years later, reflecting upon various themes for novels, she decided that she wanted to write on the subject of mother and son, and it occurred to her that there had never been an example of this relationship as tragic as that of Mary of Nazareth and her son Jesus. It seemed then that her longing to know the facts about the life of Jesus had haunted her since that evening in Galilee, and that the sermons she had listened to had only left her with a maddening sense of curiosity.

The book that had been lying dormant at the back of her mind for many years sprang into focus, inspired by her desire to understand the human Mary, the person torn between her love for her wayward son and her loyalties to her family and religious traditions as a devout Jewess raised under Mosaic Law. She wanted to put her at the centre of the narrative and to give an account of the life of Mary of Nazareth which filled in the silences about the events leading up to her son's death, as it must have seemed from her perspective. This, she believed, was what made it original in concept.

There was, however, another important catalyst for what was to become *Mary of Nazareth*. Her mother had read *A Woman with*

White Eyes and afterwards had written to May to say it upset her because it offered no hope to readers, and suggested that she consider writing a book based on the Gospels. She may have been thinking of the pious classic, *The Wide Wide World*, written by another descendant of the Whiting family, and the first best-seller in America's history, which brought true a prediction that 'Providence would take care of this book' to ensure it became widely available for the good of mankind. It, too, was a book written to save the writer and her family from financial ruin. Whether or not May had read it, she took her mother's suggestion to heart, later saying that she had written *Mary of Nazareth* for her – an indication of how much she had come to terms with their past antagonisms. This reconciliatory offering came too late, however, for in May 1933, while she was still working on it, her mother died, having been unwell for some time.

In writing *Mary of Nazareth* May had found a story which encapsulated themes of particular interest and relevance to her, and one in which her enduring preoccupation with religion found a new and precisely focused outlet. Immersing herself in research, she read everything she could about the history of the period, trying to wipe from her mind her early religious education. When she studied the Bible and the Gospels as historical documents, she became enthralled, seeing everything with fresh eyes, and finding behind the religious teaching 'clues to a political and racial drama of absorbing interest'.

With few details about Mary's life available, she invented some minor incidents and characters, but blended the imagined with biblical quotations, and material from the Old and New Testament, the Apocrypha, the Hebrew Prayer Book and the Talmud. She knew that some people might take offence at her use and interpretation of sources, particularly her presentation of Jesus as an older sibling, which challenged the age-old notion of the Virgin Mary's virginity. Attempting to pre-empt hostility over this contentious issue, she included a preface explaining her decision-making, using quotations from the Gospels of Mark and Matthew which refer to the brothers and sisters of Jesus. Justifying her stand on this controversy, which she pointed out had 'agitated the minds of theologians for many centuries', she wanted to make it clear that her purpose was not to question the authenticity of recorded facts or to compare the reliability of sources, acknowledging that she would not have been qualified to do so, even if she wished. For added weight, a bibliography indicated the scale of her background reading.

By autumn 1933 the long-conceived novel was finally ready for publication. She had invested a great deal of herself in writing it, both intellectually and emotionally, and she had enjoyed the challenge. Now she waited to see how it would be received by the critics.

12

A Catholic Commotion

If first reactions to *Mary of Nazareth* were anything to go by, its impact was all May and her publishers could have hoped for. On 23 November, she received an excited letter from Doubleday, commenting on the rather remarkable letters they had received, with interest from highly regarded people who had not paid attention to any of their books in years.[1] That morning they had had an advance copy of the next Sunday's edition of the *Herald-Tribune* with a review from the influential Unitarian minister and social activist, Dr John Haynes Holmes – someone who almost never gave their books a mention – and he had given it a lengthy and glowing write-up, commending May's treatment of her material, her careful research of place and period, and describing it as a work which commanded attention and respect as an authentic piece of historical interpretation. In his view, May had produced a work of literary quality, composed with a sure sense of beauty.

Holmes' positive review reflected the majority view in the newspapers, even if some were a little more reserved. The *New York Times* wrote an essentially approving piece, praising May's 'infinite finesse' in performing a task which few would have had the temerity to undertake, and the *Times Literary Supplement* argued that it was impossible to read the book without being lifted into a 'rarer atmosphere' and 'deepening one's knowledge of human beings'. The *Boston Post* produced a colour page feature on *Mary of Nazareth* in its Sunday edition, and further accolades poured forth.

Not only did the book spark wide comment in England and in America from the critics: it generated a flood of letters from the public, including one from the headmaster of University College School in Hampstead, London, who, by strange coincidence, was halfway through writing a book entitled *Jeshua: by his Mother Miriam*, based on memoirs supposed to have been discovered in a first-century tomb. On hearing about May's book, he decided to delay publication of his own, because, as he told her, 'it would be absurd to hope that it could compete with the work of so distinguished an author'. In the bundle of congratulatory letters came one from the Honourable Rowan Hamilton, Chief of Chambers in Bermuda, who had served as head of the Land Court in the Holy Lands, and whom May had met just before the publication of the book. In general he approved of her treatment of the Virgin Mary, but he did have one objection, adding in a postscript, 'Please, in future editions cut out the word "clean" p. 177. line 9.'[2] He was not referring to the word in its sense of purity but rather, May's anachronistic use of the American colloquialism 'clean forgotten' which had crept into the narrative.

Although the majority recognized the spirit in which the novel was written, some more orthodox believers were deeply offended. To a modern-day reader, it is hard to see that it could have caused any furore, let alone sparked a bitter religious controversy, but May's demystifying portrayal of *Mary of Nazareth* as a very human and ordinary figure, who went on to have other children, was far removed from the image of the sacred virgin, and brave for its time. In spite of her attempts to ward off trouble in her preface, on 28 October, the *Catholic Herald* published an article which accused her of historical inaccuracy and of writing in an irreverent vein, particularly taking exception to what was perceived as a questioning of Mary's virginity. Even though May had anticipated this reaction, she was furious and quickly looked around for support from more enlightened sources. A potential ally was sought in the editor of the *Church of England Newspaper*, to whom she sent the offending article, hoping he might offer advice on how she should respond. 'I have read the enclosure with surprise, if one can really be surprised at anything the R.C.'s do', [3] he replied, but although he felt the book should be 'read by all Christians', he failed to see what action could be taken. May, however, could not let the matter rest. Her scholarly integrity was at stake, and she felt she had written her book with deep reverence and stuck faithfully to the text of the Gospels on which it was based. She decided to sue, and on the 21 November 1933 a writ was served at the offices of the *Catholic Herald*.

Her solicitors believed that the newspaper's editor, Mr Charles Diamond, would respond with an apology in open court, but there was also the possibility that he would try to frighten her into dropping the action by contesting it. If the case went to court, she not only risked losing a considerable sum of money, which she could ill afford, but equally serious, doing further damage to her reputation. She was warned that the jury might be split, and that it would only need one hostile Roman Catholic, or even Anglo-Catholic, on the jury to bring this about. Instructed to prepare for the worst, she was advised to prepare a statement of evidence to counter the *Herald*'s charges against her. If she was able to find a Roman Catholic who would say that he or she regarded the book as an honest and reverent attempt to describe the life of Mary, so much the better.

At the same time as the writ was served, May's publishers in America and England sent dozens of copies of *Mary of Nazareth* to ministers of the Church, and to headteachers, inviting recipients to form their own opinions of the book, rather than listening to negative publicity. The idea for this strategy had been given to May by the London publisher Rupert Hart-Davis, who had told her that the way in which the writer Beverley Nichols reached an audience was by sending letters to anyone he thought would be interested in the subject of the book he wished to promote.

Adopting this approach for her own needs, May methodically worked her way through lists of names and addresses in *Crockford's Clerical Directory*, as well as enlisting the help of a clergyman friend who wrote to influential people on her behalf. The gamble seemed to have paid off when reassuring letters of support started flowing in with expressions of admiration for such a 'brave, daring and extraordinary psychological portrayal of Mary's inner life', which offered a 'unique contribution to religion which would stand the test of time'.

A considerable number of Church leaders wrote to say that they were so impressed with the book's content that they had lectured on it to their theology students, or used it as an aid in giving sermons, among them the Pastor of Plymouth Congregational Church, in Seattle, who wanted to use the novel as the basis for his sermon the Sunday before Christmas. The fact that clergy were treating the book with such respect was quickly picked up by certain newspapers in England and America, all of which furthered May's cause. Articles like the one which appeared in the *News and Record*, and which reported that the Reverend Chappel had given an address on the book in the New Road Church, referring to its author as one of the really great novelists of the day, were just the endorsement she needed.

Not everyone, though, was pleased to receive a complimentary copy of *Mary of Nazareth*; David Goldstein, from New York City, had been preparing an address on 'the Iconoclast and Mary' when he received his in the post, courtesy of Doubleday. 'Its attractive title', his letter of response began, had led him to 'expect to find in its pages, an antidote for the intellectual poison being disseminated that lowers the glory of motherhood by disregarding or openly repudiating the ideals personified in the Mother of the Son of David. But great is the disappointment, for the reader learns that the Mary who lived in Nazareth is nowhere to be found in the 300 pages of the book.'[4] It was the 'denial of the perpetual virginity of the Blessed Mother Mary', which had roused Goldstein to pen his diatribe, and others objected to receiving a copy at all, critical of such intrusive commercial tactics.

Not content with taking on the *Catholic Herald*, May was stirred into replying to some of the letters of criticism in order to defend the position she had taken in her book. In doing so she provoked another outburst from David Goldstein, who sent back a lengthy and scathing reiteration of his protest, ending on a resoundingly acerbic note:

> It is no pleasant task to criticize the literary production of any writer, especially of a woman who does not appear to realize that she has dealt with the greatest one of her sex the world has ever known in a manner that is sacrilegious. I do it with a prayer that the facile pen that produced the 'Mary of Nazareth' may, with God's grace, bring forth 'My Misunderstood Mary' in which reparation will be made for the offence shown to the Mother of our Lord and Saviour Jesus Christ.[5]

The possibility that the *Herald* would pursue its position was still a threat, and, contrary to what May and her advisers had hoped, supporting letters could not be used as evidence in her favour. What was needed was for members of the Church to speak in her defence in open court, something she felt unable to ask of anyone she knew. She was little comforted to discover that the editor of the *Herald* was frequently embroiled in libel cases, but her solicitor was still hopeful that he would be advised not to pursue the case, the persuasive reason being that no judge would want to get into a discussion about the virginity of Mary or allow cross-examination on the subject.

The case against the paper dragged on for another year, as each side played a waiting game; even the sudden death of Mr Diamond had no effect in the stalemate. Eventually – although not quite as favourable a result as she wanted – a settlement was agreed, with May receiving an apology by post rather than in an open court, and a proportion of her costs paid.

Undeterred by the impending court case or the adverse reaction surrounding the publication of *Mary of Nazareth*, May had started on its sequel in what she now planned as a trilogy. She had found the writing of the first volume a very emotional experience, and was not ready to disengage. She was already predicting the difficulty she would have in producing a more prosaic novel, but for the present, she had a lot more scope for her religious series. Having written about events up to the crucifixion, she wanted to keep the drama going, applying the same rational treatment to Jesus as she had to his mother's life, which had the potential to be even more contentious than *Mary of Nazareth*. Although she did not believe that the disciples and Mary Magdalene saw Jesus in the flesh after the crucifixion, she interpreted their experience as real, and a tribute to the 'tremendous force' of his character. She knew she would upset people by this disinvestment of miraculous significance, but felt it was unavoidable if she was to be honest; and anyway, she saw herself writing particularly for readers not versed in Church doctrine, who were unlikely to be interested in the story of Jesus as told by theologians. She was encouraged by the huge numbers of letters of appreciation she had had about the first book, from all backgrounds, including Roman Catholics. She was more interested in exploring the revolutionary character of Jesus' life.

Once more, she scrupulously applied herself to research, relying on a wide range of sources for background detail and to illuminate her understanding of theological debate. When she became bogged down in some of these arguments, she wrote to Canon Streeter, Provost of Queen's College Oxford, whose *The Primitive Church and The Four Gospels: A Study of Origins* she had found particularly valuable when writing *Mary of Nazareth*, and asked if she might visit him to discuss questions which were puzzling her.

Although May rarely lacked the application to write when she had an idea, by now she and Louis had bought a sixteenth-century cottage in the country, called the Old Gables, at Warfield in Berkshire, with a large garden and fields of its own, where peace and quiet was more easily found. Then, at the beginning of July, while Louis was in Kenya, Peti was struck down by a severe infection and nearly died. He had developed a form of osteomyelitis in his thigh, which had to be operated on. May rushed to be with him at a nursing home in Winchester, waiting as he underwent two blood transfusions. Not long after, Louis arrived home, only to become ill with malaria, for two days lying unconscious in the same nursing home as his son. Although both recovered, Peti needed another operation, but first he had to build up his strength, the doctors advised that he recuperate until August. To pay the medical bills, May devoted every spare moment she had to finishing *The King of Jews* in order to collect the advance, writing in her hotel or the hall of the nursing home.

When, a month later, Peti was well enough to be moved, he was taken to the Old Gables where he remained confined to bed in a room downstairs until the following June, showing great courage in facing this long and isolated confinement. May stayed with him at the cottage, writing her book.

Then one winter's day in 1934, while Peti was having his plaster removed under anaesthetic, she received a telephone call from Louis with the dreadful news that her 23-three-year old daughter Joyce had committed suicide. This was her second attempt to end her life, having once before taken an overdose of sleeping tablets in New York after an unhappy love affair. She had left a short hand-written note for Comfort which showed that this time she had made certain she would not survive, although she wrote of her sadness to leave her sisters, 'the only thing I care about'.

Cyril Connolly described Joyce as someone 'condemned by excess of sensibility, courage, and distinction of heart to suffer a perpetual kind of adolescent brainstorm of passion and disappointment'.[6] He also felt she had 'a neurotic missionary side',[7] something that resonates in her last note to Comfort which is preoccupied with the need to be good, a word she repeatedly uses with a childlike simplicity as she instructs her

May's eldest daughter Joyce – aged about 15

to influence their younger sister in this virtue so that she would know the meaning of happiness, and not become 'bad'.

May's reaction to the death of her daughter is unrecorded, but she somehow kept going, continuing to work on *The King of Jews*. By the end of November, she was able to send her manuscript to Heinemann but, impatient as she was to see it published, when the proofs were returned to her, she was not at all pleased with some of the corrections made by the 'expert', –'he may be a scholar, but he has no literary sense'. Sending them back with several pages of curt comments, she requested that most passages be returned to their original form.

The publication of *The King of Jews* at the beginning of 1935 gave plenty more provocation for her quickly roused anger, but it was also the opening for her career to take off in a new and exciting direction. Appearing with an explanatory preface and a full bibliography, *The King of Jews* generated wide interest from all sections of the press. The *Daily Telegraph* praised the author for conscientious and reverent retelling of the Gospel story, and found in her 'blend of historic truth and creative imagination' a 'deeply moving and arresting work', an opinion shared by many papers. But criticism was hard to tolerate, especially when it seemed unjustified. When a reviewer for the *Methodist Recorder* accused May of inventing her own peculiar theology, she refuted some of the points raised in a three-sided letter to the editor.

More upsetting was a review in *Punch*, which appeared on 11 February, accusing her of making a number of theological, historical and geographical errors, and citing seven of them. This required more immediate action; she picked up the telephone and put a call through to the editor, E. V. Knox. She had no quarrel with the literary opinion of the critic, she told him, but she was distressed by the impression he had conveyed that she had attempted to write a serious book about a subject that was sacred to many people without properly researching it. She was not satisfied with the editor's offer to refer her complaints to the reviewer; she wanted a printed admission from Knox to the effect that the criticism against her was unfounded, and when this was not forthcoming, she resorted to the threat of legal action at which the editor promptly hung up.

She followed up the call with an uncompromising letter, enclosing a point-by-point rebuttal of each of the seven examples cited in the review, and referring to her sources as evidence, pointing out at the end of this protracted reply that 'it is easy to attack in a word or a phrase. To defend a position is a lengthy business.' She did not have to wait long for an answer. 'I do not think that you ought to complain of incivility', began Mr Knox in his letter. 'It seemed to me that no useful purpose could be served by discussing Judaic tradition and the origins of Christianity on the telephone, and since you said that you would instruct your solicitors to proceed, I felt obliged to conclude the conversation abruptly, and await your further communication.'[8]

Although May was still smarting with indignation, enough to write again to Knox complaining of his unfairness towards her, when she received a lengthy counterstatement from the reviewer, she decided to let the matter drop.

13

Censored

Ever since the advent of the 'talkies', May had been excited by the idea of writing for the cinema and with the publication of *The King of Jews* her American agent was keen to dispose of the picture rights in America. But first she had wanted to explore the possibility of making a film in England with a new director who since the outstanding international success of his picture *The Private Life of Henry VIII* was being spoken of as the creator of a thriving English film industry. The Hungarian-born Alexander Korda had left Hollywood four years earlier, disillusioned with his relationship with Twentieth Century Fox, and determined to fulfil his vision for high-quality film-making. The British film industry, still in its infancy, welcomed him in, and having made two light but well-produced comedies, he directed Charles Laughton in the starring role of the Tudor king. The film earned Laughton an Academy award, and became the first British movie to break into the American market, generating confidence and optimism that one success could be repeated. With his reputation established, and funding for new projects readily available, Korda was dedicating himself to building up his company, London Film Productions, to compete with Hollywood.

May recognized this bright new star as just the right person to transform her book for the screen. Shortly after *The King of the Jews* was published, she wrote to invite him to lunch with her at the Ritz to discuss the picture possibilities of her book, enclosing a copy for him to read. When they met early in February 1935 they at once hit it off and Korda agreed to take on the project. He had wanted to make more worthy films, as opposed to pure entertainment, and for a long time had thought of producing a biblical story in the time of the Apostles. May's book fitted the bill perfectly; he was sure that the film would arouse interest worldwide and bring in a new audience of people who did not usually go to the cinema. Particularly exciting for May was that Korda wanted her story for his first Technicolor film.

She could not have hoped for a more enthusiastic response, and she was equally impressed by his sensitive visualisation of how the film should be made, and was convinced that he would make an inspirational picture. She was greatly buoyed up at the prospect, not least because she saw it as a means of helping her out of her worrying financial situation. As she told Charley Evans, she looked forward to the 'immense relief of being able to breathe and, for the moment anyhow, not to have to strain and struggle'. But she knew it would not all be plain sailing. On 14 February she had sent a copy of *The King of the Jews* to the British Board of Film Censors, asking their approval for it to be produced as a film. She waited with some anxiety for their reply, only too aware that a film attempting to focus on the life of Jesus would be controversial.

On 6 March a letter arrived from the BBFC which presented May with a very difficult dilemma. The board had read *The King of the Jews* and found it to be 'beautiful and reverently written', and believed 'a film produced so as to breathe the spiritual teaching contained in the book would ... prove most helpful to the Christian religion in this country'. On the other hand, the board felt that a film dealing with 'such essential features of the Christian religion as the Crucifixion, the Resurrection, and the

Ascension of our Lord, may be unsuitable for indiscriminate public exhibition'.[1] And therein lay the problem.

As it was believed that in May and Korda's hands the film would take on 'an atmosphere of religious teaching', it would almost certainly have to be classed under the category of a religious film, for which the BBFC was unable to issue a certificate; renters would have to obtain permission from their local authority to show it and adhere to special conditions. These included 'no pictorial posters, no mention of the cast, no smoking in the auditorium, music accompaniment to be of a religious character, and no other film to be shown in the same programme'.[2] Such restrictions would make the film financially unviable, and no producer would risk the expense of making it.

The problem was not insurmountable, for, as the board pointed out, everything would depend upon the treatment, but the more conscientiously Korda carried out his work, the more likely it would be that special provisions would have to be made for the exhibition of the film, in England at least. May hoped they could find a way of avoiding the religious category without sacrificing their original vision. In a letter to Korda, she suggested this could be achieved by 'emphasising the historical background and the drama of the purely human characters, and by being content to convey the personality of the dead Jesus only and entirely through the emotions and actions of these living people'.[3] They would have to leave out the voice of Christ and his appearance from the dead (which they had intended to conjure up by an effect of light). She could see that they might even have to replace the disciples with men and women 'less officially sacred'. She hoped that the changes she was proposing would not spoil the film in Korda's opinion, for 'after all' the point of the story 'is the story of a human experience, and the "power of the film version" would lie in making this experience convincing'.

She was encouraged by the fact that *Ben Hur*, and the more recent film of the Christian Martyrs in Rome, *The Sign of the*

Cross, in which Nero was played by Charles Laughton, had both been treated in such a way as to avoid censorship on religious grounds. There was even the option of making the film as they had originally conceived it for release in America and countries with less severe restrictions, and of omitting some scenes in the general release in England. If, when the film was made, the censors were still unhappy about giving it a certificate, she thought of trying to enlist the support of prominent men in the Church to agitate to have the picture included in ordinary cinema programmes. 'In fact', she told Korda in her letter, 'I am not discouraged by this difficult problem. I can even believe that the difficulty and restrictions imposed will end by making a better picture. I have worked long enough to find out that nothing is so good for an artist as to have to work within a frame.'[4]

Her optimism was enough to convince the director that the film was worth pursuing and on 12 April the contract was signed. Heinemann fully exploited the opportunity this provided, giving the *Daily Express* exclusive rights to publish the full story on a Saturday, so that it would be picked up by the Sunday papers the next day and still allow the news to run in Monday's papers, thereby keeping the story alive for three days rather than one. The article ran with the attention-grabbing headline: 'Story of Christ to be filmed. The Central Figure Will Not Appear'.[5]

May was still spending most of her time at the cottage with Peti, who after a secondary operation in the spring was finally without his plaster and moving about on crutches. She was now able to take him for drives in the countryside and by August he was well enough to accompany her to a house she had rented in the Lake District. On the day they arrived, however, he fell and broke his bad thigh, leading to another eight weeks immobilized and trussed up in plaster. It was not until autumn that he was back on his crutches and finally able to start at Eton.

She had by this time begun research for the third novel in

her planned trilogy, which would dramatize the way in which 'the spirit of Jesus' travelled west to Rome – an idea she had borrowed from Canon Streeter's *Primitive Church*. She sent the author a copy of her last book, and wondered whether she could visit him again for some advice, as in trying to reconstruct certain events she had found 'some serious snags'. She was also busy experimenting with different scenarios for the film version of *The King of the Jews*, and attending meetings with Korda and the production team. It was thought that Laurence Olivier would play the part of Judas, and it was hoped that they would begin shooting in the middle of October.

By the beginning of 1936 there was still no sign of the project starting and May was beginning to worry that Korda had lost faith in the film. Then, on 13 March, she got a letter from him bringing the news that in spite of all their efforts to write a script which would satisfy the BBFC, the board would still not give positive assurance that the picture would be passed for general release, and consequently his own board of directors at London Film Productions felt it would be too risky to undertake production of *The King of the Jews*.

May was devastated. When she had last been in communication with the censor's office, she had felt that there was a genuine enthusiasm for her cause, and that all help possible would be given. She refused to give up hope of finding some way to retrieve the situation, and pressed Korda to meet her to discuss it further, but to no avail. He had already invested a considerable sum in preparatory work and described his decision as no less a blow to himself. But he was in the process of moving into the vast new studios he had built at Denham with a loan from the Prudential Insurance Company, and his finances were strained.

The King of the Jews was one of several films which he was forced to give up that year after a costly struggle to get them made. *Lawrence of Arabia*, another grand project, was also dropped, even though he had paid £3000 for the rights. May might have taken some comfort from the fact that the director later remarked: 'My greatest films are those I announced and never made.'[6]

She had had to accept defeat, but she had learned a great deal from her collaboration with Korda and his script supervisor, Lájos Biro, and had set her heart on doing more screenwriting with them, if they could use her. It is probably no coincidence that the novel she began to work on next had particularly good cinema potential, with none of the complications which beset the previous one. She seemed to have abandoned her idea for a third story in her religious series. Instead she turned to something quite different again, producing what was essentially a court-room drama, in which the jury has to give its verdict on a trial for slander between an army captain and his superior officer. The plaintiff, Major Daviot, has been accused of cheating at poker during a weekend house party, and as events surrounding the case unravel, motives for the accusations come to light, revealing another layer of moral intrigue.

When *Action For Slander* was published in November in 1936, it was an instant success, reprinted in December, and going on to become one of her best-selling novels. Winston Churchill was one of the first to offer his congratulations on 'her brilliant book' which, he told her, 'held me from beginning to end. I lent it to several good judges who all had the same pleasurable experience.'[7]

By 1937 the extent of May's financial losses in America was fully revealed. John's desperate speculations had swallowed everything, and even a life insurance policy he had turned over to May in lieu of money owed turned out to be worthless because he had borrowed against it and then been unable to pay the premiums. For a time he had made interest payments according to what he could afford, but eventually these fizzled out too. It came as a bitter shock to May when she discovered that during this time he had been drawing a large salary from his oil company, and the close relationship they had always shared was irreparably damaged.

At least, the same year, May finally had the fulfilment of seeing a book she had written transferred to the big screen, when London Film Productions made *Action For Slander* into a motion picture starring Clive Brook, Ann Todd and Margaretta Scott.

In spite of the energy with which she had pursued her interest in the film world, the tragedies she had experienced in recent years had pushed her close to the edge, as a letter she wrote to her old friend, Noël Coward, reveals.

> As one of the accursed to another (artists) this is to tell you that I am possessed by ten thousand black devils and wanted to cry out at the sight of you yesterday and beg you to drive them out of me but couldn't show you even how glad I was to see you. But I was glad. This is to explain. You had 'em haven't you – these awful goes of black depression – I won't go crazy will I? You're happy now – aren't you? ... If you can tell me of a 'cure' for God's sake write me a line ... I need help.[8]

Louis seemed unable to offer her the support she needed, and although she loved him as much as ever, they frequently bickered, often because she stood her ground in disagreements and in expressing criticism – she would rather tell an unpalatable truth than lie to avoid upsetting him. She was careful about arousing his jealousy; and according to Ford Madox Ford she became distressed when she was photographed having lunch with him in New York because she was worried that 'the General would be upset',[9] but as both partners dealt with worries and unhappiness in their own way, Louis began to turn his attention to other women.

Nancy Maurice was waiting in the wings. She gave him the undivided devotion he craved, and her utter loyalty to him in both his work and private life was something on which he came increasingly to depend. He started visiting her in her Battersea flat, where their relationship grew into a love affair, and once she had become essential to his well-being, he refused to give her up. In spite of this, and of her horror of Nancy, May still adored him and needed him, and no matter how bad things were between the two of them, the idea of a divorce was inconceivable to her.

Although she and Louis had an often tempestuous relationship, they shared a great deal in common; one strong link was their work on behalf of the disadvantaged and voiceless. In 1934 May became involved in supporting the Cecil Houses, where homeless women and children could get a bed, hot bath, tea and facilities for washing their clothes, while in parliament Louis introduced a private member's bill to alter the Vagrancy Act so that it would not be a criminal offence to sleep out 'with no visible means of subsistence'.[10] He took up the case of a vagrant who was imprisoned and had died while still incarcerated, arguing in the House of Commons that his only crime had been 'his extreme poverty'.[11]

In 1935 Louis was re-elected as the National Conservative candidate for Carlisle, and was proactive in trying to push for international commitment to take a stand against aggression, while May's next two novels reflected her vicarious involvement with politics at home and overseas. In 1937 she brought out *The Black Virgin* – published as *Strange Weekend* in America – in which the action takes place over a family Christmas set in a large country house. Beneath the surface of the glittering festive scene there is disunity and insecurity, not just in the lives of the characters, but in the public sphere. A contrast is drawn between the old traditions of England before the Great War, and a country troubled by the threat of fascism and communism, and an uncertain future.

Most of the story unfolds through the minds of different characters who have gathered together at the home of Jock

Barnaby, a Conservative Member of Parliament, and his bored and frustrated wife Sarah who is on the point of leaving him for another man, (another of the guests). She longs to escape the confines of her life, and is resentful at having to keep her 'mouth shut' about issues she believes in, such as divorce if one is wretched, for fear of losing support from 'respectable voters of respectable England'.

Nancy Maurice makes a brief appearance as Jock's secretary who 'knew him inside and out', and both he and Sarah have a marriage in which infidelity is a means of escape from unhappiness and boredom. The House of Commons is described as 'full of fog' inside, and the government as 'a very fussy, motherly sort'. Jock has won reluctant backing from party officials only because no one else wanted to fight the 'hopeless seat' with its abandoned collieries. The plight of the unemployed is juxtaposed with the worries of the rich who feel they are 'being fleeced', and are forced to make economies. A severe lack of money is pushing Jock to sell the family home; he has already had to part with the Gainsborough.

May's sense of betrayal over her brother's financial dealings finds its way into the novel through Sarah's shady brother, one of the house guests, who has lost her inherited fortune through bad investments. He hopes to trick Jock into giving away government secrets about the oil business, which will help him buy shares cheaply and pull himself out of bankruptcy. His sister is blindly devoted to him, although in the end he tests her loyalty to breaking point, triggering reconciliation between her and her husband.

The reviews were pleasing on both sides of the Atlantic: the *Spectator* thought the novel 'exceptionally good' in all respects, and in America the *New York Times* found it refreshing for its truthful but affectionate portrayal of England.

By now, May was a grandmother. On 13 January 1935 Comfort and Rupert celebrated the birth of their first child, Bridget, who was followed by a son, Duff, in June 1936. The young couple had moved to a larger house in Highgate to accommodate their growing family and May, living in central London, was close enough to see them frequently.

Mary, the youngest Borden child, had settled in Camden, Maine, having met there while on holiday a local boy, and thus this branch of the next generation returned to its American roots and the place where May had spent the summers of her childhood.

Peti had made up for narrowly missing a scholarship to Eton by winning an Exhibition to Magdalen College, Oxford in 1938. He was shy and introverted and May worried about his lack of friends and social life; he was usually to be found absorbed in a book and his powerful intellect, which some found intimidating, was focused inwardly.

As well as writing political fiction, May kept up her work as an advocate of social causes and, in an article in the *Evening Chronicle* in July 1938, she forecast policy, proposing that wage-earners with families should have a small sum given to them for each child to make the weekly budget at the very least equal to what would be received from the dole. As an afterthought she suggested that the allowance could be paid to the mother as her own 'honourable' wage from the state for her long working hours, seven days a week.

But her concern over Nazi persecution was far more urgent. Both she and Louis were vehement critics of the government's policy of appeasement and in spring 1939 she published *Passport for a Girl,* a novel bitterly critical of the inertia which seemed to have seized the nation during the German invasion of Austria. In the aftermath of the Anschluss the passport in question belongs to the stepdaughter of a member of the British Foreign Office who has been living in Austria with her Jewish boyfriend. Hans and April manage to cross over the frontier into Hungary just in time, and from there travel back to the safety of London, but Hans's mother and grandmother face torture and death under the Nazi regime. April's mother, Christine, who looks 'frail and feminine', but has 'a vigorous, rather masculine mind', feels some 'sympathy for the nation that had been so badly treated at Versailles' and does not see the harm in carrying on her friendship with a Nazi sympathiser, who tricks Hans into returning home where he is imprisoned.

Among the political themes of the novel May wove autobiographical strands. Five years after the death of her daughter, she felt able to write about her through her reincarnation as April, a passionate and tender-hearted person, who is always in search of freedom of the 'mind' and 'soul', and lives by the creed of giving and being good. Like Joyce, she is often too distracted by life to bother with necessities such as a good meal, and she attaches no importance to her appearance. She writes poetry, speaks French, Italian and German fluently, and Christine finds it 'delicious' when she recites from 'her beloved Dante'.

In this very personal evocation, there is an anticipation of tragedy. 'It was true that there was a heartbreaking sound in some of her little verses, and a sense that was frightening in anyone so young', thinks Christine. In an almost identical retelling of the vignette in *The Technique of Marriage*, Christine finds her daughter sitting cross-legged in the middle of the drawing-room floor, 'papers strewn all over the place, ink spluttering on the rug from her fountain pen and a lighted cigarette balanced beside her on a matchbox'. When the scene is played out here, though, Christine is furious that her daughter has made such a mess of the carpet, and that she is writing a political pamphlet to be circulated throughout Austria, to warn people of the coming German invasion, which Christine dismisses as nonsense. The relationship between mother and daughter in the novel is fraught because of Christine's intolerance of the way April leads her life. This is not something which comes through in May's portrayal of Joyce in *The Technique of Marriage* – where her words are invested with new and poignant significance: 'She is an artist, she has a spark of the divine fire; I must not put it out.'[12] Yet there is something very wistful in Christine's reflection that if she and her daughter had not been so different, 'they might have been such great friends.'

To research the novel, May travelled to Vienna to discover for herself what life was like there after its annexation. The critics admired her courage in pulling no punches in her criticism of the British over the crisis in Central Europe. The *Saturday Review of Literature* thought it was a book that should be read, and that nothing else had 'so savagely stripped the padding from those in England' who had believed Hitler was protecting them from the Bolsheviks. Much was made in the newspapers of her trip to Vienna and the risk she had taken in her efforts to paint the truth. She made it clear in interviews that the atrocities she described in the novel were not invented and were taken directly from what she had been told. These insights had made her all the more horrified by the Munich Pact; during a dinner party she argued her reasons for not bargaining with a Nazi regime by 'giving a few horrible facts learned in Vienna' but was stopped by one of those present, a Member of Parliament, who could not bear to listen. 'So I did stop', she wrote afterwards in a diary she kept during the crisis, but 'with the remark that this inability and unwillingness to face or even know such disagreeable truths permeated the whole Cabinet'.[13]

She was writing *Passport* throughout the events leading up to, and following, the fall of Sudetenland, and her anger, frustration and pessimism over the handling of the crisis no doubt gave added fuel to the cynicism in her novel. When England seemed on the brink of war, May felt a 'curious sense of loneliness and isolation'. Comfort was subdued, worrying about Rupert having to enlist. 'This is her tragedy', wrote May. 'I feel nothing. Have lived too long. It means nothing to me personally.'[14] She visited Peti at Eton where the boys were 'in squads building ramparts of sandbags'. In Hyde Park she saw an anti-aircraft gun and men digging trenches.

On September 28 she went to a recalled House of Commons and was taken aback by the Prime Minister saying he was convinced that Hitler meant what he said about Sudetenland being his last territorial demand. When the next day she and Louis listened to the news of the Munich agreement with 'the new sacrifices demanded of Prague' his eyes filled with tears. He told May he had never felt so ashamed and that if he could afford to leave the country he would. She was disgusted that the news of the latest appeasement was greeted with such hysteria – 'You'd think we'd won a victory', she wrote. The *Chicago Tribune* rang her to ask if she was out in the streets rejoicing. 'I told them no. I don't feel like rejoicing.'

Both she and Louis were made uneasy by the Nazi threat long before most people in England, but although May was praised for her political insights in writing *Passport*, she had in the eyes of her sister Joyce behaved extremely naively – she was living in Berlin at the time Hitler assumed dictatorial powers on 21 March 1933, and had been profoundly shocked when May flew out to interview him for the *Daily Mail.*

In the year she published *Passport for a Girl,* her nineteenth book, May turned fifty-three. The young girl who had so earnestly cherished an ambition to make her mark as a writer had achieved her goal and kept her reputation. Since *Jane Our Stranger,* with the exception of 1934 and 1938, she had published a book a year, choosing themes as diverse as her life and producing books which were widely reviewed around the world. If she was disappointed not to have achieved literary greatness, her popularity was undisputed, with her novels translated into numerous languages and lending libraries as far away as Australia writing to tell her that her new books were always those most eagerly awaited. Then came the news that Europe was once more at war.

* * *

Listening to the sombre voice of Neville Chamberlain from her London home that Sunday, 3 September, May experienced a strange condensing of time as memories of the past swept her back to her hospital in France, filling her with the same old longing to play an active role. But now that she no longer had her inheritance, she wondered what, if anything, she could offer. There seemed little chance that Louis would be called upon by the War Office, and both tried to reconcile themselves to taking a back seat in the coming conflict.

At the very least, though, she could volunteer for duties on the home front, and she wasted no time in joining an ambulance unit based in a garage in Fulham. Here she worked up to eight hours a day, reluctantly facing the hazardous drive back in the black-out, her eyes straining to pick her way through the unlit streets. Staying up long enough to have a bowl of soup as she listened to the BBC news at midnight, she would finally collapse into bed, only to wake the next morning for her shift still feeling fatigued.

The weariness was as much mental as physical during the monotonous days of the phoney war when everything was thrown into an uneasy limbo. When she had the energy, she tried to record her impressions in a diary, sometimes taking it with her to the ambulance station to pass the time as she sat behind sandbags waiting for an air raid warning. Her jotted notes express her sense of disorientation: 'Only slept three hours last night. I lose track of the days and time. It seems years since Germany invaded Poland. As if with all one's habits violently broken and not only the fabric of one's little life – but of one's world – space time all the rest of it – was shattered.'[15]

The atmosphere in the capital as everyone waited for the bombs to start falling was tense with expectancy, although May noted the lack of preparation where she worked. When volunteers from St John's Ambulance came to lecture them on what they must do in an air raid (everything from artificial respiration to stopping haemorrhaging of the main artery[16]) they were warned that the stretcher bearers would never be able to cope with the expected numbers of wounded, and that they would have to do a lot of the work for them, prompting May to wonder how the very young girls on her shift watching the demonstration would meet the occasion.

Sometimes she met Louis for lunch at the House of Commons where it infuriated her that people asked why she was not in the country, 'as if it was strange that a woman who writes should stay in town'.[17] She was intrigued by the shift in roles since all the young and active men had enlisted, observing how those left behind took on the housekeeping while their wives went out 'to drive ambulances and milk wagons etc … I suppose it's because the women want to – it's a change for them, & the men don't. It's beneath their dignity or something. In any case something must be done about offering humans a theatre or the population will take to drink and melancholia.'[18] The Carlton restaurant provided a diversion of sorts for although she found the mood there subdued, at least 'there were people', she wrote in her diary, and Noël Coward had joined her, 'facetious and affectionate full of a mysterious and unfortunate intelligence job in Paris'. As he kissed her goodbye, she wondered why he did not 'simply join up and do a little work with a rifle',[19] before reflecting wryly that she could not imagine him staring down a gun barrel.

Then out of the blue came a fantastic offer which transformed May's horizons. Her old friend from the last war, Lady Hadfield, got in touch to say her husband, a Sheffield steel magnate, had given her a sum of money for war work and she wanted it to be used for the French, and to do something with May. For May, this meant only one thing. They would use the money to set up a field hospital and take it to France. There was of course the old problem of bureaucratic red tape, but Louis knew General

Gamelin, Chief of Staff to the Minister of Defence, who might be persuaded to act as an intermediary if May wrote to him offering to equip and organize a mobile hospital of one hundred beds. In acknowledgement of the strange repetition of her past, she began her letter to him, 'Twenty-five years ago I wrote to General Joffre ...'

She did not have to wait long for a response. A few days later, she was dining again at the Carlton when General Lelong, Head of the French Military Mission in London, came in with a large party of soldiers, and stopping at her table, told her that her offer to run her own hospital had been accepted. Louis was delighted for her; but her own reaction was a mixture of elation and dismay. 'I had undertaken to create a hospital out of nothing', she wrote later, 'I had nothing to build on, save a sum of money and a bit of experience a quarter of a century out of date.'[20]

14

Journey Down a Blind Alley

It was in a mood of some trepidation that a few weeks later, May boarded a train for Paris for a meeting at the Service de Santé. She had once known the place well, having many times travelled there from the front to receive orders of where her unit was to move next, but that was long ago, and she had no idea how she would fight her way through all the bureaucracy after so many years of absence. The confidence with which she had dealt with officialdom in the last war now seemed utterly deflated as she told herself that it was sheer madness to think she could pull off her plan. Yet the moment she arrived at the Gare du Nord among the throngs of French soldiers, the old routines came flooding back to her, and once again she had the curious sensation of being propelled back in time as though the intervening twenty years were no more than a dream. Even the Service de Santé headquarters were unchanged, the same 'yellow forms, the long dirty pens that spluttered and scratched, the grimy corridors'.[1]

Any residual nerves were dispelled by the warm welcome she received on her arrival. Her work in the First World War had not been forgotten, and General Gamelin had given instructions that everything was to be done to facilitate her task of setting up a new mobile hospital. This, she learned, was to be stationed in Lorraine, ten miles behind the Maginot Line which ran along the north-eastern border of France and Germany. By sheer good luck, her unit had been assigned to the Fourth Army commanded by General Réquin, a friend of Louis's from the last war. She left the building overflowing with excitement and bursting to share the good news with Lady Hadfield.

Over the next few months May travelled frequently to Paris, organizing all she needed in the way of surgical and sterilizing apparatus, X-ray, tents and heavy trucks. At the London end, equipment for the wards had to be assembled and shipped to France, and female personnel recruited. She was rigorous in selecting a good team, weeding out those she suspected of wanting to 'joyride at the front' with no real concept of what the work would involve. She needed tough and hard-working volunteers and was fortunate in finding them, for nurses appeared like magic in response to her appeal, and in spite of offering small wages in return for a job description that deliberately emphasized dangers and hardship, she ended up with ten whom she believed to be of the highest standard. There was no difficulty either, thanks to the Mechanized Transport Corps, in finding women drivers eager for adventure overseas who were only too happy to volunteer to go with May, and to provide their own cars.

At the beginning of the New Year, she travelled to Paris for the last time and took up temporary residence in an apartment on the Quai Malaquai to deal with last-minute problems. The claims on her time were reduced by the help of the newly recruited head of the medical team, Jean Gosset. Tall and passionate-looking, he had presented himself to May dressed in a leather jacket and riding boots, and quickly impressed her with his charm and intelligence. He was mercurial and highly determined, and reputed to be a brilliant surgeon. By

February the final countdown had begun as the rest of the staff congregated in Paris: four French surgeons, a medical clinician, an X-ray specialist, administrative staff, twelve military drivers for the heavy trucks and last but certainly not least the select and hardy group of English nurses, who arrived by train from London, tired and dishevelled after a rough Channel crossing, but in exuberant spirits, and the volunteer drivers in their cars: Ford station wagons, a Buick, two Sunbeams and the 'clown' of the bunch, an old Bedford shooting brake which could carry thirty French orderlies. Just four months after May's plan had been accepted, the Hadfield–Spears Unit was ready for action.

With its assortment of new and old vehicles, from heavy lumbering military lorries to the luxurious Renault limousine which Lady Hadfield presented to May for her personal use, it was an eccentric-looking convoy that set off from Paris on a bitterly cold February morning. In the eyes of some of the French contingent, the cars brought across from England with the MTC drivers gave an undesirable impression of a tourist outing, especially with the oversized suitcases belonging to the women crammed inside them. It had to be said, that appearances aside, the cars were not entirely practical. For a start, they had no chains to prevent them getting stuck on the snow-bound roads around Lorraine – an oversight on May's part. Another more general peculiarity of the convoy was that speed of movement was restricted to the pace of the slowest vehicle; and the entire concept of a mobile hospital which carried everything one would expect to have in a fixed one, was something that many found a puzzling anomaly, not least because installation, packing up and moving were inevitably a time consuming business.

In spite of shortcomings, the convoy got off to a good start. Travelling 250 miles and navigating treacherously icy roads without mishap, it made its first night's stop at Nancy. The next day, General Réquin invited all the unit staff to lunch at his headquarters where he told the assembled English girls, the nurses kitted out in grey uniform and the drivers in khaki, that they were the only British troops in his army and that he intended to make the most of them, a gesture which May realized was absolutely sincere. He was in fact to prove himself a loyal friend to them all over the coming months, always solicitous in his care for their welfare.

Their arrival later that day in the snow-covered village of St Jean le Bassel, where one wing of a large convent had been requisitioned by the Service de Santé for a temporary hospital, was a depressing start to their hospital work, for the makeshift wards had been left in a sordid state by the outgoing unit, and below the ground floor, in a huge dark vaulted hall, May was horrified to discover patients too ill to be moved who had been left behind. The general state of neglect reminded her of the casino at Malo-les-Bains, and it was a case of all hands on deck, as over the next two weeks the entire staff team worked in a frenzy of activity, cleaning, redecorating and organizing the rooms, while beyond the hospital quarters the silent figures of the nuns carried on their daily lives, a shadowy presence behind the scenes. May's sense of style imposed itself on creating wards which were bright and welcoming, with attention to detail such as covers for the bedside tables and good-quality bedding, all of which were in place by the time the patients were at last carried up from the gloomy hall. It was an uplifting moment, as they reacted with surprised delight to being placed in beds made up with new linen, soft blankets and coloured bedspreads which May had bought in Paris in a moment of extravagance.

The unit was finally up and running and ready to deal with large numbers of wounded, but instead of working to full capacity, it seldom took in more than twelve patients each day, just enough to keep the team occupied but never stretched. As May later wrote, 'there was no war that could be called war' in the sector of the Maginot Line to which they were assigned. Fighting was limited to minor skirmishes; the land and sky around them were quiet and peaceful, and as they settled into an easy, almost carefree existence, she found it somewhat disconcerting. Réquin, who came regularly to visit the wounded, liked to spoil his 'English troops' and endeavoured to make life as comfortable for them as he could. He provided new and relatively luxurious sleeping quarters for the nurses in wooden huts in the garden, and for May, a small house for her offices where she could receive her military visitors, more sturdy than the one she had had when she was nursing at the Somme, 'a ridiculous but pretty papier maché house with a roof which was for ever being blown off'.[2]

Like her, Réquin enjoyed painting, giving her two of his own watercolours to hang on the walls of her new rooms. Since it was quiet, she gave her nurses French lessons here, an hour a day. The convent became the unlikely venue for cinema screenings, receptions and dinners, put on by the commander to entertain the staff and patients, and General de Lattre de Tassigny organized concerts at his divisional headquarters to which the unit staff were invited. Peti even came to stay for part of his Easter holiday from Oxford, and Louis was invited by his old friend Réquin to see the ambulance at work.

Pleasant as all this was, May was not the only one to be made wary by the strangely indeterminate existence. Réquin confided in her that he was concerned about the effect that such a long period of inactivity might have on his men and as a way of keeping up the morale of the troops he regularly took groups of the English nurses with him on his tours of inspection of the Maginot Line. From her point of view, May felt that the soldiers seemed softer and more vulnerable than those she had nursed during the First World War.

She noticed other changes too. With scientific advances over the last half century, medicine had moved forward, and she was fascinated to observe Gosset and another of the surgeons, Boutron, using the antibacterial sulphonamide intravenously during an operation on a soldier brought in with peritonitis and

May with her unit at St Jean Le Bassel during Louis' visit.
General Réquin is standing next to May with Louis far right

multiple intestinal perforations. The antibiotic saved his life and this was noteworthy for the drug had only been used for the first time in 1936; human trials of penicillin had not yet taken place and scientists had not learned how it could be mass-produced. At any rate, the medical inspector of the Fourth Army, General Wörms, was 'full of good will and gratitude' for the work of the unit.

By May, the village that had been covered in snow when they arrived was instead buried in greenery, and the first sprigs of apple blossom were beginning to show. Those patients well enough to get up lay out on the grass in the sun, and in the peacefulness of rural Lorraine in the full bloom of spring, there was little to suggest the calamity awaiting France. May found it hard enough to imagine the desolate no man's land beyond the section of Maginot Line from where the wounded French troops were brought to the hospital, let alone the events unfolding as

Hitler invaded first Norway and Denmark, and then Holland, Luxembourg and Belgium. In spite of the gloomy news, the world at the convent seemed far removed from the stories they were hearing. Eternally optimistic as usual, May quarrelled with Gosset, who infuriated her with his predictions of the defeat of France and England.

Such was her inability to grasp the magnitude of events taking place that she treated as an exciting adventure an outing to choose a dinner service for the mess from the famous china factory in Sarreguemines, where there was a chance they would 'get a look at the Germans' who occupied one half of the town. It had been evacuated at two hours' notice on 3 September and its entire population cleared out in just one afternoon, along with some ten million others in eastern France. As they drove down a broad avenue, their high spirits were suddenly subdued by the eerie quiet of the deserted city that made May think of it as 'under the spell of some awful enchantment'.

The hot sun shone down on silent, empty streets from which people had fled their homes in such haste that they had not had time to draw the curtains or pull the blinds. In one house the doors and windows had been left open and the remains of a lunch served nine months before were still on the table, with hardened string beans in a dish, and wine in the glasses. Shop doors had been left gaping. At a bakery abandoned loaves of bread lay rotting, and further down the road the butcher's shop had been cleared of its meat, but in an inner room at the back, a desk was littered with papers indicating a frenzied search for vital documents. At the china factory they walked through endless deserted corridors. A shell had fallen through its roof damaging one wing and leaving the floor littered with broken cups and plates, although there were still shelves stacked high with beautiful untouched china.

Driving further on they parked the car at a point where it was screened by houses, and walked in single file past a flimsy barbed wire entanglement to the end of the street, where one end of a bridge was blocked off by a wall of sandbags. Less than fifty yards away, on the other side of the River Saar, the Germans had control of the town. Occupying the last house before the bridge, a French company of soldiers were cooking their dinner in the open, screened by sandbags, and above them clothes hung from a line, a surreal scene of domesticity. They greeted May and her companions cheerfully, and allowed them to climb a ladder to an observation post, from which they looked through a hole at the bank opposite. There they observed the same absence of life and uncanny quiet: a deserted café bar, its outdoor tables and chairs scattered about, with long grass pushing up between their iron slats. The corporal told them that they had never seen the German soldiers on the other side, and that he and his colleagues even ventured out in the evenings to fish from the riverbank. 'Why not fish?' he asked May. 'They were good chaps the Germans, they didn't fire.'[3]

May's birthday on 15 May brought another note of disquiet. At the army headquarters, where she had gone to talk to Louis on the telephone, she overheard snatches of conversation about battle plans, noticing the uneasy atmosphere, and saw that Réquin looked anxiously pale. The next day she learned that the Allies had been ordered to abandon the line running south from Antwerp. Her entry for that day records the change in her mood: 'I am frightened. I wasn't ever in the last war – I don't think it is fear for my life. Fear for France – for England – for everything and one I know – The news this morning was cheering but tonight it is bad – Gamilin's order to his troops – To die rather than give way a foot of soil sounds desperate – and the horror of the battle of machines – sheer horror … I only get flashes.'[4]

A radio announcement ordering civilians not to evacuate the towns as they would interfere with the movement of the troops, led her to understand the confusion and chaos that must be taking place across France. War was certainly beginning to feel more real, and a letter from Comfort, complaining about

Rupert's weekend being spoilt because the War Office had summoned him to London on a Saturday to offer him a forces job, shocked her. 'She understands nothing', wrote May in her diary.

But she too was left in ignorance. The rumours filtering back to her often lacked specific and crucial detail, as an entry in her diary reveals: 'Gosset tells me that every mobile in the north similar to ours has been wiped out or evacuated to the rear. Horrible stories of nurses he knew being drowned trying to cross a river under fire. What river?'[5]

She invested 2000 francs in a good wireless so that she could hear England even if she could not go there. 'The boom of Big Ben is wonderful', she wrote. Yet it did not really cross her mind that she should evacuate her unit and try to head for home. Wishing to instil an example of calm, she dressed up for a Sunday service in the convent chapel, noting in her diary the irony of making an effort with her appearance at such a time. 'I am 54 – the greatest battle in history is raging to the north of us. I still worry about the length of my apron. Make up carefully. But this last is part of my plan. To be immaculate & look as nice as possible – part vanity part fooling.'[6] Even so, the nurses singing hymns made her weep, reminding her of the songs she had sung on Sunday evenings as a child with her father, mother and brothers.

She was cheered to learn that Louis, newly appointed as Churchill's representative in France, had spoken to the French nation by radio, but the comfort of this news was soon eclipsed by the announcement that the Germans had reached Boulogne on 25 May, and two days later, Calais, followed by the capitulation of the Belgians on 28 May. At Dunkirk, Operation Dynamo was taking place with the desperate scramble to evacuate some twenty-five thousand British troops from the port. Writing in her diary, May wondered from which port she could get home and felt 'afraid in a new way'. General Réquin was expected for a gala arranged that evening, and all day she waited for word from him to cancel the event, but as no word came, she went ahead with the preparations. At six she had just changed into clean clothes when she received a telephone call from him to say he was unable to come to dinner as he was leaving in the morning and taking the Fourth Army with him. She set off at once by car to see him, and drove through the countryside in the dusk, the darkening fields and sky matching her fearful mood. She had felt safe while Réquin was there to warn them if the war spread to their sector, but now she was very afraid of what might happen to them. He met her with a pale and rigid face and she felt guilty for bothering him as she admitted to feeling '*un peu perdue*' and asked if her unit could follow his army. He told her he would send for them if possible, but nothing could be guaranteed; the safety of her girls was uppermost in her mind during the drive back to the convent.

Later that evening she received an unexpected telephone call from Louis who had arrived in Paris and was angry to learn that she had been driving around the countryside at night. It was a difficult conversation, with neither able to speak openly. He was alarmed by her hints that she might move, for he believed she was safer where she was, within the protection of the Maginot Line, and with relatively easy access to Switzerland or the Mediterranean as an escape route. As she was unable to explain on the telephone her reasons for wanting to leave, they argued about it, but hearing his voice brought her a semblance of normality and she felt somewhat comforted when she said goodbye to him. Not wanting to frighten her, he had not let her know that 'he envisaged the total collapse of French armed resistance'; in her ignorance, she made up her mind that regardless of what her husband thought, she was right to stick with Réquin and his men.

The next morning, 31 May, she received orders to evacuate all the wounded, and to pack up ready but with no precise information of when or where they might be going. When she spoke to Louis again that evening he said he was returning to London in a few days' time and wanted her to come at once for Paris. She told him it was impossible. They had already stripped the wards, loaded the lorries and at any moment might receive orders to move. Yet several days went by and still no word came. Louis rang repeatedly and with increasing urgency, begging May to join him; but she, afraid that the unit might be forced to depart without her, refused to come. In their part of Lorraine the surrounding countryside was as peaceful as ever, and she felt relaxed enough to head off into the hills with her watercolours to paint, seeing little wrong in going on a sketching expedition within a few miles of the enemy. That evening, Louis again spoke to her on the telephone, and ordered her to come to Paris, a conversation she later described:

'It's no good talking like that. I can't leave, I tell you.'

'Why? What are you doing?'

'Waiting. As a matter of fact I've been painting with Elaine up the Saverne road.'

'What?' roared Louis. 'Did you say painting?'

'Yes – watercolours.'[7]

In the end she agreed to go to Paris for just one night, against the advice of Gosset and the other officers who warned of the dangers of the road being cut off by German night raiders. Travelling there with her driver Barbara, and with little clue that 'German armour was dashing forward from a Somme bridgehead making for Rouen and the Seine', she arrived safely and saw nothing which suggested any new menace to the capital, although the city itself was uncannily empty, and the government had ordered all civil telephones to be cut off. At the British Embassy, Louis came out of a meeting to greet her and she was taken aback by how exhausted he looked. She realized she had been picturing him as he was in 1916 when she first saw

May enjoying a relaxing painting expedition in the Lorraine countryside shortly before the fall of France

him at Bray-sur-Somme, yet it was not just that he was twenty-two years older: rather, the expression on his face told her just how hopeless was the fate of France.

Louis joined her late on in the evening in her room at the Ritz, and as she discussed with him her worries about her hospital and the plans she had made, he was acutely aware of how little prepared she was. 'Her terms of reference were those of 1917', he later wrote. '1914 had been before her time, she had never seen the retreats, refugees, armies and populations rolling back together.'[8] He experienced the same helpless fear for her that he had on so many other occasions, for he knew that 'the Hadfield–Spears unit was about to be launched like a cockle-shell into the torrent of the battle'. He had utter faith in her toughness and resolve, writing that only 'one thing was certain: my wife would not lose her head, or fail to fulfil the task assigned to her'.[9] It was not that he was ever doubting of her courage, but that 'it was, in fact, of too positive a kind ever to be reassuring.'[10]

Nevertheless, as always in times of crisis they were cheered and comforted by each other's presence, and almost able to relax as they sat down to share a supper of cold chicken and ham. Then a call came through on the embassy extension to say May had to return at once to St Jean le Bassel. Orders to move had come. Ignoring her husband's protests, she promised she would leave by midnight to be there the following morning at eight. Bolting down her food, she was about to send a message to Barbara when she appeared at the door, the bearer of bad news. She had run into a roadblock in the dark on the Champs-Élysées and the Buick was wrecked. May was frantic with frustration but there was nothing to be done; they would have to wait until the following morning when Louis was able to arrange for a car to drive them back.

Next day, after a bad night's sleep worrying about the unit, May said goodbye to her husband. She did not know when she would see or hear from him again. All communication between them was snapped from the moment she walked out of the hotel. He was talking on the telephone as she left and 'waved a distraught hand'. It was 7 June: one week later the Germans would sweep in to Paris, but as she sped away from the capital, she had no way of knowing that she would not return there for five long years.

All May's drivers soon discovered that she liked to be driven fast, but her hair-raising journey to join the convoy that morning was like nothing she had ever experienced. Told to hurry, the two military drivers pushed the car to its limits, covering 250 miles in less than five hours. They reached the convent as the convoy was setting off for the village of St Chéron, close to General Réquin's new headquarters, back the way they had just driven at breakneck speed.

May still expected that the front would be stabilized, and on this assumption, she continued to concentrate her efforts on establishing a base somewhere as close to the battle zone as possible. Thus when General Wörms suggested that they move to a large military hospital in Troyes, over a hundred miles away, she flatly refused. They were a field unit and to be based such a distance from the lines would defeat the object of their existence. Only later did she realize the general must have known that the Fourth Army had little hope of holding the line on the Aisne, and that once it was lost, the Germans would push forward.

Even when, on 10 June, she heard rumours that the French government had left Paris for Tours, she failed to grasp the gravity of the situation. By then she was far too preoccupied with the immediate concern of organizing the unit in a small chateau in the picturesque village of Rosnay, on the main road south, but after only two nights there, and before they had received any wounded, they were ordered to pack up and move off again. As it turned out, this proved to be their longest stop anywhere as the Fourth Army was pushed relentlessly back during the fall of France. In the chaos that followed, the unit was left to fend for itself as it tried to navigate a path of escape with the advancing German army close behind it.

As the main unit waited for ambulances at the chateau, a medical team, which included the surgeons Boutron and Guénin, had responded to an appeal for help at a military hospital in Chalons, some 50 miles to the north of Rosnay. When they sent an urgent message to May for more helping hands, medical supplies and candles, she was nonplussed as to why the latter were necessary.

A dreadful scene greeted them. Hundreds of badly wounded men lay on the ground outside, and inside the building there were hundreds more. The electricity and water supplies had been cut off, there was no sterilizer, and all but two of the previous staff had left. As May later wrote:

> All down the long corridor the dead and the dying and those who need not have died lay silent in the dark. We seemed to

walk for miles down those corridors. We turned left, then right, and the motionless silent procession passed with us, unending. And there was almost no sound. Almost none of the bundles moaned or whimpered.[11]

She found the surgeons in despair at the hopelessness of the situation, and as they went between the wounded with candles to separate the living from the dead, 'lifting a blanket to look at a face, fumble for a pulse',[12] she was only too aware of the inadequacy of the medical provisions they had brought with them, and all the time more ambulances were arriving. Once again she set off with a driver to collect more dressings and bandages from Rosnay but by now it was the middle of the night and, having lost their way in the dark, they did not reach their destination until dawn. They had lost vital time, and before they had a chance to turn around, they received word that her team had been ordered to leave Chalons. She learned later that the Germans entered the town at noon.

With orders to also leave Rosnay as well, May led an advance party to the town of Guigny, off the main road and to the north, where they set up a dressing-station in a deserted cheese factory next door to a railway siding. She spent the morning unpacking surgical baskets and looking for billets, but the houses were packed with refugees and the search for rooms proved fruitless. An improvised operating room was ready, but 'there was no sign of an ambulance nor of any living human being' save themselves, wrote May later, recalling the desolate stillness of their surroundings, the pervading smell of cheese, and the pent-up frustration of the surgeons as they paced the floor of the empty building and station platform waiting in vain for casualties. As the day wore on, and the thunder of guns grew nearer, the idea of bringing the rest of the staff and all the equipment north, when the German Army was advancing southwards towards them seemed madness, but Gosset was insistent that the dressing station stay put. Eventually he agreed that the rest of the unit should move south to Amance, but that the surgical team remain behind. Throughout the long night the wait for ambulances continued as all around battles raged, but the only patient was a small child, hit by a bomb, who died in Guénin's arms.

With the devastating speed at which the allied armies were retreating, coupled with a barely functioning communication system between Army Headquarters, May had lost touch with Réquin and his army. She imagined they were probably far ahead of them on the road south. All idea of finding a suitable place to set up their hospital was finally abandoned; now it was simply a case of travelling as far south as possible before dark. Their petrol reserves were low, and looking at the dusty road ahead of them, May had a sensation of blindness, not knowing where the road led. As they pored over a map of France, the town of Tonnerre was mentioned as somewhere they might find petrol before nightfall. It was a place May knew well, having stayed there with Louis some years before at the invitation of their friend, the Duc de Clermont-Tonnerre, who owned a Renaissance palace on the outskirts of the town. May was sure that they could be billeted there for the night, and setting off at once ahead of the convoy to make arrangements, she felt a surge of hopefulness. It was a blow, therefore, to find the duke away in the south of France and his chateau and grounds already taken over by General Huntzinger and his troops. Not put off, and with a show of boldness that she did not feel, she insisted on seeing the general, eventually persuading a very reluctant young officer to take her to him. He led her up a flight of stairs and down a long corridor to a closed door, where he abruptly fled, leaving May standing alone outside. What happened next she described in her book *Journey Down a Blind Alley*:

> I knocked. A voice said 'Entrez,' rather angrily. I opened
> the door and walked into a crowd of generals. Three stars,

four stars, five stars. I'd never seen so many stars together in such a small space. Nor so many peering eyes. My head swam. Everything blacked out save a circle of astonished eyes, staring as if at a ghost. Then a small spare, sandy haired man stepped forward and I said:

> 'I am Madame Spears, and I have lost my Army.'
> What Army is that, Madame?'
> 'The IVth Army.'
> The general looked at me gravely in silence.[13]

She had interrupted a military conference 'of desperate urgency'. A few days later General Huntzinger would become one of the signatories of the Franco-German armistice, joining the Vichy government as the Minister of War. Whatever his feelings toward May at the time, and regardless of the inconvenience of her sudden appearance, he treated her with civility, and requisitioned another chateau close by for her unit to use for the night. He also advised that she cross the Loire as soon as possible. This, though, proved harder than expected as the bridges were blocked by escaping traffic and the roads filled by the torrent of refugees whose faces, contorted with fear, would haunt May in the weeks to come.

After trying several alternative routes across the river at the town of Nivers without success, they took the risk of manoeuvring the convoy over a light suspension bridge. May watched with dread as the structure sagged under its weight, and when it was safely over, her relief was short-lived. Having been under the impression that the French army would retreat no further, and that a battle for the Loire was about to take place, she now found that they were heading straight into the path of the German Army, which was approaching along the left bank. A collision was prevented by the lucky arrival on the scene of General Wörms, who happened to speed past in a military car. Recovering from his surprise at seeing them, he stopped long enough to send them in the opposite direction towards the town of La Palisse, where he said they would find the Fourth Army.

The next day, 16 June, the French laid down their arms, but May had no presentiment of the surrender. Early in the morning, she set off to meet Réquin with her driver, Rosaleen Forbes, and Dr Bernard. The general's words to her were bleak. He no longer had an army, he told her, and could only advise her to head for Gannat, and on no account to go to Moulins. This last piece of advice she was forced to ignore, since this was exactly where the rest of the unit had been heading when they parted that morning, with instructions to wait there until further notice. Gosset was supposed to be acting as a go-between but had failed to reappear, and although it seemed likely that he had found his way blocked by traffic, and had gone back to collect the others and set off on another road south, there was no question of not looking for them in Moulins. Just as they anticipated, this 60 kilometre excursion towards the enemy and against the flood of refugees was in vain, for the unit had already moved on.

As they doubled back through the dark, May was uncertain of what to do next, knowing only that their mad trek across France could not go on much longer. She hated to be separated from her English staff, her conscience stricken by the fact that she was responsible for their fate. She had brought them to France, and now the country was disintegrating. Her anxiety was heightened when there was no sign of the unit at Gannat – only scenes of chaos and panic in a town filled with lost and frightened people. Then, in another strange turn of fate, just as they stopped at the Bureau de la Place to ask a young lieutenant whether he had seen the Hadfield–Spears unit, a telephone call came through from Gosset. He was waiting at a town called Le Thiel, some 40 miles away. Having made plans to meet early the next morning, May managed to find beds for the night in a small monastery where, although she was utterly exhausted, sleep eluded her as she lay worrying that something might happen before they were reunited with the unit.

Next day her fears seemed well founded when they arrived

at Le Thiel to find themselves in a large industrial suburb filled with factories and warehouses, and no sign of the convoy. A frantic search of the surroundings was of no avail. There was no news at the Bureau de la Poste or the Military Hospital and, running out of ideas of where else to look, May found her helplessness and frustration verging on hysteria. But suddenly a hopeful thought occurred to her. Perhaps there was another Le Thiel in the region. There was, and they had passed close to it the night before. It was 60 kilometres away, and they had to get there before the unit moved off. Their car was out of petrol, however, and the only place in the area to buy some was at the barracks where there was a long queue of military trucks in front of them. As they waited their turn in silence, too anxious to speak, an announcement came over a loud speaker that Pétain had asked for an armistice.

May tried to think clearly; she knew she had to keep her head and plan how to get her girls out of France, but they were hundreds of miles from the nearest port. It was the afternoon by the time they reached the other Le Thiel, where they were overjoyed to find the unit still waiting for them in the square. Reunited at last, the convoy set off again with a plan to travel west through the hills of the Auvergne. If they could make it as far as Brive, they would be in easy reach of Bordeaux, but failing that, they could turn southeast and head for the Mediterranean.

With frequent stops to fill up with petrol, and without a map covering the part of France in which they were travelling, they continued on their way, stopping wherever they could at night, and willing their cars to hold out as the engines boiled on the steep hills and the Bedford, 'hoary with age ... creaked and groaned and lurched along' with its thirty orderlies inside. To May, the sight of the convoy as it wound 'its slow laborious way up hill and down dale through the beautiful country', was a moving spectacle:

I suppose it was the valiant girls at the wheels, the sense

of their complete reliability and courageous good humour that twisted something in my left side, but the vehicles too seemed to be taking part in our crazy drama by doing their best. And I remember, perhaps because I was tired, looking back down a steep hill with breathless suspense and misty eyes the old Bedford flounder like an elephant across a stream and begin the ascent.[14]

When they at last reached the outskirts of Tulle they were informed that nearly all British units had left France – news which made May's heart sink. They had almost certainly left it too late to get away. Their only hope was to start at dawn the next morning and try to reach Bordeaux.

They slept that night in their vehicles and at daybreak, over mugs of coffee, Guénin and May agreed that she and all her girls would leave the formation as soon as they found petrol. They could just about squeeze into six cars, and needed 500 litres of fuel in case they had to divert to the Spanish frontier. At Brive, while Guénin went off in search of petrol, May tried to find an officer to help her get a message through to the British Embassy. No longer could she rely on the favours she had called in as the Director of a French Ambulance, and as the wife of a British General. In fact, the opposite was true. She was now treated with 'cold animosity', a change in attitude she found amazing in its swiftness. Whereas before the armistice she had been looked upon by the French army as benefactress and friend, she was now 'an enemy in their midst and was looked upon not only with detestation but with the gravest suspicion'.[15]

Hours passed and darkness fell as they waited for Guénin to return. It was not until the early hours of the morning that May saw the lights of his truck. She did not know how far he had travelled, but he had returned with enough petrol to see them through. Now it was time to disband the Hadfield–Spears Unit, a sad and sombre moment as they said their goodbyes in the moonlight by the roadside. One by one she shook the hands of all the orderlies. What would happen to the surgeons and Dr Bernard she did not know, but all the equipment that went with the unit had to be left behind: the X-ray trailer, the sterilizing truck, the mobile kitchen, and all the bedding. Personal luggage too was abandoned for there was room in the cars for only one suitcase each.

All went well until some 80 kilometres beyond Brive where they were stopped at a military checkpoint. Gosset had given May a movement order paper, signed by General Colson, which she handed to the guard, who having studied it in silence, told them that Bordeaux was closed, and that they would not be allowed to enter the city. 'Nevertheless I must', said May, boldly. 'These ladies are all British. We are obliged to leave France. It is by order of the Chief of Staff, General Colson.' Her bravado paid off. With a shrug of the shoulders, the guard let the cars go.

Then just after dawn, a fan-belt on one of the cars broke. There was no time to repair it, and so abandoning the vehicle, they divided its passengers between them. A few hours later they approached Bordeaux, May feeling sick with apprehension. Whatever she was told, she decided, she would insist on being allowed through. As it turned out, however, there were no barriers or roadblocks, and they were able to drive into the middle of the town and park the cars right by the British Consulate. Pushing her way through a crowd of people, May walked into the building, where in an upstairs office she found two young Englishmen. 'I am Mrs Spears', she announced. 'We've been so worried about you', they replied.

Louis had left Bordeaux for England two days earlier by plane, but she was in safe hands now, and was assured that the ambassador would get them all home. They were to leave from Arcachon, a name which brought back memories for May of her last visit there in very different circumstances, when during a holiday cruise with Louis and the children they had gone ashore to eat oysters. Now they were forced to spend two tense days there until at last, in the middle of the night, they were ferried away from shore on a couple of sardine boats, their cars abandoned at the end of the jetty, the last remnants of the Hadfield–Spears Unit. Next came what May considered to be, without question, the worst moments she had endured on the entire journey – a three hour wait, being tossed about on a nausea-inducing sea, until they were picked up by the British navy ship the *Galatea*, and from there, transferred to a passenger ship, the last British transport to leave France.

When they finally docked safely at Plymouth on 26 June, they found themselves the centre of attention. The newspapers had reported them lost without trace for two weeks, and now, their safe return after the drama of their flight across France just a few kilometres ahead of the German army, was cause for celebration. They had had an extraordinarily narrow escape, and picture captions of the girls throwing themselves into the arms of their friends and relatives as they arrived in London made an uplifting story.

15

A New Beginning

May arrived home to the discovery that Louis had taken on a new war job. On 18 June, a week before her ship sailed into Plymouth, he had flown to England from France, bringing with him General de Gaulle, who had briefly been the Under Secretary for war in Paul Reynaud's government. After the armistice, a warrant had been issued for his arrest, and a dramatic escape plan was put into action. With the pretext of seeing Louis off at the airport, de Gaulle had jumped on board the plane at the last moment, and travelled back to England with him. The two were now united by the goal of persuading the French to continue fighting.

May had never heard of de Gaulle, which was not surprising, as neither had the majority of people in England, or even France at that time, and for those in his own country who did know him, he was seen by many as a traitor. Louis explained to May that because the French nation would be subjected to continuous German propaganda, it was feared that they would take up arms against the British unless there was a French force fighting too. De Gaulle was the only minister prepared to come back with Louis to form a resistance, and although the Prime

Minister and the War Cabinet would have preferred someone from the French government who was better known and of higher standing, in the absence of choice, they had given him their backing. Now installed in an office next to Louis' in St Stephen's House in Westminster, he had established himself as the leader of the Free French, and through regular broadcasts was trying to recruit troops. The French soldiers who had been rescued at Dunkirk, and those who had made their own way to England, had been given the choice of serving under de Gaulle or returning to France.

May found the atmosphere of London strange and tense as the country waited for invasion, but what she found strangest of all was that her husband had such faith in a man they knew so little about, and that the two had set themselves a task which seemed to her hopeless. She felt her husband had lost all sense of reason – yet Louis and de Gaulle were convinced that it was possible to bring over to the Allied side the French African colonies, believing that they would not give in to the terms of the armistice, or take orders from the Vichy government. Whatever her own feelings, she realized that she was expected to take an active role in supporting the French Resistance, and without further questioning, she committed herself to the new organization with her usual brio. Within twenty-four hours of arriving back in England she opened a canteen in Olympia beside a recruiting centre. A week later she and a team of helpers opened another canteen at White City, and later on, a third one at Euston. In July, when an army training camp for new recruits was set up in Aldershot, May moved there with the Free French, taking on the role of general welfare officer. So involved had she become in the cause that she found herself offering to equip and organize a new field hospital to accompany de Gaulle's troops overseas, a proposal she put to him in a letter. Her conditions were the same as before: while emphasising the unit's Anglo-French character, she insisted on absolute authority over the female personnel as the directrice.

She had no doubts that her unit still had a purpose, but her feelings about de Gaulle were more ambivalent. He represented the country she had always been proud to serve, but she found him cold, unapproachable and hard to fathom, and she did not think she would ever grow to like him as a friend. On their first meeting, she felt a curious discomfort, almost fear, noticing how he 'stalked into the room', and how expressionless his face remained as he talked. She met him many times over the next few months, sometimes travelling from Aldershot to join him and Louis for dinner, and she continued to find these encounters disturbing. 'De Gaulle could be eloquent', she later wrote. 'He could make himself very agreeable if he felt so inclined. But he was often biting, scathing in his criticisms of England and the English, just as much or more so of France. His long lips would grimace as if he were drinking gall and wormwood when he talked of France.'[1]

May was under no illusions about the task ahead of her. She had to build the hospital from scratch, and this time she could not rely on financial help from Lady Hadfield, who was ensconced in her villa in the south of France and seemed unwilling to leave. As good fortune would have it, however, another source of money materialized. The British War Relief Society in New York answered her plea for help, sending a cheque for £25,000 as an initial payment, and agreed to send further monthly instalments to maintain upkeep. Although her financial worries were largely resolved, she had a more complex organizational task this time, since the hospital would be travelling a much greater distance, and in the desert. They would need to house all the staff and patients, as well as equipment, in tents, which would have to be transported in desert-worthy trucks, and she wanted drivers who could double up as orderlies. The difficulty was where to find such men, as there was no possibility of using troops from the Free French who had no one to spare.

One by one, volunteers emerged. The American Field Service

in New York promised to supply a group of drivers, and in England the Friends' Ambulance Unit said they could find men with hospital experience. Next stop was the Transport Section of the War Office. The kindly major who dealt with her there was at first nonplussed by her vision of a self-sufficient hospital with its own operating theatres, and at least a hundred beds, complete with mattresses, linen and pillows, all of which could be moved anywhere at any time under its own steam. This did not conform to either a field ambulance, which only used stretchers, or to a casualty clearing station, which was not mobile. What May wanted was a combination of the best points of each, and it was this that made her field hospital not only unconventional, but unique. For the extra comfort of the wounded she insisted upon pyjamas and soft blue blankets, neither of which could be described as essential, but which from past experience she knew would be appreciated by the recipients. The theatre tents required a full complement of surgical instruments and sterilizing drums, as well as hydraulic operating tables lit by lamps

May with de Gaulle

run from generators. To carry everything, May and the major calculated that they would need fifteen 3-ton Bedford trucks and as many fifteen hundredweights, plus five Ford V8s to transport the nurses and officers, which with the tents, beds, cookers and ward equipment, could be bought from the War Office.

Once again there seemed no shortage of women prepared to volunteer as nurses and drivers, in spite of May's warnings of the perils they would face in terms of tropical diseases and extremes of temperatures. In addition to the new recruits, seven of the original team members had wanted to stay on, including Barbara Graham, Kit Tatham-Warner, Cynthia Toulmin and Rosaleen Forbes of the MTC, and three of the nurses, Evelyn Fulroth, Nancy Wright and Josie Pearce. Far more difficult was the search for a medical team. Only one surgeon of note, a Colonel Fruchaud, had volunteered for de Gaulle's Medical Service, but he was not able to join them until later. Eventually, a temporary medical director was found, Commandant Durbach, and also one of the first women, if not the very first, to be employed in the French Army as an anaesthetist, Louise-Marie Asquin, with her doctor husband, and one other medical officer.

Although May was prepared to serve in the war overseas, it seemed not to occur to her that Louis might too. His news, when it came, landed like a bombshell. She was at home in bed when he returned one evening in the middle of August, in a particularly tender and loving mood, and with something clearly on his mind. He told her he was going with General de Gaulle and his forces on a secret expedition, and was unable to say more than this. She had presumed he would be staying in Whitehall, and not even the appearance of some mysterious packages in his room at Strathearn Place had done much to arouse her suspicions.

Her sense of dread increased by his very visible preparations for going away; spread out on the floor of the drawing room was his luggage, with tropical kit and an array of different medicines. At the end of August the time came to say goodbye. She went with him to Euston Station, where they both managed to keep the mood light and cheerful for each other's sake. All she knew about his mission was that he was taking with him some two thousand Free French troops, as well as British, including fifty officers and specialists, to some place in Africa. It was not until quite some time after the event that she heard that the Free French had fought at Dakar in Senegal, with British support, encountering such strong resistance that they were forced to retreat. The whole thing had turned out to be an abysmal failure. The possibility of further awful defeats haunted her as she studied maps of Africa, trying to second-guess Louis and de Gaulle's next plans. What particularly worried her was the possibility that after this fiasco, they lacked the support of the British government, and that Louis was about to launch himself on some 'further hopeless quest'. She drafted a telegram to tell him to return home and 'get the facts'. Never had she been 'more wretched & futile', she wrote in her diary:

> Feel ill with nerves – incapable of attending to anything – The truth is that I am lost without B and feeble – All the time I was in France he was behind me – supporting me – now he is gone – I am at home – and should be supporting him – But how? In my heart – yes – with my whole heart and mind – yes – But in practical, actual ways? How can I?[2]

Three days alone with Peti at her cottage, eating supper on their laps by the fireside and listening to her son's talk, restored her equilibrium. She redrafted a telegram to Louis: 'Peti and I well but I feel you do not understand situation since Dakar and should come home.'[3] This version was sent off, but the difficulty in communicating with each other exacerbated her misery. She was distressed by a letter from Louis wanting her to reply to a telegram he had sent, but she was only aware of one that Nancy had received from him, and it had not occurred to her that she should answer it. Now she felt dreadful that she had not been able to send him an affectionate message back. She understood that he trusted Nancy to defend him from his enemies in Whitehall, but her role as his indispensable assistant was a bitter pill to swallow. She 'is sensible & very loyal to him', wrote May gallantly in her diary, 'but she is there between us physically so placed that she gives me news of him & sends him news of me.'4

When a telegram arrived from Louis with the news that he might soon be returning to report to the government, she read between the lines to surmise that he was intending to remain in North Africa, an unpleasant thought which was soon confirmed by General Maurice, Nancy's father, when they met.

Throughout the autumn, while May waited for orders to leave England, she resumed her work at the canteens. The country was suffering the most intense period of the Blitz, and her diary records the surreal quality of life in London as familiar landmarks were reduced to rubble during night raids. 'Was to have met Lavinia at Punch's club but it disappeared in the night', was one diary entry. 'The north-west corner of Berkeley Square is gone, fine house disembowelled, a piece of red stair carpet waving in the wind from what is left of an upstairs landing.'5

The devastation in London reminded her of Ypres, and she was now 'beginning to realize that we are living in a world where everything dreadful that we put from us, as "this couldn't happen," is more than likely to happen. Such as? Being killed with one's soup-spoon in one's mouth. Dying alone – cut off at the cottage – as completely as if in the middle of the Sahara.' An air raid brought destruction even closer to home, demolishing the two houses next to May's in Hyde Park Square, and badly damaging her own. All the windows were blown out by the blast and the ceiling of her bedroom landed on the bed. As she surveyed the rain and mud cascading down the stairs from the holes in the ceilings, her response to the desolation was a lyrical one: she saw 'a kind of poetry' in 'the eloquence of trivial objects, contents of cupboards strewn about, whitish dust inches deep over everything, like ashes, and the view from the stair landing is like the last days of Pompeii'.[6]

Louis came home for Christmas and she went to meet him at Poole Airport, arriving in time to see his plane circling over the harbour. De Gaulle joined them at the cottage on Christmas Eve after visiting the camp at Aldershot for midnight Mass, and May observed a softer side to his character as he chatted to Peti, who was so taken by the French commander that he announced his wish to serve under him. These slightly warmer thoughts towards the general did not allay the growing unease May felt about the plan to take the unit to North Africa, and she began the New Year with dread and inertia. Over the last few months she had been going through the motions of getting the ambulance ready without the enthusiasm which had motivated her before. There was still a lot more to be done, and it took an immense mental effort to apply herself to the details.

Over dinner with General Le Gentilhomme, discussing provisions, she realized with a nasty jolt that she had greatly underestimated how many water trucks she would need for the desert. Told that she must allow enough water to last for five days at a stretch, at the rate of 2 gallons per person per day, she calculated that with one hundred patients, and another one hundred staff, they would have to carry 2,000 gallons. The trucks held only 230 gallons each, so they would need eight, and she only had enough money for four. She would have to buy more and trust that funds would be found, rather than risk being stranded without water. Again she asked herself what on earth had impelled her to let herself in for the venture. 'I don't know the answer', she wrote in her diary. 'Vanity, curiosity, sense of adventure, the will to keep young, defy time … all these bogus & shameful reasons come into it and muddle up the decent impulse to do what one can in this war.'[7]

She desperately needed reassurance that she was doing the

right thing in joining the 'ragged band' that made up the Free French. Working at the draughty canteen through the long and cold winter evenings, she served the young French recruits feeling concerned and sorry for them. They had put their faith in de Gaulle, but they seemed a disorganized and incoherent force, and she worried how they would ever succeed in their aims. French Resistance recruitment had been disappointing: at the time of the first offensive in Dakar, Free French forces numbered about three thousand men, including soldiers, sailors and airmen.

Louis was immersed in dealing with one crisis after another, far too preoccupied to listen to May's worries. Whenever she tried to see him at his office, she was unable to catch him for more than a few minutes, and it was hopeless attempting a conversation with him as it was constantly interrupted. All she had managed to get out of him was that she must make up her own mind, although he would rather she did not go. Beyond this, he could not advise her. He continued in his belief, right or wrong, that the only hope of keeping the French nation from fighting the British was to have a French force on their side, however small. His commitment to de Gaulle was absolute, and it seemed that nothing would alter this until France was liberated.

In the end, it was her husband's passionate conviction which persuaded her to follow his example, and on 22 February 1941, de Gaulle signed a document agreeing to the creation of the Hadfield–Spears Ambulance under the specific terms requested by May, and this unequivocal endorsement of her authority over the women personnel was something she would be extremely glad to have in her possession. Then, at the beginning of February, the hospital began its exodus, setting off in a convoy for Cardiff, whence it was shipped on a steamer to East Africa. Taking up two and a half miles of road, it seemed to May an impressive sight, although she wondered what would happen to all their cars and equipment if the fighting in East Africa was all over before they arrived.

16

Doubt and Disillusion

She found the wait exasperating, and in the meantime, Louis was leaving on another secret mission of which she knew nothing, except that he and de Gaulle were to fly to West Africa. When the time came, she saw him off with a heavy heart, only to have him back in her arms a few hours later when his flight was delayed. 'The anguish of the first day's goodbye couldn't be repeated', she wrote after they had parted once more. 'One can't suffer or register beyond a given point – so we were compassionately cheerful.'[1] Then, a few days later, her turn to be off finally came. Carrying a bundle of papers with her instructions marked 'secret', she and her British girls, the French commander Durbach, and three thousand Free French troops, embarked at Glasgow on the SS *Otranto*.

The six weeks they spent at sea, following a circuitous route to avoid the German and Italian navy in the Mediterranean, were something of an endurance test for May. She felt none of the excitement that she had when her old unit set off for France a year before. She missed her old team members whose companionship would have been a comfort as she stood on the brink of a new adventure; now she was mostly surrounded by strangers who were untested and might prove inadequate for the task – a concern that seemed well founded judging by the behaviour of her second-in-command, Miss Fischer, who had quickly revealed a bad temper, and was making no effort to get on with anyone. This boded ill if she was expected to have any authority in May's absence. Mulling the problem over in her diary, she decided that the path of diplomacy was the most advisable. 'My line for the moment must be exquisite politeness', she wrote. 'But I foresee endless bother.'

Out of all the girls she had brought with her, and in terms of reliability, ability and humanity, she ranked Barbara first, followed by Cynthia, Rosie and Kit Tatham Warner (who became known as TW). Although to outward appearances she seemed calm and resolute, inside she was still tormented by terrible doubts about the wisdom of what she had taken on, and the burden of responsibility made her feel isolated. 'I am lonely on this crowded ship', she wrote in her diary. Living quarters were particularly confined in the first week when it was too cold to sit outside. Passengers sought refuge in the lounge, where, in spite of the crush and the blaring jazz band, May attempted to organize after-dinner games in the interests of group solidarity. Yet her hope of getting the different members of staff to gel seemed at times a losing battle. The French and English were reluctant to mix, and her second-in-command consistently rebuffed May's invitations to join her for bridge – a further black mark as far as her boss was concerned.

When at last she could be alone at night in her cabin, May was kept awake by thoughts of Peti and Louis, missing them unbearably. She tried not to think of how cut off from them she was, and the effort made her apathetic. To her staff, however, she gave the impression that she was enjoying her time on board the ship as much as they were; for once they had left winter behind the voyage could have been mistaken for a pleasure cruise as they sailed south past the Azores and down the west coast of Africa, lazing on deck in warm sun, drinking cocktails before dinner, and afterwards dancing, playing bridge or watching the stars in the night sky. The war seemed strangely remote, even though by this stage the Axis had control of most of the Mediterranean and were preparing to invade Greece.

A highpoint of the journey for May was her first taste of Africa when they stopped off at the British naval base of Freetown, in Sierra Leone. Before she had even set foot on land, she was rallied by a letter from Louis, wired through to the ship. He had passed through a few weeks earlier and had made sure May was looked after when she got there. First came lunch with the admiral, an invitation extended to some of her girls, and that same night she was the guest of the Governor, with a room at Government House. 'It is all lovely & exciting thanks to B – whose long arm is reaching out to protect us', she wrote in her diary. His letter had 'taken away the loneliness', and with her sense of adventure restored, she embraced the 'wonderful sensation of seeing something quite new and entirely different' from anything she had before.

Back on board the ship, though, her spirits plummeted as grim news reached them of the Allied retreat in Libya. In February 1941 General Rommel had been made Commander of the Axis forces in North Africa with a mission to support the Italian troops in Libya and to threaten the British in Egypt. His first offensive was launched in March 1941 and having begun by forcing the British out of El Aghelia, by May he had recaptured all the territory lost by the Italians. It was a particularly bad time for the Allies with the simultaneous loss of the war in Greece.

Hearing of this last news, May was gripped again with dread for Louis and horrible regrets about the decisions she had taken. With nerves on edge, she found it difficult to muster the energy to stay in charge, and her staff were becoming increasingly unruly. She took a firm stand, breaking up a noisy late-night party the girls were having on the upper deck, dancing to gramophone records. She knew it was all harmless fun, and did not like to make herself unpopular, and even wondered afterwards if she had behaved a little peevishly at not having fun herself.

Far more tiresome was her second-in-command whose rebelliousness defeated her. She tried everything, from frosty civility to bullying and threats, and was at a loss to know what to do next. The more Miss Fischer played up, the more she inspired May's hostility, which took an increasingly personal slant. If she managed to conceal her feelings in public, she gave full expression to them in her diary, finding fault with her deputy's looks and manners, her mode of speaking and her ignorance; she was appalled when the hapless girl asked the padre why he had never married. Eventually matters came to a head when May felt forced to ask for her resignation – perhaps unwisely for the demand not only sent Miss Fischer into an apoplectic vengeful fury, but enabled her, once freed from her employment, to cause even more trouble, without fear of reprisal.

As if all this was not wearying enough, when they stopped to go ashore in Durban, Father Kelly twice had to be carried back on board after becoming too drunk to walk. 'Is this an ill-starred enterprise?' she asked herself in her diary. 'It has begun badly … I could lose my nerve about the whole thing – But won't.' Resting on a small bed in a hotel in Durban, she gave herself a pep talk, summoning the determination to face the future, whatever it might bring, although, as she later wrote in her diary, 'instead of gnashing my teeth and chewing my pillow', she fell asleep. 'Don't seem up to much physically', she reflected. 'That too is a worry.' Then, when she tried to return to the ship, she was dropped off at the wrong place by a taxi, and became lost in the dark and the rain, trudging for what felt like miles along the docks past railway trucks. But after this unnerving detour, she was restored later by the sight of the ships of the convoy steaming out of the harbour, 'all the troops cheering'.

When on 2 May the *Otranto* came to the end of her voyage and anchored at Suez, May was thrust into an atmosphere of surprise and excitement. She was greeted by officers from the Spears

Mission, who came aboard with the news that her unit was to join the Free French division in British-controlled Palestine; but before that, she was to meet Louis in Cairo at the British Embassy for a few days' rest. She had had no idea that he was in Egypt, and had convinced herself that by now he would be on his way back to England with de Gaulle. As she absorbed this wonderful news, her new medical chief, Fruchaud, turned up, back from the Eritrean campaign where he had run a forward operating theatre, and with him Mr Stokes of the American Field Service, who had recently arrived with fifteen drivers from New York. He was able to tell her that the hospital equipment had been safely disembarked at Port Said, and all the composite parts of the unit were now united. It seemed almost too good to be true that everything had worked out as planned.

Hardly catching her breath, she was hurried off the ship and into a car waiting on the quay to take her to join Louis for two 'delirious days'. She found him absorbed in planning the Syrian campaign which was seen as necessary to prevent the Germans gaining control of the region. Although distracted, he was attentive and 'very sweet' to her, and to be looked after by a maid was 'wonderful'. She noted the absence of any sense of the war in Cairo, where they dined together on 'delicious food as in peacetime' and the hairdressers had 'every luxury'.

It was not all pleasure, though; at a meeting with General Sir Archibald Wavell, the British commander in the Middle East, she discussed plans for her unit, and the threat to British positions if the Vichy French in Syria allowed the Germans the use of their airfields. Another day she was invited to have tea with the powerful and much-feared wife of General Catroux, and the meeting heralded the start of an uneasy relationship. She was 'even worse & more dangerous than I expected', wrote May. Attractive and chic, and with a steely will, Madame Catroux had had considerable experience in the Red Cross, although at that point in time was unoccupied and May suspected that she would love to take over her hospital. Indeed, she had her own views on how it should be run. As they exchanged civilities, Madame Catroux made it clear that she thought it inappropriate for English nurses to care for the French wounded, and suggested that French staff could be recruited in Egypt. Although prickling at this interference, May knew better than to quarrel, and continued to sip her tea in silence before replying carefully that she was perfectly willing to employ French nurses, provided they were fully qualified and prepared to accept English methods.

With so much to occupy her thoughts, she paid little attention to the fact that she was feeling unwell, and had developed a sore and flaming spot on her shoulder. By the time she rejoined the unit at Suez, she had a high fever, and the onward journey to Palestine passed in 'a daze of heat and pain'. A large infected boil was the source of the trouble, severe enough to have her transferred straight to a British field hospital where she was laid up for four weeks, much to her frustration. It was small consolation that the hospital was a luxurious one, with electric fans keeping the wards refreshingly cool – but to begin with she was far too ill to appreciate anything much. In a letter to Nancy, Louis referred to her condition as extremely serious.

From her hospital bedside she received solicitous visits: General Koenig, recently returned from the Eritrean campaign, in whom she put her trust, kind and 'consoling' General Le Gentilhomme, who had commanded the French troops in Somalia and who talked to her frankly about preparations for Syria; and on her fifty-fifth birthday, Louis came to see her. She thought he was 'looking very fine and handsome', but he was concerned about her state of mind, finding her 'v nervy and overwrought'. He told her that she must show a calm façade and 'not give the unit the impression that she was forever worried to death'.[2]

She had good reason to be anxious, for once she started to feel physically better she was depressed by stories of tensions between the French and English within the unit, stationed not far from her at a camp in Sarafind. Barbara, who spoke French as well as Arabic, having been brought up in Cairo, had taken charge in her absence, but there seemed a complete lack of cohesion. In fact, it was such a disparate group that May felt it could hardly be called a unit at all. Her demoted second-in-command had caused ructions by whipping up bad feeling against her, Father Kelly was proving to be nothing more than a drunkard, and even Fruchaud was adding to the general furore. He came to see her most days, always bringing the problems of the unit to her bedside and one day turning 'very nasty' and reporting that General Koenig had said she could look after herself and he had no need for her hospital. This outburst left her 'utterly dumbfounded', and she had no idea why Fruchaud had suddenly turned on her. She found him hot-tempered, but admired his enthusiasm and commitment to his work, and when he was in a good mood, he was wonderful company, but on his visits to see her in hospital, he was withdrawn and troubled, and she suspected he was hiding something from her.

As for Commandant Durbach, he remained aloof and unfriendly, and she sensed that he resented her position as Directrice and having to work with her British volunteers, and no doubt shared the attitude of Margot Catroux. Lying in her hospital bed brooding over these problems, she debated transferring her English nurses to a British hospital, where they would cause less friction. But the idea of breaking up the unit was too awful to contemplate, and in any case, she had signed a contract with de Gaulle. She had also been warned by Louis that the British authorities did not want her hospital to go into Syria with the Free French, as it was not their policy to have a medical unit so close to the front. All this made her feel miserable and helpless, for she was in no fit state to sort the problems out, and when she learned the unit was to be moved from its present comfortable camp, surrounded by orange groves and with every amenity, in order to make way for troops, her low physical state baulked at the prospect of 'roughing it'. She began to wonder seriously whether it was not just that she was too ill to contemplate these things, but 'too old for this job altogether.'[3]

When May was finally discharged from hospital, she went to recuperate at the King David Hotel in Jerusalem, where she had a room with a terrace and a view of the old city. The top floor of the hotel had been taken over by GHQ as Free French, British and Australian forces prepared to cross the border into Syria and Lebanon for Operation Exporter. Louis joined her for a night, her brief time with him marred by the panic-inducing prospect of him leaving in the morning, with no idea when she would see him again. The next day, still not at all well, she accompanied him to the airport, struggling against dizziness and fatigue. Once he had gone, she gave in to her misery. They had been married for twenty-four years, she wrote in her diary. 'A quarter century that has passed like lightning – and now I am waiting the last of it out here away from him.'

She feared for Louis' physical safety, but also – quite rightly – that he had made enemies among the commanders at the Middle East headquarters who resented his special relationship with Churchill. A pleasant lunch with George Bernard Shaw and his wife at their rented house in Palestine was dampened by Barbara bringing the news that TW, head of the MTC Unit, had left her post to take off with a French officer in one of the cars without permission, or even a message, and had failed to return. May was furious with her for letting 'the whole show down' and determined this would result in her dismissal – a decision she rescinded once she had calmed down, and the driver had returned to explain her actions. But with so much trouble in the ranks, her confidence in her ability to run a good ship was sorely tested.

Since arriving in Palestine, while the French division reformed after the Eritrean campaign, the unit had functioned briefly with three wards and one theatre, receiving a total of fifty-eight patients for medical and post-operative treatment. The quiet time allowed the staff to check stores and reorganize for the next move. This was expected at any time and would signal the start of the Syrian campaign. As everyone waited, May discussed contingency plans with Louis and what she should do if things went wrong and she had to get the girls home quickly. She was alarmed by his reply that they would have to return by way of India and America.

When word finally came to pack up and be ready to move within thirty-six hours, a buzz of excitement went round the camp, and on 7 June the convoy set off northwards, May with her shoulder bandaged up, just well enough to take to the road with her unit a year to the day since they had begun their retreat across France. She found herself thinking of the 'old lumbering motley collection' of vehicles which had made its way through the Auvergne hills, now replaced by new trucks, and heading off into a very different terrain.

Their first night they stopped near the Transjordan border, where, too tired to put up tents, they slept in the vehicles. The next day they reached Irbid, close to the place where the battle for Deraa, a town just inside the Syrian frontier on the road from Jerusalem to Damascus, was in progress. The fighting had begun that morning, the invasion force made up of 30,000 men from the Indian Army, Free French, British and the Transjordan Frontier Force, who confronted a Vichy army of between 35,000 to 40,000. As the desert around them swarmed with trucks and troops, May's staff struggled to pitch the hospital tents against a 'tearing wind' and 'blazing sun', and by the time the wounded began to arrive the operating tent was ready, X-ray was working and thirty-two beds made up – 'Not a bad effort', wrote May.

One of the first casualties to arrive was the commandant of Deraa who upset some of the nurses with his haughty demeanour. May had a policy of never turning anyone away, but the need to nurse Vichy and Free French side by side inevitably generated considerable tension. Far from the two opposing French forces refusing to fight each other, as had been hoped, the animosities seemed intensified and the conflict was particularly brutal. Nevertheless, May agreed to meet General Catroux at the fort of Irbid, five miles across the desert, to act as an interpreter for a group of Vichy officers taken captive, who were to be given the chance of joining de Gaulle. This proved an experience she wished never to repeat, and her complicity in the bitter affair made her acutely uncomfortable and miserable. It was only too clear to her that there would be no sudden change of allegiance from the officers, and it seemed illogical to expect otherwise when only the day before they had fought so hard against de Gaulle's forces.

She returned to camp to find the unit packing up for the third time within the week, having received orders to move forward to Deraa and prepare to receive the wounded from the Battle of Damascus. In the European district of the small town, the outlook was inhospitable: 'The Khamsin was blowing like a wind out of a furnace, clouds of yellow dust were rolling down the street to envelop the ugly houses, the few starved trees and straggling troops in billows of yellow fog, and the windscreens of our cars were thick with flies.'[4]

On the other side of a deep wadi lay the Arab quarter, a cluster of flat-roofed houses on a plateau, and beyond it, mile upon mile of flat, arid desert stretching away into the horizon. Scanning the area, May could see no place to set up camp. All the houses had been taken by the troops. Then she saw a small figure making its way towards her through the dust, an apparition that seemed to be literally heaven-sent. The mother superior of a recently evacuated convent school had come to offer its building and grounds as a base for the unit, and this proved to be an almost perfect setting for the hospital. The classrooms were easily adapted as wards, the vehicles took over the courtyard, and in the field adjoining the convent, there was ample space for the staff tents. There was even a well for water, the only one in the town which had not been blown up by the Vichy: it had been saved by the defiance of the mother superior who had sat upon it, declaring that they would have to blow her up with it – clearly a challenge judged too daunting to take up.

From the moment the hospital opened it took in a steady stream of wounded, with the operating theatre running twenty-four hours a day. There was only one other field hospital in the area, and all the most serious cases were sent to the Hadfield–Spears Unit, which during the three weeks of fighting, received around six hundred serious surgical cases. This included British and Colonial casualties needing urgent treatment for although the British medical authorities did not allow hospitals like May's to be so near the line, particularly one with female staff, without it the wounded would have to travel two or three days before they could be treated.

Later, May would think back to the 'suffocating, fly-infected schoolrooms smelling of blood and gangrene', and the beds filled with the 'refuse of shattered bodies'. What the nuns thought of the havoc unleashed there, she could only wonder, but they did their share of work, each morning collecting the piles of bloody sheets to scrub clean. When the fighting intensified during the big battle which started on 15 June and continued for four days, the flow of wounded became 'an avalanche', with May writing in her diary of 'the nightmare of suffering', and the torment, not just of the 'dreadfully sick men', but of the hot desert wind, which blew mercilessly.

One day General Le Gentilhomme was brought in, having been wounded by a machine-gun bullet and his presence turned the hospital into 'a sort of secondary G.H.Q.', according to May. 'You never saw such a fuss', she wrote of the crowds attending him. 'The Salle des Entrées like a race meeting', but the patient himself she thought 'very sweet' lying on the operating table, 'small and frail' and 'exquisitely courteous'. A few days later, a more alarming pandemonium broke out as Deraa itself came under attack, and the hospital was suddenly flooded with patients from the nearby Indian Ambulance, which had been ordered to evacuate because a column of the enemy had broken through the lines. May was told to be ready to move too, and already the village had filled with troops taking up battle positions around them.

Then in the afternoon the hospital was bombed. May and her staff were quite accustomed to a lone Vichy plane flying over early each morning spraying machine-gun fire, but as the tents were widely spread out, no one had ever been hurt. If the bullets seemed to be coming close to May's tent, she simply rolled out of bed to shelter beneath it. On the day of the bombing, however, many of the nurses were resting after lunch, and her abiding memory was the sight of them all 'legging it across the fields' as they made for the shelter of the convent building. One bomb landed between two of the trucks but fortunately failed to go off, but another fell on the ammunition dump near by, creating a massive explosion. None of the staff was injured in the raid, but others were not so lucky. A bomb hit the railway station, killing all the patients waiting to be transferred to a base hospital in Nazareth.

As explosions shook the town, May went off to speak to the area commander at the army headquarters to see if she should evacuate her unit, but was told to stay put. Enemy troops were reported to be just a mile away.

May's shoulder flared up again forcing her to remain in bed for several days. By the time Damascus was taken she was recovered enough to travel there the next day with Cynthia, driving in blistering heat along the bombed road and into the strangely quiet streets of the city to find General Koenig installed in his new headquarters. She had been sent by Fruchaud to find a new base for the unit which he believed was now too far behind the battle lines to serve any useful purpose. His insistence that surgical operations should take place as close to the front line as possible had earned him something of a reputation. 'Your Fruchaud is a madman', General Koenig said of the intrepid Frenchman to May at their meeting. 'He wants to operate under the mouths of the guns.'[5]

This time no one objected to them following the troops, and May felt satisfied that the new Hadfield–Spears Unit had finally become an 'integral part of the French Brigade'.[6] It had proved its worth in the height of battle at Deraa and received praise from the base hospitals in Nazareth and Jerusalem for the treatment of the patients sent on to them. Even the British command was forced to recognize the unit's importance as a field hospital.

New quarters were found for the unit in an Italian hospital in time for it to receive the wounded from the Battle of Beirut, and May took up residence on the ground floor of a nearby house which she shared with her drivers, Barbara, Rosie, Cynthia and TW. It had a terrace and a small garden with a stream running through, and each day they sat outside to eat breakfast of fresh eggs, orange juice, butter on bread and coffee, a welcome relief from their usual army rations. Compared to the deprivations of camping in the desert, their life seemed idyllic. May had immediately come under the spell of Damascus, 'a stern city, old, proud, moody and violent; its beauty was cold, or again it was hot; the colours in the bazaars were like running flames'.[7]

She found endless delight in wandering through the souk in her free time, soaking up the vibrant atmosphere, and returning with odds and ends to decorate her temporary living quarters. The daytime heat of the city in July, though, was something she had to get used to, the 'floor red-hot under your feet, the sky a white-hot metal lid covering the world', but at least 'the air was dry, the evenings were cool and the minarets of the mosques were frail silver at night under the stars'. To escape the intense daytime temperatures, she liked to drive into the countryside or to visit 'a crazy café that hung high above the road at the top of a steep and uncertain wooden stair.'[8]

One night they held a small party on their terrace, where they danced to the wireless by candlelight. Another evening May was invited to join the Indian regiment for a picnic supper in an olive grove, where the party sat on cushions, their surroundings illuminated by lanterns hung from the trees, to eat chicken curry, rice and chapattis to the accompaniment of Indian music. 'A wonderful body of men these Indians', she wrote later of the troops, thoroughly enchanted by the whole 'lovely party', and by their Major Buich about whom she felt she could write a story – 'his extraordinary ability' and his 'disastrous sex-appeal'.[9]

During her three weeks in Damascus, Louis came several times to report on the Syrian situation for the War Cabinet and stayed with May, allowing them what felt like borrowed time together. Not long after he left, word came that the Vichy troops had withdrawn from Beirut, the road there from Damascus had opened, and Louis was already there from Cairo. May took off at once to see him, taking Rosie as her driver, and she would never forget her first sight of the breathtaking views, with the 'long smooth sweep' of the Bekaa Valley, the 'winding climb over the mountains' and 'Mt Hermon white as crystal in the far distance'.[10]

Her arrival in the Lebanese capital on 14 July coincided with the state entry of General Wilson and General Catroux, but her diary records Louis' frustration over the proposed terms of the armistice from which the Free French were virtually excluded, and their right to seek recruits from the Vichy side-stepped. Although a compromise was eventually reached, thanks in large part to Louis' intervention, de Gaulle's pride was deeply wounded and his resentment towards the British reached a new low. May observed the tensions between different factions: the Syrians 'full of discontent', the Vichy behaving like 'vanquishers' and de Gaulle's actively hostile attitude towards the British – a volatile situation which inevitably grew worse. To gain local support for an advance into Syria, Louis had proposed to London that Britain and the Free French should give a guarantee of independence for the Levant states of Syria and Lebanon – the two largest French colonies in the Middle East — and on the first day of the Syrian campaign, Catroux had duly issued one which was endorsed by the British and backed up by a separate disclaimer of any territorial ambitions in the region. In spite of this, the establishment of independence was characterized by suspicion and rivalry between the French and English, and was the main cause of a complete breakdown in relations between Louis and de Gaulle.

At least relations between May and Madame Catroux seemed to have taken a turn for the better. The French general's wife invited May to dine with her at the French residency in Damascus and the meeting was full of bonhomie from the moment she entered the house – a 'bit of authentic France' with its Louis Quinze furniture in the elegant drawing room, and the 'fresh shadowy garden', all a happy reminder of rue Monsieur. Her hostess had turned on her utmost charm, talking intimately about how she and 'Georges' had first met, and she even offered May and Louis the use of her house in the mountains at Aley, half an hour's drive from Beirut. The combined effect of this offensive was enough to seduce her guest.

Madame Catroux had seemed to want to offer May her hand of friendship, and she 'walked on air' as she said goodnight, but before too long she was brought back down to earth. First came the discovery that the house in Aley was in fact the official summer residence of the outgoing high commissioner in the Levant, and had been put at the disposal of General Catroux, whose wife had let it go in preference for something grander. Madame Catroux 'was the first lady' in Beirut, May noted wryly, and she was clearly relegated to that of second.

All the same, she was delighted with the house which overlooked olive groves and a deep valley. Close enough to Beirut for her to travel in each day, it provided a cool and peaceful retreat from the bustle and heat of the city, although when Noël Coward came to stay during a round of troop concerts, he found the change in temperature too extreme, and the house itself 'slightly sinister'.[11] In the evenings, May liked to eat her supper on the terrace, watching the changing light on the mountains, and the ships sailing in and out of Beirut harbour on the distant horizon. It was from here that she watched the Vichy forces of some 35,000 men set sail for France, leaving just 3,000 Free French troops and the British Eighth Army to defend the Syrian frontier.

The Hadfield–Spears Unit was installed in what had previously been a German hospital, with bright and sunny wards, and wide verandas looking out over the bay to the mountains beyond. Louis was made temporary head of the British Mission to the newly liberated Levant States, and had his headquarters next door. When, in the autumn, colder weather set in and rainstorms lashed the hills around Aley, May and Louis went in search of a more benign winter home, moving into the old Japanese Consulate in Beirut, 'a large house with a fine hall, vaguely reminiscent of Venice',[12] which stood not far from the centre of the town. They did not expect to stay there long, but it was to become their home for the next three years.

Keeping house for Louis in an official residence was not at all what May had envisaged when she left England, but she was by no means averse to it, quite the opposite, for it was the first time in many years that she was 'mistress in his house' and the relief of this was 'enormous'. With her rival Nancy far away, she felt more valued by Louis: 'I think he realizes that I am after all quite a useful person', she mused in her diary. 'That sort of thing being separate from the fact that we are bound by memory – purpose – love. I at any rate have never admired him more.'[13]

Yet even if Nancy was out of sight, she was not out of mind for Louis who wrote to her regularly, and his letters reveal how much she meant to him. He worried for her safety and was made quite desperate with panic whenever he did not hear from her. Nevertheless, in her absence, it was a particularly happy existence for May. In the future she came to think of this time as 'a hiatus between two periods of strenuous endeavour'.[14] For the time being her hospital work was not too demanding, and she had the opportunity to become acquainted with the city and its people.

Beirut she found, 'soft, luscious as ripe fruit', but lacking the character of Damascus:

> No elegance of the desert swept through its tortuous streets; the Arab chiefs who swaggered through the suhks of Damascus with flowing cloaks and clanking spurs gave place in Beirut to pale Jesuit Fathers and dusky bearded Bishops of the Maronite Church or the Greek Orthodox; the languid camels that wound their stilted way from the market place toward the hills seemed not to be at home.[15]

On the other hand, the Lebanese people were easier to befriend, being more used to living in a Christian community and many were themselves Christian. It was not surprising that May became a habitué of the privileged sphere of the 'rich cosmopolitan set' who welcomed them into their lives. May found this group of Lebanese superficial and not 'very weighty' in conversation, but they were 'gentle and sensitive' and could not have been more generous in responding to her requests for help in providing food parcels for the British troops, or whatever else was asked of them. There was also the community of Lebanese, French and British politicians and diplomats whom May and Louis met at official receptions and dinners. Other friends were Bayard Dodge, president of the American University in Beirut, and his wife Mary, with whom she became involved in a number of work schemes. One of these ventures was initiated by the boys from the Friends' Ambulance Unit who came up with an idea for a health project more in sympathy with their Quaker philosophy than working in a military hospital. They had talked to some Syrian doctors who wanted to help their people living in remote areas, where through lack of transport medical services had broken down during the war. The boys suggested using trucks belonging to the Hadfield–Spears Unit which they could take to outlying villages and there team up with local doctors. May had quickly set to in getting permission from the necessary authorities, while Louis persuaded the Eighth Army that it would be worth their while to allocate some of their funds to the scheme, which would be a cheaper and more effective propaganda tool than all the paper distributed at great expense by the publicity services – an irony of which the FAU boys might not have been aware.

Madame Catroux had not given up trying to recruit French nurses to work at the Hadfield–Spears Unit, and May had succumbed to the pressure, employing two. This decision she soon regretted when they refused to work night shifts and acted as spies for the general's wife, reporting to her on any faults they found. The incipient friendship between the two wives was rocked, and May's guard went back up. They invariably met at official dinners and receptions, where May waited with apprehension, anticipating trouble, which eventually materialized in the form of a '*note de service*' bearing General Catroux's signature, and introducing new rules into May's hospital, including one concerning night duty. She swiftly retaliated by sending copies of her original *note de service* signed by de Gaulle and giving her complete control of the female personnel, and threatened to leave the French Health Service if this was undermined.

Madame Catroux had met her match, and she made no further attempt to take over. Instead, she started up her own field hospital, which May had the graciousness to describe as 'excellent'. After this stand-off she felt they became better friends, even if a sense of competition remained: 'If we were rivals it was friendly rivalry; if she outran me in the rapidity with which she moved across continents, we far outdistanced her in the number of men we looked after.'[16]

But these conflicts were small fry compared to the tensions building up between Louis and the British military authorities, and his relationship with de Gaulle had become openly hostile. Recuperating from a bout of bronchitis, he returned to London on leave at the end of the year. He was still officially a Member of Parliament for Carlisle, and it was uncertain how much longer he would remain as Head of Mission in the Levant, or if he would return at all. His departure brought a sudden interruption to the genial way of life into which May had settled.

Waiting anxiously for news from home, she sought the company of her Lebanese friends, uncomfortably aware of the self-indulgence of playing bridge 'in luxurious Lebanese houses', eating 'chocolate cake from a groaning table loaded with pastries' and listening to the 'gay childish chatter of these people who haven't yet realized that the world is at war'.[17] This guilt and anxiety-laden limbo came to an abrupt end when she received orders to pack up the hospital and move to the Western Desert with the First Brigade of the Free French under General Koenig, who had been asked to support the newly formed British Eighth Army.

She would not see Louis before she left and her unhappy thoughts on the subject show how truly dispensable she felt where he was concerned: 'If and when B gets back I shan't be here. He will have Miss M instead to look after him & run his house – All wrong.' Yet there was no way to avoid this outcome, unless she was to 'stay at home to try and keep B's affection', a solution which she could not seriously entertain when her hospital needed her. To add to the hurt, she knew her actions would be judged by people who had no idea of the true facts. 'The gossips will say I've left him', she anticipated, and 'he too may well imagine a grievance. Whereas the truth is that he neither needs me nor wants me when she is at hand.' She thought of the last few months they had had together, 'such a happy time with Miss M removed to the other side of the world'. But now it seemed her bête noire was to take her place. 'That at any rate is what she and he are determined shall be – and I go. So once again I have made a beautiful house for her to enjoy with him. The queerest part of it all is that he is fond of me.'[18]

May was right to presume that Nancy would return with Louis, for although she was the only person he could rely upon to look after his interests in England during his absence, and alert him to political betrayal, his need to have her safely by his side was even more urgent.

The year ended with May feeling cut off from all those she loved; her far flung family, half of whom were in America (including Comfort and her children who had evacuated there while Rupert was stationed outside London) and Michael, who she felt really needed her, unlike Louis, from whom she had had no news, 'no personal message of any kind'. She tried to think positively about the coming year, to 'live decidedly and do what is given me to do'. Then, on New Year's Day, she set off once more with the Hatfield–Spears Unit.

17

Factions in the Desert

'It is a mystery to me how we got there', she wrote later of the journey to their destination, Safafi West – a statement which epitomized the general air of ignorance and naivety with which she and her English girls launched themselves into the Desert War. After a gruelling drive to Cairo from Beirut, they spent their first week at a camp at El Daaba, on the coast road between Alexandria and Tobruk, where they waited for further movement orders. Nobody seemed to mind the delay, for it gave them a chance to acclimatize and at the same time to enjoy a fairly constant round of parties, hosted in dugouts spread about in the sand. The presence of May's girls, the first women in the place, spiced up life no end for the troops stuck inside their gloomy burrows, who wasted no time in inviting them in for drinks, food and singsongs.

By the time the unit moved on from Daaba and set off into the 'vast region of sand', its members felt like seasoned veterans, but as initiations go, it had hardly prepared for the reality of desert war. Only in retrospect did May realize how little they understood then of 'its vast ebb and flow, its great encircling movements, its sudden cyclonic changes of fortune'.[1]

An amateur attitude was compounded by their topographical blindness, for at that stage they lacked any real sense of the geography of the area, and thus could not really appreciate the significance of developments in the new British offensive.

Even for those with a knowledge of the area, it was hard going travelling along rough tracks in the sand, with no landmarks to orientate oneself. 'If you don't know where to look for Safafi West, no more did I', May later told readers in *Journey Down a Blind Alley*; for, having left the coast road at Buq Buq to head south, they found themselves in a wide and empty world consisting of sand and wind, and where the so-called road ahead of them was 'a switchback across the desert' covered by great sand drifts. These, the drivers soon learned, had to be charged head-on, ignoring the instinct to change gear; it was the only way to prevent the cars becoming bogged down in the sand.

Having eventually traversed the barely perceptible road to Safafi, they found nothing to prove they had arrived. All that marked the place was a rocky escarpment, with nowhere obvious to camp; a catastrophe was narrowly averted when they were prevented from seeking refuge in the ruins of some Arab huts which turned out to be mined. As May watched the Quaker boys wrestle in vain to put up the tents in an icy wind, she saw approaching a funnel-shaped cloud like a tornado. This was their first encounter with a sand blizzard which swept across from the west at great speed, engulfing them in dense cloud, and making May think of 'the end of the world' with man as 'helpless atoms' pitched against the 'inimical powers of nature'.

With nowhere to take cover, they arranged the vehicles in a semi-circle and huddled in them for a long night, their spirits cheered by plentiful stocks of whisky and gin. They were presently joined by a lost army truck whose four very tough-looking passengers materialized out of the 'gritty gloom' to offer drinks in exchange 'for the hospitality of our sandpit', wrote May in her diary of their woeful desert camp. 'We were a queer looking lot in the morning', she added, but 'the old rolling kitchen produced hot coffee', and soon after they moved off in search of a more suitable spot. Finding a better place to pitch their tents and prepare for the wounded, they were greeted with amazement by officers who could not conceal their surprise at seeing 'ladies in the desert'. May heard one of them say 'it's crazy', and she was inclined to agree. 'If he meant our driving across the desert through a sandstorm alone – he was right.'[2]

The unit had been sent to Safafi to receive the wounded from the offensive to take Halfaya Pass. This was rendered unnecessary by the German retreat and instead the hospital was ordered to move to Timini, beyond the strategically important port of Tobruk, from which Rommel had been forced to withdraw in early December. May set off ahead of the unit with her female personnel to find new quarters, happily oblivious to the fact that Rommel had chosen that very same morning to counter-attack, and in the ensuing general confusion, with Rommel's army making rapid advances into Allied territory, she found herself, just as she had in France, blindly travelling a path, that if pursued, would have taken her ahead of the brigade troops and slap into the Axis forces. When she turned up at the Area Headquarters in Tobruk to seek further instructions, she could not understand why she was greeted with such a look of shock. 'I understood, when I told them that I had sixteen women with me, that it was awkward for them', she later wrote of her reception that day. 'But I didn't know that we were the only women in the desert west of Mersa Matruh, and it took me some time to realize that they not only didn't know what to do with us or where to put us for the night, but were profoundly shocked at our being allowed in the desert at all.'[3]

No-one, it seemed, wanted responsibility for them, but eventually they were granted permission to camp beside Tobruk Beach Hospital. They woke next day to find themselves in the midst of another sandstorm which extended far and wide. After several frustrating days of being marooned, May was anxious to

May in the Western Desert

make contact with the unit, and as soon as she was able, she set out to look for it. She was relieved when she managed to track down General Koenig on the road to El Adam, but he could not enlighten her on the whereabouts of her hospital. Like everything else, it had become lost in the sandstorm, Koenig informed her, showing his exasperation with the forces of nature, but then he broke into laugher as he asked, 'And you, chère Madame, is it correct, do you think, to advance ahead of your troops?'[4] In fact, it was becoming something of a habit.

The chaos of war was compounded for May by orders from the Commanding Officer of the Free French conflicting with those of the Eighth Army, a situation which culminated in the worst of possible scenarios when, having eventually rejoined the unit, she was told to head for Timini, where the French Brigade, under General de Larminat, had an advanced post. As they travelled there, May observed, in worried silence, the British coming towards them in the opposite direction.

'The stream of convoys going down toward Tobruk, and the fact that none were coming up, had puzzled me, but it was only now that I became uneasy', she wrote later of her gradual realization of the problem she was facing.

> The road was one unbroken procession of vehicles moving east and it was made up of every kind of unit and it was travelling fast. Guns, supply columns, ambulances, signals, all were making east as fast as they could go. And nothing was going west save ourselves. Barbara was driving me and I was sitting beside her. She said nothing. We watched fascinated. At last I spoke. 'It looks singularly like a retreat to me. What do you say?'[5]

A full-scale retreat it was indeed, but this did not prevent them from executing their original plan to travel to Timini, some 60 miles beyond Tobruk. Here they erected the hospital tents in a suitable-looking field which unfortunately happened to be the very site that the Eighth Army had chosen to position their guns the next day in preparation for battle. To make matters worse, May had lost contact with Larminat; Fruchaud, as a French officer under his command, categorically refused to obey British orders to retreat, insisting his orders were for the unit to stay where it was, and for him to join the Brigade in Mekili with a light section in the morning.

Although the aim of the unit was always to be as close to the front as possible, to be practically on top of it was clearly foolhardy, and much as May hated the feeling that they were 'running away' and feared the repercussions from Fruchaud and Larminat, she saw she had no choice but to obey the orders of the Eighth Army who by now were frantic to see them on their way. She had been told quite plainly that their presence was embarrassing, and besides that, they would not be able to evacuate the wounded or have supplies brought to them for the situation was 'pretty grim'. As a compromise, it was agreed that while the bulk of the unit returned to Tobruk, Fruchaud would join Larminat in the advanced post at Mekili. May loathed breaking the unit up, but it seemed the only solution, and by dawn they were retracing their steps along a road now empty of traffic.

She felt in better fettle as their new camp began to go up on a strip of beach they had been allotted outside Tobruk. It reminded her of Cornwall, and at least they were to have a chance to settle somewhere. But any sense of contentment was short-lived. As she sat down to eat supper, a message came from Larminat ordering the unit to return at once to Timimi. This command was shortly followed by a note from the Eighth Army stating that they were not to move from Tobruk and that 'this order supersedes all other orders'. May decided to obey it, but next day she set off to speak to Larminat to try to explain her actions. With TW driving, they travelled back through the still retreating convoys and beyond, toward the advance camp at Mekili. Out in the wide sandy wilderness, there were a bewildering number of tracks to follow and with no idea whether they were even going in the right direction, they saw a French truck and flagged it down to ask the way. The driver turned out to be the brigade's postman, who, by happy coincidence, was able to produce two letters addressed to May, one from Louis in London, and another from Peti.

Pushing onward, they eventually found the French Brigade camp, whereupon May approached the general's caravan, her 'knees trembling'. As she stood anxiously before him, his icy manner did nothing to relieve her discomfort. It was clear that he was extremely angry, and her attempt to explain her predicament of conflicting orders did little to appease him. As far as he was concerned, she should obey him, otherwise she might as well take her hospital back to England. She was too afraid of him to argue, let alone mention the fact that he was under the Eighth Army himself. The thought that Fruchaud might feel the same resentment toward herself, and to the British staff members in the unit, made her feel wretched. She decided she could not return to Tobruk until she had talked things over with her Médicin Chef. Learning that he was somewhere further toward the front, she was so impatient to speak to him and so distracted by her horrible dilemma, that she did not listen to the directions given her, or think to ask for an escort. Instead, she and her driver set off again into the desert, with only the 'vaguest of notions' as to where they were going:

> It was a silly thing to do. Mekili was a very advanced post. There was nothing between it and the enemy save a stretch of empty sand. We only realized how empty it was when we had left the fort some miles behind us. Not a track anywhere on the horizon. Nothing moving in all that vast expanse save ourselves. No sign of any living thing. And the sun was down, the sky was crimson beyond the darkening sand.[6]

May's impulsive decision to go charging off in the fading light towards the enemy on something of a wild-goose chase was, as she herself realized, somewhat reckless; and if she was in any doubt about lurking dangers as they continued on their way, their predicament was brought home to her when TW abruptly stopped the car and announced that they were in the middle of a minefield. Somehow managing to reverse carefully the way they had come without detonating any explosions, they pushed on a little further down a track, May with growing misgivings but bowing to TW's refusal to give up.

Their persistence was rewarded, for camped between a sand hill and a dry stream bed, they found Fruchaud and the advance team, and had timed it just right to join them for a camp fire supper. Afterwards, she took the surgeon aside to tell him of her decision to stay in Tobruk, and was heartened to see that he appeared to appreciate her situation and respect her decision. For her part, although she understood his reasons, she had grave concerns about him being so far forward, and was also extremely unhappy at having to split up the unit.

May now had to turn her attention to the next pressing task of establishing the main body of the unit in new quarters at the General Hospital outside Tobruk. It was certainly needed there, for although the military hospital was well staffed by doctors and surgeons, its nurses had been evacuated away from the front in keeping with British army policy, leaving it very short of hands. May no doubt took army officials in the garrison by surprise when she interrupted a meeting to announce the arrival of herself and her nurses, and when told they could not stay, refused to take no for an answer in her usual indomitable way. Being Louis' wife undoubtedly lent her confidence and helped her cause, but from a practical point of view, she could see that the unit was needed there, and she was charged with an impatience to get to work and prove that they were perfectly capable. Her persistence won the day and they were allocated a wing of the hospital with eighty beds, while the staff camped in tents on the beach: the colonel dealing with them could not 'have been nicer', as wrote May effusively, but the conditions at Tobruk were more 'squalid' than anything she had seen before.

Without staff to do the laundry, bedding had gone unchanged and new patients had been placed in sheets stiff with old blood. Appalled as she was, May was a tactician as much as she was obstinate, and she did not want to rock the boat when she knew her team were there on sufferance. She gave her nurses a lecture, warning them they were not to complain about anything; they had to make the best possible impression and show their worth to the British military and their surgeons. Her staff were used to her fights with bureaucracy, but they also knew how important it was to her that she break down prejudices against women working at the front through whatever strategy it required, and compliantly they got on with the task at hand, transforming the wing within twenty-four hours of moving in.

As soon as she was able, May went to visit Fruchaud and the forward unit where they were camped in a lonely part of the desert at El Azrac. She shared a cup of tea with Nick Alderson, head of the Friends' Ambulance Unit, a tall and very handsome officer with 'fair curly hair, pleasant blue eyes, and charming manners', with whom she had sailed on the *Ontranto*. Now he told her of his journey from Mekili under the cover of darkness. It was the last time she would see this gentle man, for a few days later a bomb from a German plane landed smack on his slit trench, blowing off his head. He was only in his early twenties and his death was ironic for a pacifist. May had sometimes lost patience with his views, and she had been quick to judge him when she first got to know him. She had thought him weak, and a 'trifle smug', but she came to realize how mistaken she had been, and to appreciate that to stand outside the herd took a special kind of courage. She saw his sensitivity, and understood what it must have cost him to mix with the other officers on board ship. He had proved himself to a brave and very good person, and his death pained her deeply.

Dividing the unit into two caused May great distress and although she had found the forward team in good spirits, she was no less anxious about their safety so near the front line in the particularly unpredictable conditions of the desert war. She also did not want it ever to be said that she expected her staff to go where she did not. Mindful of this, as much as for her own peace of mind, when the forward unit moved again she went to see it at its new base some 80 kilometres south of Tobruk, at the desert outpost of Bir Hacheim. What, pre-war, had been an Italian fort was now the most southerly point of a line of defence held by the Eighth Army stretching some 60 kilometres across to the coastal town of Gazala. The Free French had been given the task of holding Bir Hacheim with the support of British, African and Indian brigades; and the fortress, on the outer edge of the windswept Libyan desert, with its sand sea stretching for hundreds of miles, was by any standards a desolate spot.

The hazards of reaching it were not to be minimized either, for the whole length of the Gazala Line was heavily mined. Also, the route from Tobruk to Bir Hacheim ran through an area that hardly featured on the map; and as May and her driver travelled it for the first time, there were few signs to guide them. Making their way past the burnt-out tanks, vehicles and planes, bits of twisted metal and the ubiquitous petrol tins littering the landscape, they finally reached the fort, a slightly raised area of rocky sand extending over several acres, and fenced by barbed wire, where they were amazed to find that the '3,600 troops dug into the great sandy bow were all but invisible'.[7] Their impressive camouflage disguised a warren of small trenches; arriving as a sandstorm blew up, they took an hour to locate the Hadfield–Spears Unit.

The storm was still raging as she went to talk to Fruchaud in 'a dingy, ice-cold tent' where she found him absorbed in writing his book on war surgery, the surface of the floor covered in several inches of sand which had 'whirled in under the flapping canvas'. They had 'an intelligent & amicable conversation' but he was determined to stay put, and only wished for May to obey Larminat. She could see she would have to pluck up the courage to speak again to the general, and a few days later she returned once more to try to sort things out, and prepared for another dressing-down. This time, though, the atmosphere was quite different, and their meeting, conducted with an air of informality as she sat on his bed in his caravan to discuss the whole problem of her unit, was more congenial. Koenig joined them and a decision was reached that what was needed was someone to take her role at Bir Hacheim. This job she entrusted to TW.

Even so, every few days May travelled to the fort to make sure that all was running smoothly, a journey she never took without some nervousness, especially as Barbara liked to use a direct cross-country route, and found it amusing to use her Boy Scout compass to guide them. May was good enough to indulge her whims while looking out anxiously for the wreck of a Stuka which served as a useful landmark. En route, they often stopped to talk to the men living in their trucks scattered far out in the desert, who were glad of the company to break the long lonely hours, and of the chance to talk about their families far away, pulling out photographs to show off as they shared a cup of tea.

Although 'life in the forward unit was austere' May was 'exhilarated' by her visits to the Bir Hacheim camp. Even 'shut in by minefields', there was 'a wonderful feeling of freedom and camaraderie', and here she believed she had finally found 'the old spirit of the French army of 1914–1918'. She could always guarantee a lunch far superior to one she might expect at 'any Corps Headquarters', and so avoided the usual 'cold bully beef with pickles and tinned peaches'. From the kitchen set up in a sand pit, Père Boileau, the Catholic chaplain, and the Lebanese cook, Hajali, served mouth-watering feasts of 'succulent stew with onions, hot pease-pudding, pommes frites, crème-au-chocolat, red wine and beer', and finishing off with 'large steaming mugs of strong coffee with thick condensed milk and sugar'. However, there was no escaping the heavily chlorinated, brackish-tasting water brought by truck from Tobruk.

Sleeping quarters were waist-deep holes in the sand, just wide enough to take a camp bed, with belongings stored in shelves dug into the sides of the shelter, and the roofs, at ground level, made of canvas. May was amused to see how these subterranean dwellings ingeniously evolved, with members of the unit digging increasingly elaborate, and surprisingly cosy, underground houses, some 10 feet square. Scavenging the desert wreckage for home-improvement materials was a useful diversion from boredom, and there was little that could not be used in some way. Scrap iron reinforced the roofs and petrol cans strengthened and insulated the walls. The Friends' Ambulance Unit boys even managed to rig up electric light. Their burrows gave protection from the burning sun during the day and the bitter cold at night, but after sandstorms which blew in from the Sahara, sometimes lasting four or five days, the entrances could become completely blocked and the occupants had to wait to be dug out. The brief rainy season created bog-like conditions, but also produced an astonishing array of wild grasses and flowers which suddenly sprouted forth, filling the air with scent.

Dividing her time between the garrison and the Beach Hospital, May was always strangely glad to catch sight of Tobruk as the car swept down towards the bay.

She liked to talk to the men who had remained all through the siege of the port in April to December 1941, enduring the air attacks and bombardment from three sides of land, living in houses they had built in 'deep wadis by the shore, tiny hidden villages invisible from the air that went clambering down steep narrow paths to the sea'.[8] They told her stories of their survival, but alarmed her with their conviction that they would not hold Tobruk for a second siege.

Although the fighting in the Western Desert died down between February and May 1942 as both sides prepared to strengthen their armies for the next big push, Tobruk was still subjected to constant aerial attacks by Axis forces which continued to wreak damage. On one day of particularly ferocious bombardments, an explosion brought down part of the ceiling in the unit's wing of the hospital. But in a sterling display of the British stiff upper lip, a member of the FAU who was making tea for the patients at the time continued to serve them even when they had taken cover under their beds, crawling between them on his hands and knees, until it was pointed out to him that the air raid was over. That same day, twenty British sailors were admitted for third-degree burns from the attack on Tobruk, and May saw this as a turning point in changing the attitude of the British surgical staff towards the work of the unit. From then on it was allowed to receive the most serious surgery cases among the British.

In early March May had a meeting with de Larminat who asked her to prepare the unit for its greatest challenge yet; she must select only those who were able to endure great hardship, for they would be travelling far with the planned advance. She put the question to her girls. Were they prepared to follow the brigade across 3000 miles of desert in blazing heat?[9] In the meantime, Louis was on his way back to the Middle East. He had been appointed Minister to Syria and the Lebanon with ambassadorial status. He had also been awarded a knighthood – news about which May had mixed feelings: 'I'm glad his hard work has been recognized in this small way', she wrote in her diary, 'but I hate Lady Spears – it will take a lot of getting used to.'[10] She made plans to return to Beirut and stay until she was called for the start of the next offensive. Others were leaving the unit: Barbara to join Freya Stark in Baghdad and Cynthia to visit her mother in America. By the time May returned on 11 June, however, the war in the desert had taken an unexpected turn for the worse.

Rommel had surprised the British by outflanking the southern end of the Gazala Line and advancing north. Against all odds, the garrison at Bir Hacheim managed to hold out for seventeen days in the face of relentless bombardment, refusing to surrender until the night of 11 June.

Much to their annoyance, the women attached to the advance unit were evacuated at the end of May, and two weeks before the onslaught, Colonel Fruchaud transferred to a military hospital in Alexandria, but the second surgeon, Thibaut, who had come from Damascus to join the team, proved himself worthy of the same reputation for front-line heroics. He stayed on at Bir Hacheim with an assistant and two orderlies, continuing to operate until the bitter end. On the last day, when it had become clear that the garrison could no longer hold out, and Koenig prepared his midnight exit, Thibaux performed twenty-one operations as bombs fell all around him; tragically, all his efforts were in vain, for as these last patients lay on stretchers in a hollow in the sand, to be moved under the cover of darkness by ambulance, a bomb fell on them, killing them all.

When May returned from Beirut on 11 June, the main unit was no longer in Tobruk, but at Sollum, where the next day rumours began to reach them of the surrender of Bir Hacheim. These painted a bleak picture, with reports of few survivors and the atmosphere in the hospital was thick with tension. Then the wounded began to arrive and the mood changed dramatically to one of triumph, as May recalled: 'soon all the hospital was filled with the sound of jubilant voices calling to each other from beds and stretchers; greetings, curses, shouts of defiance, and laughter and groans all mixed together'.[11] As each new arrival was greeted with questions, gradually the story unfolded of the remarkable resistance to Rommel's offensive – how they had followed Koenig out of the garrison, and 'fought their way through the German lines with hand grenades and bayonets'. The 'reception tent was out of control' with excitement, wrote May, and when Koenig visited them, he was given 'a hero's welcome', something unprecedented in her experience. One unsung hero was Susan Travers, a driver who sometimes worked with May's unit, and had piloted General Koenig to safety through the barrage of enemy fire and all the surrounding minefields.

There was little else to rejoice about and the unit was soon on the move again, swept up in the retreat as Rommel pushed the Allies back towards Cairo. A replacement for Fruchaud had arrived – Colonel Jean Frédéric Vernier – and although he and May shared a tendency towards optimism, their partnership was initiated in the direst of times. She was shocked to the core when Tobruk fell on 21 June, hardly able to believe that this 'largest supply base in the desert', that had for so long held out, had been captured. Forced to leave Sollum Bay, the unit moved back to a new position not far from the Egyptian watering town of Mersa Matruh, where in peacetime the wealthy had their villas, and from there they were moved on again to Ikingo camp outside Alexandria on the road to Cairo. The week they spent here May found the most disagreeable of the entire war. The heat and constant dust and noise from the convoys passing through, was bad enough, but they had lost contact with their brigade, and had nothing to occupy them as the retreat continued, apart from the unwelcome, daily visitations from officers arriving to inspect, and then condemn, their latrines.

Because of the peculiar Anglo-French character of the unit, it avoided being evacuated out of the combat zone. If anything, May had a problem finding someone from whom to take orders. As they were swept along in the chaos, they were passed from General de Larminat to the British medical authorities, where, when May presented herself, officers were amazed to learn that the unit had managed to get away from Tobruk without the loss of any of its vehicles or equipment, the only one to have done so. They were even more astonished to be told that, once they gave the order, she could have her hospital set up and running within three hours. Informed that she was now under the newly formed Reese Force for the defence of Cairo, she was allocated the task of providing medical services for the troops defending the bridge over the Nile.

When Rommel did not advance that far, they passed the rest of July waiting in blistering heat at Kilo 4 camp on the dusty Cairo–Suez road. The only positive memory May had from this time was an invitation to meet Dick Casey, the Minister of State in the Middle East, and his Australian wife, Maie, at their villa close to the pyramids – the beginning of a close friendship, particularly between the two women. When the German advance finally stopped at El Alamein, the unit was transferred to a Franco-Egyptian school at Heliopolis, a relatively luxurious place, with cool wards and plenty of space. Here May left it to return to Beirut, covering the 500 hundred mile distance in one day with a live grenade under the back seat, given to her driver Rosie as a souvenir, which she had promptly forgotten about. None the wiser, May arrived safe and sound at her cool mountain home at Aley, in time to join Louis and his dinner guests, including Freya Stark, just back from Baghdad, on the terrace.

May (centre) with Louis (left) in 1942 in Lebanon on the steps of their residence

18

Two Centres of Gravity

May was perfectly used to change and contrast, but her life in the desert could hardly have been more different from the one for which she now swapped it. The summer bathing season was at its peak and the day after she had arrived back in Beirut she met Louis for a picnic at the Bain Militaire, a lagoon by the sea built long before by the French army of the Levant for the exclusive use of those with a military connection. She and Louis had the use of a beach hut there, and as they ate their lunch laid out on a white cloth and relaxed on deckchairs in the sun, May observed the somewhat surreal scene taking place at this 'relic of a by-gone time': the faded beach huts, scantily dressed French women tottering by on high heels, the head of the military section of the Spears Mission sunbathing on a rock – 'a fine looking chap, Robin, such good legs' – officers supine on their backs in the lagoon. The war in the desert seemed a world away.

Later, she roused herself for a series of meetings, including one with Bayard Dodge about the mobile clinics, which were proving so successful there were plans afoot to expand them, and another with Madame Catroux, to organize a charity ball which was to be a major event. May always enjoyed the chance to relax and unwind, but without the interest of her various commitments in the Levant she would have felt bored and restless. Before August was out, she was on her way back to Cairo, this time by air, in order to inspect some new recruits to the English team of drivers. One of these was Rachel Millet, a trained children's nurse who had realized that there was a greater chance of serving overseas as a volunteer for the Mechanized Transport Corps.

She awaited her first encounter with her new boss with a degree of alarm for she had heard all about May's reputation as a passenger from the more experienced MTC girls. That The Gee, as she was known by her staff (shortened from The General), liked to be driven very fast was daunting for someone not at all familiar with Cairo or its surroundings. She had also been warned never to allow May to sit in the front as she would then take over the navigation, leading to 'wrong turnings and late arrivals', and under no circumstances to ever let her get behind the wheel, as she was 'lethal'.

Rachel later recalled May's rather strange appearance, with heavily applied make-up, and mascara smudged around her still 'beautiful grey eyes' and 'lipstick smeared over her mouth', and her 'wavering husky voice', and 'slight head tremor'. Rachel soon discovered that May was the easiest of passengers 'as long as she was firmly ensconced in the back seat, where she would happily bounce up and down over the pot-holed roads engrossed in the latest detective story'.[1] In fact, in all the time Rachel drove her, she never witnessed her flapped or fazed by any mishap, of which there were many: her only concern was to reach her destination as quickly as possible. Rachel was full of admiration for her boss and from their first meeting the two women forged a close and lasting friendship.

The Countess of Ranfurly, who defied the War Office to follow her husband to the Middle East, was equally enamoured when she met May for the first time in September 1942 at her house at Aley. Writing in her diary, the countess described May's diminutive height, snub nose and 'large humouress mouth', before enthusing about her knack for storytelling: 'Her voice is high and she speaks very slowly but one never gets impatient because she is so interesting … I could have listened to her forever. In three phrases she paints a man, in two more she gives the background, and then, with her kind crackly laugh she sets them in motion, they talk, gesticulate and move about. This afternoon I met Colonel Koenig, General Catroux and General de Gaulle … they came and went on her high thin voice and so did the mobile hospital, the smell of blood and burning tyres, the chatter of girl drivers and nurses. Lady Spears has a lot of courage - that sticks out a mile.' [2]

In October May returned once more to the unit, now in a large military hospital in the delta at Buselli, in time for the great battle of El Alamein. Again the wounded poured in. It was a particularly sad day when one of the men who had been with the Free French since Camberley was brought in blinded and with such horrific injuries that he was not expected to live. Against all expectations he pulled through, and even insisted he could see a little. May, though, knew better. 'He had no eyes', she recalled. 'I saw the empty sockets.'

After the battle was over, May went to the forward unit to visit Vernier at the front and over lunch in his dugout he regaled her with stories of Rommel's retreat, which, with the Anglo-American landings in French northwest Africa, heralded a decisive turning point in the war. Then once again it was time for her to leave, a parting she found hard. Barbara, who had returned from Iran, was to run the unit in her absence, but May's need to be in two places at once was making her feel increasingly torn. She had 'two distinct spheres of activity', with their own 'centres of gravity',[3] and their physical distance from each other was to grow as the hospital moved further away from Beirut behind the advance across north Africa. If she was forced to choose between the two she had no idea which it would be.

She knew some people might think that her first responsibility was toward Louis and her role as the wife of the British minister, but he had always encouraged her in her hospital work and took obvious pride in her achievements. She was self-effacing about these, and believed that most of the time her hospital could get on perfectly well without her, but its staff depended upon her leadership more than she perhaps realized. She possessed a firm, yet sensitive, authority, which could instil confidence and calm in a crisis. When morale was low, she liked to gather everyone together and in her distinctive, gravelly voice, deliver a rousing pep talk, her tiny five-foot frame commanding complete attention as she looked at those around her with a serious expression.[4] She also seemed to be the only person able to soothe tensions between different nationalities, and if these reached uncomfortable levels, she would be summoned to smooth things over, taking the trouble to speak to all those involved: 'She had time for everyone and everything and accomplished more in twenty-four hours than anyone else I have ever known', Rachel Millet wrote about her.

> Her brain worked like quicksilver and her conclusions and decisions were invariably right. She was afraid of no-one and quite prepared to beard the Commander-in-Chief of the Eighth Army and did so on more than one occasion when her hospital was threatened. Her prestige in the French Brigade was enormous and she was admired and esteemed by everyone.[5]

Others appreciated her singularly penetrating and perceptive intelligence and her extraordinary tenacity. With the possible exception of one or two of the Quakers, who felt that her lack of sympathy with their views showed arrogance, there is no doubt that she inspired great affection and loyalty from her staff.

For her part, she loved the unit's 'elastic, tough, Bohemian soul',[6] and was proud of the willingness of everyone to pitch in together and confront whatever had to be done. The disparate body of staff, with its English nurses and drivers, French doctors, Quakers and orderlies, had come to represent her surrogate family, and one whose unconventional character was part of its appeal, earning it the affectionate nickname of 'the circus' from its crew. For example, there was the flamboyant Vernier, 'a short thickset sturdy little man with pleasant blue eyes' whose father, a Protestant missionary, had looked after Gauguin in Tahiti when the artist was dying. Vernier, usually referred to as 'the Col', liked to practise performing operations with the minimum of instruments possible, and perfected this art to manage even complex ones with a single knife or scalpel – or so it was claimed. May had taken to him immediately, finding 'a warmth about him, a frank friendliness and enthusiasm' that won her confidence. A far more ebullient character than his predecessor Fruchaud, if lacking his urbanity, he was an 'ardent Gaullist' and remained head of the unit until the end of the war. He had an even worse reputation for driving than May, managing to write off a considerable number of cars. He also shared with her a passion for bridge, and they never wasted an opportunity to settle down to a game when things were quiet, though their sessions were often sabotaged by Father Boileau, who possessed an unfortunate phobia of loud explosions and on black-out nightwatch, particularly in the desert, his vigilance was such that he would put out the storm lamp at the slightest sound, much to the indignation of May if she was in the middle of some clever card manoeuvre.[7]

The FAU boys were relied upon for many jobs which contributed to the smooth running of the hospital, working tirelessly, but it was the nurses, and perhaps the drivers in particular, to whom May was most devoted. She loved their defiance of female stereotype, their tough and fearless attitude to any task at hand which would be done with cheerful and bawdy humour, and their confidence as mechanics, able to keep the battered old cars going – not easy in the desert where sand constantly choked and clogged the systems. They did not ignore their feminine side and in their tents, boxes doubled as dressing tables where pots of cream and make-up jostled for space with engine parts. Clothes were washed in petrol, which unlike water, was in plentiful supply, as was paraffin, which the girls used to wash their hair.

In Beirut she swapped her Bedouin routines and protective tin helmet for a more sophisticated role, hosting parties and entertaining the steady flow of diplomats and ministers, many of whom stayed at the residence. If she felt a greater affinity with her hospital colleagues she was always supportive of her husband's work and played the part expected of her with charm and warmth, and even Nancy, now installed at close quarters, could never compete with May's social ease and panache.

By autumn 1942 the work of the mobile clinics had expanded to five permanent centres, each with its own catchment of villages and Bedouin tribes, in places where there were no other medical services available. The nearest of these centres was in the Bekaa Valley at Chtaura, halfway between Beirut and Damascus, where some of the FAU boys lived in a simple mud cottage. Each day they went out in one of the ambulances to different villages where it was the custom for the headman to lend a room in his house in which patients could be seen, many of whom travelled a long way on foot or by donkey. May loved the chance the clinics gave her to get to know the people of the country with whom she felt a natural empathy. She gratefully accepted the invitations of the younger women to enter their cosy houses, with their soft blue distempered walls decorated with 'plates of gay design'. They would give her coffee, and if she offered cigarettes, 'the old grandmothers were delighted' and would sit beside her, 'puffing with deep enjoyment'.[8] Although there was great poverty and misery among the people and malaria, dysentery and trachoma ravaged the country, she remembered 'the scene was always full of colour and gaiety as well as pathos'.

Sometimes, especially in the winter when snow or fog held them up, May and her fellow travellers broke their journey to Chtaura at a favourite hotel, where the owner, Masabki, had become a friend. If forewarned that they were coming, he prepared a special feast of mezze, fish, game, dessert and wine from the local vineyards. Sitting to eat in his private dining room with its warming log fire and walls lined with Persian rugs, May was relaxed and invigorated. When it was time to leave, Masabki sent them off with 'jars of honey, baskets of apples and in the spring great bunches of asparagus' to take to the FAU boys.

The clinics at Chataura, and at Sidnaya, north of Damascus, were relatively easy to reach, but the one at Tel-Tamer, in the far north near the Turkish frontier on the Khabur river, took several days travel across the desert. This medical centre, two hours from any hospital, had a small operating theatre, and drew in large crowds of Bedouin, Kurds and Assyrian Christians.

May had dreams of founding a nursing college in Damascus, seeing it as both a way of both meeting a great need for hospital-trained nurses and of providing an occupation for Muslim women. She knew how hard it would be to recruit nurses from this community, but hoped that 'if one could persuade the Arab women to think of nursing as a holy vocation, then even Moslem girls of good family would be free to adopt it as a profession'.[9]

May found her war experience so 'exacting and so satisfying' that she had not only stopped writing but felt she had stopped being a writer altogether – too busy with the business of living. But she was channelling her creativity into other dimensions: when she had time to herself, she liked to escape into the mountains or along the Barada river to paint, feeling a 'compulsion' to do so that she understood in terms of a strong physical identification with a landscape which she had taken to her heart:

> For I was in love with the land and the sky. I was fascinated
> by the old crooked trunks of the olive trees and the great

A hazard of mobile clinics was getting stuck in the mud (above)
The mud-built medical centre in Tel-Tamer in north-east Syria (below)

eucalyptuses with fronds hanging down like the tresses of Gods in the sun, and the deep mysterious valleys and the queer sinister shapes of their rocky sides, and the light. I was in love with the wonderful soft full light that poured down round me and through me and seemed to fill, not only my eyes with beauty, but my body with an essence that was life-giving and had something to do with the source of pure happiness.[10]

She had found a painting companion in Maie Casey with whom she had forged a deepening friendship. They saw each other frequently, either in Beirut or Damascus, or when May was on her way through Cairo to visit the unit she would sometimes break her journey to stay with Maie and her husband Dick. It was always a heart-warming moment when her plane circled the airfield at El Maza, and May looked down to see her friend waiting to greet her, 'a small figure standing in the sun with the wide sands of Egypt spreading round her'. The Caseys lived without pomp or ceremony, in a relatively small and simple house, and although it was 'unbearably hot in summer' and 'infested with mosquitoes', May found their relaxed informality refreshing. As she later wrote about them, 'they were breezy and gay, they were generous and free, there was a touch of recklessness about them, something youthful and daring and true that made them very endearing'.[11]

In February 1943, when May rejoined the unit when it was camped at El Adam, near Tobruk, Maie went too, donning an Australian trooper's hat out of respect for the division that had held the town during the siege the year before. May was glad to be back with her old friends. 'Like going home', she wrote in her diary, though she was not altogether approving of the informality that had taken hold in these quarters. The hospital tents were camped on the escarpment above the harbour, while the girls and the FAU boys were on the side of a wadi overlooking the sea. Two of the staff, Jean Williams, a nursing sister, and Pat

Barr, one of the members of the FAU, had recently married, and, sharing the aspirations of most newly-weds to possess their own home, they had built themselves a house by scavenging from an Italian dump. It had its own front door and windows (albeit paneless) through which one could see the harbour, and even a small garden. Rosie had joined the development, making her own humble abode out of petrol cans with a roof so unstable that it blew off every day, and the boys, too, had made more elaborate dwellings of ill-defined shape. From a distance May thought they gave the impression of 'squatters' huts', but the camp was festooned in a dazzling array of wild flowers which had recently sprouted forth from the desert earth, making it easier on the eye.

The hospital had arrived at the end of January with the First Division which was now retraining and re-equipping in preparation for the Tunisian campaign and May found an almost 'festive' air about the place with officers of the Free French in 'a state of hope and excitement'. While the unit was on standby to move north with the troops, the hospital was relatively quiet, and the mood relaxed. One evening the patients were wheeled outside in their beds, wrapped up against the bitter cold in warm blankets for an open-air screening of a Charlie Chaplin film. Other evenings May played cards or drank whisky in Rosie's 'incredibly untidy tent', and talked late into the evening. 'What a good life', she wrote in her diary of her time there, 'lazy – easy – free – the acme of luxury – no worry – no telephone – no problems that can't be solved in a few minutes – no fuss over clothes – They are all happy.'[12] This time there were no tensions or difficulties to deal with, and she too 'was happy again', with the familiar 'special brand of happiness' that, as she confided in her diary, she only found 'in this life and among these people'.

There were sombre moments too. She went on a pilgrimage, retracing her steps through the war-torn desert to visit Nick Alderson's grave, and the camp at Bir Hacheim, now eerily quiet. She found it sad; the 'utter silence, the solitude, the scraps strewn in the sand; forgotten relics of boisterous fighting men'. The 'wreckage of war was everywhere', she wrote later, 'Tobruk in ruins and the old hospital reduced to rubble', and the harbour, 'with its mute tragic burden'. She went out in a naval launch, weaving slowly between sunken ships, some partially immersed, and others rising well clear of the water, on their sides, 'as if with great weariness'. Her party looked into the 'water-washed cabins' and followed the gangways 'down into the obscurity beneath the shimmering surface'.

May's divided life continued. The unit's next mission was to be in Tripoli and she regretted that she would not be going too. Yet although she was happier with the unit than anywhere else, she felt the inescapable longing to be with Louis – a state of affairs she found puzzling. 'Is that curious? To prefer the life that is not the happiest?' she wondered in her diary, before answering dispiritingly, 'No – Any jealous lover would be happier away from his love – and I am seldom very happy with B.' He was always 'too tired – too preoccupied to talk' to her, but that she could cope with were it not for the 'constant undercurrent of distress – distrust – division – because of N.M.' She was reading 'Marcel Proust and Swann's story of jealousy', but if literary examples provided some insights, the reality of her situation was increasingly hard to bear. The unpalatable truth was that Miss Maurice had become a permanent fixture, a demoralising presence that overshadowed everything good in her life.[13]

May and Louis had moved into an attractive new house in Damascus, but she found the community 'small' and the Europeans 'drab'. She was even sorry to learn that Madame Catroux was leaving with her husband for Algiers, for she 'is at least alive – and a woman of the world, although "a vulgarian"'.[14] In Beirut her weekdays passed uneventfully, with Sundays at the races or out sightseeing with Louis, when he could spare the time. He encouraged her to relax and have fun, and she was happy to give way, but life was so easy and so luxurious that she sometimes felt in danger of forgetting the tragedy of war,[15] and she was always glad to return to a more active role with her unit. It was Barbara, however, who took the lead when the unit moved off in the middle of April, the largest convoy they had taken part in, with the entire division wending its way together. Their final destination turned out not to be Tripoli after all; at the last moment they were told to push on to the Tunisian front to relieve the New Zealand Division. May rejoined them there in the middle of May, cadging a lift part of the way with the Middle East American Air Force commander in his 'magnificent plane'. She found the hospital camped outside Sidi Bou Ali, perched on a rise with stunning views of the mountains, the tents dotted about beneath shady olive trees, and the surrounding meadowland ablaze with wild flowers – quite the nicest place they had been given. Everyone was in exuberant spirits since hearing the news that all Axis resistance in North Africa had ended with the unconditional surrender of nearly a quarter of a million men. But even after the fall of Tunis on 7 May, the fighting had been intense and the hospital stretched, receiving 130 casualties a day. The forward unit had come under heavy fire at its camp just below the mountains, earning Pat Barr the Croix de Guerre for his bravery.

Back in Beirut again during June, with Louis away in London, May found herself missing him intensely, writing in her journal that she felt 'only half alive', but when she went to meet him in Cairo on his return, their reunion was not happy, prompting her to write that it was a mistake to have come, for they 'made each other wretched'. It was a relief to return once more to the unit in October 1943 in Tunisia, but as the Free French troops waited to be seconded to the American Fifth Army, the Eighth Army had crossed to Sicily and from there, to mainland Italy in the northward push through Europe, and there was a sense of abandonment in the division at being left so far behind the front. To May everything felt somehow flat. Even a military ceremony in which she and Barbara were decorated with the Nichan-If-Takar by the Governor of Tunisia, General Maast, felt dreary and empty.

Another loss was that Barbara was leaving to get married. She had been a rock-solid member of the team and a good and wise boss to the female personnel. Her going left just three of the original staff who had been with the unit in France in 1939: TW, Jean and Evelyn, and there was no obvious person to fill her shoes. In the end, May handed the responsibility to a reluctant Vernier.

On her way back to Beirut she broke her journey at the Caseys, but her time there was turned into a nightmare by letters from Louis, 'almost the worst' she had ever received from him. Yet when she got back, 'ill with misery', he was 'glad to see me', she wrote with surprise. But the atmosphere in the house was no better, with Nancy's ominous presence feeling like an 'intangible web of ill will'. Louis was absorbed in work worries and if he found the tensions in the house uncongenial, he was neither able to understand the depths of May's distress nor willing to send Nancy away. 'The Greek triangle seems even worse than the French', she wrote in her diary of her wretched and precarious position. 'There appears to be no solution – i.e. none that can mean, normal happiness for me – for B perhaps if I can conceal the fear – the sense of a force sinister & unnatural always at work.'

The quarrels over Nancy and the strain of work seemed to be taking their toll. John Stokes, Louis' ADC in Beirut, was shocked by her haggard appearance on her return from Tunisia. She unburdened herself to him about Nancy's growing possessiveness, and her journal, when she had the stamina or inclination to write in it, was as much a record of her ailing marriage as a memory jog for writing her war memoirs at some later date. Asking herself why she found it so hard to keep it up, she thought that the answer was 'laziness', 'or my personal, private unhappiness that spoils everything'.[16]

At the same time, an explosive political scene was unravelling in the Levant over the issue of independence. The Vichy former ambassador to Turkey, Jean Helleu, had replaced Catroux, an appointment which was inevitably unpopular with Louis and exacerbated already heightened tensions in the area. At the end of July, the elections in Syria took place and the nationalists had a large majority win. This was followed by a smaller majority win in the Lebanese elections in November, a campaign characterized by Franco-British enmity as Louis championed Bishara al-Khoury, with his closer ties to the Muslim community than the Helleu-backed candidate, whose leanings were more European. Such was the mutual suspicion that the military were brought in to guard the ballot boxes. The nationalist, Read Sohl, was made prime minister, well known for his anti-French feeling, and the Foreign Secretary, Selim Tacla, represented the Greek Orthodox Church. May saw the newly elected government in Beirut as hopeful, uniting men of different faiths through the common sentiment of patriotism in a country where religion had been a disruptive force for many years; but the French suspected British imperialist motives.[17]

On the night of 11 November the French staged a coup, arresting the new president and most of his cabinet, dragging them from their beds as they lay sleeping. Louis was woken by the president's eldest son, who appeared covered with blood as he was dragged away by guards who had lashed out at the boy with their rifle butts. Concerned for the president's wife and her children, May brought them back to stay with her. On a visit to the Prime Minister's wife, French troops fired at the crowds gathering outside, and in the panic people climbed on her car 'seeking British protection'.

When the Lebanese ministers were eventually released on 22 November, and Louis went to call on the president, he received a rapturous welcome, lifted up by celebrating Lebanese and hugged by al-Khoury, who was full of gratitude to May for being 'like a sister to his wife and a mother to his children'. Stokes wrote to his wife that Louis was the 'absolute hero of the whole country'.[18] By others, though, he was viewed with extreme hostility and suspected of inciting trouble from the nationalists, and his pro-independence stance seen to be born of self-interest.

Inevitably, all this put an even greater strain on May, who felt extremely apprehensive for Louis. But when she 'cautioned him not to sink his life in this country', he accused her of showing a lack of support. Aware that her advice only depressed him, she wondered in her diary what she was supposed to do. 'Should I do nothing more than console and praise him? I can & do give him all my admiration & respect – Perhaps I don't repeat it often enough.'[19]

She was seriously considering severing her relationship with the Free French, but was torn by conflicting feelings. Louis was now despised by de Gaulle, his one-time ally: she was aware of his campaign to get rid of her husband, and had heard the rumours that Louis was about to be recalled to London and the Spears Mission closed down. It seemed a betrayal that she was still working for de Gaulle, yet there were all those who supported the unit, and had done from the start: those in London, organizing everything from that end, those in America who kept the money rolling in, and all the hospital staff so committed to its work. How could she let all those people down? She felt wretched with indecision.

Then Vernier made contact saying that she was missed and that he needed her support with some staffing problems. When she asked Louis' advice about going, he was adamant that she should stay true to her commitment, and reminded her that she was doing it for the fighting troops: this was her contribution to the war effort, and the war was still in progress. She must try to separate her work at the hospital from the personal feud between himself and de Gaulle.

The matter seemed resolved, but she was unable to leave straight away. She had all the Christmas parcels to prepare for the British troops, and she had taken on the presidency of the British Red Cross for Syria and the Lebanon, as well as serving on the Ninth Army's United Services Welfare Council, responsible for all welfare of the service women. Besides these preoccupations, the FAU boys at the Spears clinic in Tel-Tamer had written to say they were having serious problems with the French authorities who had taken over the hospital and that a campaign to get rid of the Syrian surgeon had been whipped up among the Kurds and Bedouin.

The New Year brought little respite from worries both professional and personal; and to make matters worse, the Caseys were leaving Cairo for Bengal. This news was 'a shattering blow' to May who felt 'grief-stricken' at the news, writing in her diary of the calamity this was for both her and Louis, from the official as well as the human side, for 'no-one will ever back B. as Dick has done', and she would miss Maie 'more than words can express'. Maie was her 'one friend here – we love each other and are completely candid to each other – Her generosity – devotion – welcome in her home & her life – all the warmth – the sense of security for the heart will go from the M.E. when she goes.'[20]

Feeling more alone than ever, May turned to Stokes, who complained to his wife that 'the Lady S-Miss M friction has reached unpleasant heights and I have to listen to Lady S pouring out her woes to me by the half hour'. [21] Only too glad to escape the antipathy between them and the 'strange and uncomfortable' atmosphere in the house, in February 1944 May rejoined the unit on the shore of the Bay of Tunis, where she found a catalogue of problems waiting for her. There was no doubt that the unit was in a bad way, and suffering particularly from an outbreak of infighting, which, without Barbara to sort things out, had been allowed to ferment. Everyone seemed thoroughly bad-tempered and out of sorts. The colonel, too, was on edge, and quick to take offence when May remarked that the hospital looked shabby. It was not just that it was installed in a 'derelict hotel of indescribable dinginess', but the bedding was worn and stained, adding to the general drab effect, and May felt chagrined when told that on his last tour of inspection, the medical inspector had not been pleased with what he saw. Morale was low, with the staff feeling redundant away from the front, and two new nurses from England expressed their disappointment that they had been sent out on what seemed to be false pretences. A state of dejectedness hung in the air, with people feeling the British army had 'washed its hands' of them, and until the Americans took them over, they remained in a strange limbo.

It took May a long time to work through the complaints, talking to people one by one to try to sort out the problems; the officers were particularly alarmed by the colonel's involvement in a scheme to expand the hospital to four hundred beds, which they all felt would be too much to manage. Vernier insisted it need not compromise the hospital's mobility, as it could be divided into a forward and a second-line formation. He expected to receive equipment from the Americans, which were re-equipping the whole division. As a compromise May agreed to a maximum of two hundred beds and flew to Algiers to see what equipment she could beg from the American Supply Service, staying for two days with Duff Cooper, the newly arrived British representative to the French Committee of National Liberation, and his wife Diana at their house above the town. Then it was time to leave the unit again, promising to rejoin them in Italy, and with the knowledge that she was going to miss the 'best part of the war'.

Her return to Beirut clearly did not please Nancy who according to Stokes was 'becoming quite intolerable and possessive in a demoniac sort of way'. He also observed the bond between May and Louis as they discussed poetry and writers and their memories of the past. In a letter to his wife written in June Stokes appeared infatuated with both of them: 'Lady Spears is in marvellous form these days, looking really lovely when she makes up well at night (and that is so extraordinary because she normally looks appalling but sometimes at night she looks radiant) and talking with a brilliance that I've never heard anywhere else before.' In contrast, he thought Nancy 'a dull, extremely unsympathetic woman', but May and Louis were 'most remarkable people, great faults and yet very loveable, terrible errors of judgement in simple things and yet such brilliance'. He saw them as having 'tremendous vitality' and 'infinite charm' although 'insincere and selfish … but oh how interesting'.[22]

In early May the unit left North Africa with the brigade for the last time. The equipment, transport and male members of the team had crossed to Naples on two American Liberty ships but as USA policy barred women, the colonel hatched a plan to smuggle the drivers aboard dressed up as French soldiers. This ruse was unfortunately foiled, but not before Susan Travers, Koenig's intrepid driver, had successfully mingled with the troops to climb the gangplank, her disguise undiscovered, in spite of the fact that she was wearing her gaiters the wrong way round with the ankle hooks and buckles displayed on the outside.

May set off in the middle of June to join them, flying from Cairo to Naples in a Dakota courtesy of the Middle East air marshal. In Italy, with impeccable timing, she was met by TW, who had set out that morning to motor the 250 miles from their camp at Lake Bolsena, just north of Rome. As they drove back together past the ravaged towns and the bombed-out remains of Monte Cassino, its monastery in ruins, May was given an idea of the ferocity of the battles which had taken place. The division had suffered particularly heavy losses in the fighting around the hill town of Montefiascone, built on the volcanic ridge of Lake Bolsena, where the hospital, camped on its sandy shores, had been machine-gunned from the air, the bullets ripping holes in the tents. But arriving there from Naples, May found calm and order reigning.

The unit's low morale had been banished with the need to pull together for the Italian campaign, and everyone had stories to relate of the hard and bitter advance. The unit had shadowed the division so closely that at times even the colonel had thought it was rash. With the front moving forward at such a pace, they were moving every few days to keep up, each time going through the process of evacuating patients and dismantling tents, and often by the time they arrived at the next place rows of ambulances were already waiting to unload their wounded. At St Georgia, across the Garigliano river, they were positioned as far forward as possible to give them a head start and to eliminate the need for an advance unit, just three miles from the clearly visible German lines.

Surrounded by the division's own artillery, with two of the heavy guns placed within yards of the hospital tents, their position was extremely exposed and on several occasions was the target of enemy strikes. Once a shell landed in the middle of the open-air mess table during lunchbreak, moments after people had left it to help unload a newly arrived convoy of ambulances; and another flew straight through the theatre tent during a major abdominal operation. As the lights went out, everyone dropped to the ground, whereupon Thibaut coolly continued the surgery with the aid of a hurricane lamp, spreading the patient's intestines out beside him on the grass as he checked for perforations. In spite of the fact that his insides were nearly stepped on, and possibly put back in with bits of earth attached, the man made a full recovery.

Listening to the different accounts of what had been going on in her absence, May believed the unit had done its 'best job of the war.' Her stay was now punctuated by meetings with various military. In General Alphonse Juin, in charge of the troops from the North African and Free French Divisions, now united in the single French Expeditionary Corps, she discovered a directness that matched her own, and over lunch she raised with him a matter which was bothering her. Her hospital was now known by the more official and anonymous designation HCM3, introduced, she was told, because the Americans would not equip voluntary hospitals. She understood the reason, but wished to have 'Ambulance Hadfield–Spears' suffixed in brackets. This was the name by which it had always been known, and it was at once recognizable to ambulance and lorry drivers when put up on signposts to point out its ever-changing sites and routes during battles. More than that, it was important to her that the hospital retained its special identity; its trademark yellow lorries and tents continued to be used even when the Free French Forces had to adopt the green uniform of the desert campaign, and its abbreviated name 'Spears' had become legendary. The general agreed to May's request, and showed his appreciation of the work of the hospital by making a public statement of thanks in front of the patients, a gesture de Gaulle had never bestowed.

She was also invited to stay the night at Eighth Army headquarters overlooking Lake Trasamene as guest of General Oliver Leese. There her sleeping quarters were well above the standard to which she was used: she had her own caravan with a proper bed and hot and cold running water, and dinner was an elaborate affair with all the general's staff assembled in a large tent, the dining table adorned with 'white tablecloth and napkins, flowers, silver, cut glass and china'.[23] She slept to a cacophony of artillery and crowing cockerels disturbed by the gunfire and the next morning shared breakfast with the general who showed her the map room with up-to-date news of the battle.

May was still with the unit when they received the orders they had been longing for; to prepare to move south and then overseas. This, they knew, meant France, and the mood was euphoric. 'To be with the troops again was enough in itself', wrote May, 'but to be this time with French troops who were approaching France, was wonderful.'[24] When at the end of June the unit travelled with the division in a night-time convoy to Albanova, 20 miles north of Naples, May went too, staying with them as they waited for further movement orders. At night, from her camp bed beneath the lime trees, with her tent-flap open to the 'soft and warm' air, she watched 'the moonlight drift through the tree-tops', and each morning the girls would arrive with baskets of ripe peaches collected from a local farm. It was an immensely happy and exhilarating time but as always, tinged by regret that she would have to part from them.

Her staff tried to convince her to stay, but she was needed back in the Levant. It was particularly hard to miss this last part of the unit's journey, but she had the solace of knowing that in spite of all the upheaval and change that the hospital had gone through, with people leaving and new staff coming, the 'alchemy' was the same: 'The spirit of the Hadfield–Spears Unit, that special mixture of gallant toughness and ribald mirth and quarrelsome loyalty and high undaunted purpose, was still going on and would prevail, I knew, to the end', she wrote later.[25] Her 'band of steady British girls' had come a long way and she was immensely proud of them. The recent Italian campaign had been particularly testing, dangerous, tough and arduous in the extreme, as well as very exciting. It had 'meant great effort, little or no sleep, a complete lack of comfort, and splendid team work', but, as she knew well, 'it was what they liked best and they were at the top of their form.'[26] She had had a wonderful month with them all, and promised to join them in France as soon as she could.

19

Demobilization

Not long after her return from Italy to Beirut, Louis left for London, taking Nancy with him, and leaving May to hold the fort which was in a hotbed of unrest. Concerns in the Foreign Office about Louis' increasingly Francophobe stance had put pressure on Churchill to call Louis back to report, and almost as soon as he had gone, May had to face gossip that her husband would not be returning. That these rumours caused unease in official Lebanese circles alarmed her, for 'what hope had they of winning a long struggle for true independence if they depended so much on this one man?' The French, however, hoped that Louis' days in the Levant were numbered, and May's friends were quick to warn her of stories circulating which they told her were being put about to stir trouble: 'The British were working to get the Levant for themselves', she wrote later, and 'Spears was the prime mover in the plot. His secret agents were at work all through the country. If they could get rid of Spears all would be well. I seemed to hear the malicious gossip coming up the valley from Beirut like the buzzing of a swarm of bees.'[1]

She tried her best to rise above it all but at the end of each day she went home to Aley feeling tired and depressed, and even the progress of the French campaign, which should have been cause for celebration, was for her mired by local discord. Listening to the French-controlled Radio Levant broadcast news of the liberation of Paris, she was stung by the fact that there was no mention of the Allies, and that there was no cheering on the streets of Beirut. Public opinion was divided with some people saying, 'Were there no British troops in Normandy? No Americans to march on Paris?' May thought of how her English girls had advanced north from the south coast of France, risking their lives to help in the campaign to liberate the country, and felt extremely bitter.

It was as much for her unit, as it was to represent Louis, that she attended a 'pathetic celebration', organized by the French to mark the liberation of Paris, which was turned into something of a debacle when a crowd of men, whom May had heard were hired by General Beynet to stand outside his gate and shout de Gaulle's name, stormed his house and stole the spoons and electric lights arranged for the party.

When the strain of fielding the constant flow of rumours about Louis became too intense, she sought refuge with Bayard and Mary Dodge, whose house she found 'quiet and serene' and where she could focus on matters of importance to her, such as the future of the Spears Clinics and how to keep them going after the war. Her work with the Ninth Army Welfare Council also needed post-war planning as there would be a lengthy period of transition as troops were repatriated.

Louis returned in early September, knowing that his time in the Levant was about to run out. Churchill had allowed him just a few months more, at the end of which he would be expected to be relieved of his post. The atmosphere in the house was worse than ever, with Louis in a bullish frame of mind and May short-tempered and waspish, and increasingly at loggerheads with him over Nancy. But when he was forced to offer his resignation, she softened, and put aside her anger and resentment to support him. Looking back on their last few months in the Middle East, she recalled the good times they shared together, such as their afternoon walks, when they would drive around the city walls of Damascus and head out east along the river through the Guta, then leave their car to follow paths through the autumn landscape, enjoying the beauty and peacefulness of their surroundings, and making promises to come back in the future. They took the Lebanese president's wife and children away with them to the great archaeological site of Petra – something they had always told her they would do – and there May was more enthralled by the open land above the city than the archaeological remains, finding the empty tombs 'forbidding, desolate reminders of the emptiness of death and man's futile vanity.' But at least the excursion gave her a chance to say an informal farewell to Madame Khoury and her family, away from the spotlight.

Although there were great cries of relief among the French that Louis was leaving, their Lebanese friends were downcast, some of the women crying when they heard the news, and when Louis told the President, he also wept. The official goodbyes given in Beirut and Damascus showed the extraordinarily high esteem in which the couple were held in some Lebanese circles, and demonstrated their popularity on the streets, with receptions on a scale usually reserved for royalty and heads of state. John Stokes observed the boost this gave to May and Louis who lapped up the adoration. But as they left Beirut on 15 December, seen off by a ceremony of a British guard of honour, it was the landscape which imprinted itself upon May, a stormy sea in the 'winter sun, the date palms by the shore lashed in the wind, the mountains of the Lebanon covered' with snow.

In England for Christmas, the first time back since her departure from Glasgow in 1941, she could barely wait to rejoin her unit after nearly six months' absence. Since it had landed in the south of France on 30 August, it had followed a zigzag route across the country, travelling to Lyons and Dijon, then to the west coast at Royon and back east again to Hohwald in the foothills of the Vosges where May now prepared to join it in January, travelling first to Paris, her feelings in a state of flux. She 'had longed to go back to France', but with a sense of unease, for she knew that it would not be the same, and had no idea what she would find. To be in the capital again was a disturbing experience, for it brought back so many memories of the past. As she later explained, 'It was my life, the part of me that I had left in France, and the monstrous war that had come between me and the other self.'[2]

It could not have helped to know that de Gaulle was also in Paris, having been made the head of a provisional government, but May was not going to let the deep divisions between him and Louis interfere with her work with the unit, and simply hoped that she could keep a distance from him. She might have suspected trouble ahead, however, for Colonel Vernier had written to tell her that he had received orders to remove the name of Spears from the unit – a gesture he had interpreted in a formal letter of complaint to the commander of the First Free French Division as the 'openly hostile attitude adopted officially by the High Command toward the founder of the hospital'. She would deal with this affront at the first opportunity, but first she had to sort things out at her hospital, which was once more in a state of turmoil. One point of contention was that an advance unit, of which Rachel was a part, had landed with the French Commandos on 14 August, and because of the need for secrecy, the rest of the staff had been kept in the dark about what was happening. Vernier had been very proud of the fact that when the division arrived under General Brosset, Ambulance Spears was already there, but when the others, including Thibaux, found out they had not been included, they were so angry that they resigned.

Trouble had also flared up again because Vernier had gone back on his promise not to increase the size of the hospital, which had since doubled to four hundred beds, and an influx of new French staff, recruited by him, were refusing to take orders from Jean Barr, the head sister, who had subsequently handed in her notice, with Rachel and TW following suit.

'La Generale was in high dudgeon', wrote Rachel of her boss's reaction. The atmosphere was certainly more fraught than May had ever known it and she could see that it was going to take a lot longer to put right this time. Although initially upset with Vernier, she blamed herself for being absent for so long, and could understand the reasons for his breaking their agreement. The division was heavily engaged, and with inadequate medical supplies in the local hospitals and the French Medical Service in France in chaos, there was no where else for the division's wounded to go. Everything was different now, and she was pragmatic enough to recognize the need to adapt to the inevitable changes. She held interviews with her British staff, counselling them to see that it was impossible to retain things as they had been in the past when they had been a 'small compact' mobile hospital, and appealed to them to see things through. In the end all agreed to stay except Jean who insisted on leaving and with May in situ again, the unit regained its equilibrium.

Her own well-being was not so easy to find in the country of her past. She was taken to see the German concentration camp at Struthof, 'a small affair compared to Belsen', but where in its gas chamber, 'like a large frigidare with smooth white walls', twenty thousand Jewish women and children had been exterminated. The young woman who showed them round lived on a small farm 'within earshot of the tortured' and admitted 'with a sad apologetic smile' that after a time they became so used to the screams of terror which went on day and night that they ceased to hear them. They had seen the corpses, too, when delivering vegetables, but had had to close their minds to what was going on, as they were afraid of losing their own lives. The woman's aunt owned a hotel requisitioned by the commandant of the camp. She 'lived well', wrote May, her disgust implicit.

As she travelled a country 'torn by dissension', catching

'glimpses into the life of a people that had purchased peace at any price', she was shocked by the indifference of those she met who seemed not to care who won the war, or to have any interest in it - an inertia she found hard to forgive. Occasionally she heard pro-German sentiments: 'The people are rotten', she wrote, recording her impressions of 'a fragmented and sick nation', which by coming 'to terms with the enemy to avoid destruction' had, she believed, been 'inwardly destroyed'. Slowly she 'put the fragments together', feeling her way 'back into the past, searching for buried treasure, for the France I had known; here and there I found it'.[3]

When the unit followed the division to the Mediterranean in March, she was even more outraged by the sense of detachment that she found there, with the lives of the wealthy untouched even by the proximity of the wounded pouring in to the hospital. This was now installed at the once grand and opulent Bristol Hotel at Beaulieu, its faded glory reminding May of the converted casino at Malo-les-Bains in 1914. The final campaign for the division was proving to be one of the heaviest of all. Nearly three thousand wounded were brought in, and the death of troops who had survived so many other battles now took on a new poignancy.

A more trivial matter, but one which still left her feeling infuriated, was the change of her unit's name which she saw as a provocative order. She was directed to discuss the issue with General Guerriac, the inspector of the Service de Santé of the French Army, with whom she had always been on friendly terms, and who had been a frequent visitor to her home in Beirut. He welcomed her warmly, and claiming to know nothing at all about the affair, he gave his authorisation for her to order a new official stamp with the Hadfield–Spears name reinstated. When she returned to the unit to announce her success, however, Vernier flew into a rage of indignation before producing the original order, which he had not wanted to show her before, and which had come from General de Lattre de Tassigny, the First Army commander, and Monsieur Diethelm, the Minister for War for de Gaulle, when they had visited the hospital, and had been signed by none other than Guerriac with his official stamp. In professing ignorance of it he had lied to May, but she had the last laugh, for the new stamp he had promised her was duly ordered and remained in place until the end of the war. A hollow victory as it turned out.

Churchill's announcement of peace in Europe was broadcast on 8 May. In Nice, the division took part in a celebratory parade, but May stayed in her sitting room with Rosie, both feeling 'only a sense of dreary anti-climax' and wishing they were somewhere other than the Riviera, like 'brave' Tobruk, where the war had been fought so hard. The next day she had a meeting with Vernier to discuss a date for disbanding. There were still many wounded in the wards, but they would soon be transferred to base hospitals, and staff wanted to know when they could leave, as they were needed elsewhere. But the colonel had other ideas and surprised her by asking whether she would take the unit to the Far East with the French Expeditionary Forces. He had already seen officials at the Ministère des Colonies who had said the hospital was wanted and he believed they should stick together and carry on their work. He needed her English nurses, if they would agree to volunteer.

May's initial reaction, as far as her position was concerned, was to say no. She had too much to do in England. A general election was imminent; she had her house to sort out, and her family to see. The colonel, however, would not take no for an answer, insisting that there would be time for her to go home and deal with the election before leaving for overseas. He implored her to think about it at least, which she agreed to do, and by the end of the month she had made up her mind to do as he asked, although she certainly did not share his enthusiasm. 'I didn't want to go', she later wrote, but 'perhaps that was the reason. An old lesson learned in childhood from some puritanical forebear or Spartan Nanny. If you hate the job, do it; if you are afraid, stand up to it.'4 She was not looking forward to it, and it could not have been easy to write to de Gaulle offering to continue to serve his troops on the basis of their original agreement drawn up in 1941, but she duly sent the letter off. In the meantime, the unit received orders to pack up and prepare to move to an unknown destination, with still no date for closing down.

In early June the convoy moved with the rest of the division to the village of Trilport on the Marne and the next day, May went to the British embassy in Paris to consult Duff Cooper, the ambassador. She had not heard back from de Gaulle and was impatient for an answer to her proposal. She also wanted his advice about whether to take part in the victory parade in Paris on 18 June arranged by de Gaulle. Cooper had little to say about her decision to take part in the Pacific War but he was adamant that the unit must attend the parade. He handed her a letter from Louis which said the same, reiterating his view that the antagonism between himself and de Gaulle had nothing to do with her long service with the division.

May was uneasy about their presence at the parade, but her staff were honoured by the invitation to take part, and there was a hive of excited activity as the least shabby of the cars and trucks were repainted with the hospital logo, incorporating both French and English flags, and best uniforms pulled out. The day of the procession was sunny and bright, and the mood festive as crowds lined the avenues to watch the parade. As the unit convoy reached the Place de la Concorde, some former patients, whom Koenig had brought along from the military hospital in Paris, and who had pride of place in the grandstand reserved for de Gaulle and VIPs, gave a rousing shout of encouragement, calling 'Vive l'Ambulance Spears'. This was appreciated by the hospital entourage, but de Gaulle was livid to hear the name of his enemy called out and to see the British flag flying alongside the French flag, and turned to Koenig in angry protest.

Two days later, when May was away in Paris, Vernier gathered the staff together to break the news that de Gaulle had ordered that the unit was to close down within forty-eight hours and its British members repatriated. Vernier had learnt this the day after the parade, but had not known how to tell May. Although the official reason for the closure was that it had been planned for some time, few doubted that the flying of the British flag had provoked de Gaulle to this action. May wrote to him at once, complaining in strong terms about his brutal order, which he had not even had the courtesy to give her personally. He denied that he acted in spite, but his decision remained unchanged and the row was widely reported in the newspapers as accusations flew back and forth.

May had never felt that de Gaulle had appreciated the dedication of the unit. Once when she had met him in Beirut at a lunch reception, and perhaps fishing for some sign of his gratitude, she had told him how her hospital had treated the wounded after Bir Hacheim, but he did not give her the response she might have hoped for: 'Neither then, nor any time during the war, did he say anything that could be construed as a tribute to the work we had done',[5] she wrote later, and to end on such an inglorious note was deeply wounding.

20

Home is in the Heartland

May returned to England at the end of June 1945 still reeling from the shock of the unit's disbandment and its reverberating implications – not least that she was suddenly plunged back into civilian life without time to prepare for the change. Since she had expected to go to the Far East with Colonel Vernier, her immediate future had seemed settled. Now those plans were exchanged for uncertainty about what to do next. After being constantly on the move throughout the war, leading a full and stimulating existence, she found it hard to adjust to life in bleak post-war England, and to begin with she felt very restless.

One obvious diversion was to return to writing, and with her head crowded with her experiences of the last five years, she set to work on an account of these times in *Journey Down a Blind Alley*. Although she found it 'child's play' compared with writing a novel, and the book virtually 'wrote itself', it proved to be her only volume of autobiography.

In it she re-lived the journey she had taken with the Hadfield-Spears Unit, from its enthusiastic inception in 1939 to its abrupt and humiliating end in Paris. She also covered her parallel life in the Levant as wife of the British minister. Although she had been inconsistent about keeping a diary during the war, her journals provided the foundation she needed, and at times she quoted directly from them to capture the immediacy of the moment.

The narrative is often lit up by an unrestrained freedom of expression as May's impressions and feelings, still fresh, and in some instances painfully raw spilt onto the page. Her hurt and bitterness toward de Gaulle laid itself bare, as did her disappointment in France – and the fact that it was a nation she had loved and served passionately made her disillusion all the greater. She asked herself why she had not believed the signs that the fall of the country in June 1940 was inevitable: 'It was all there for those who had eyes to see and ears to hear. The defeatism, the corruption, the treachery that had been eating away the foundations of France and was to bring about the collapse of her armies.' The attitude of defeat she saw as ingrained in the country, for it had exchanged its 'old fear of Germany for the new pre-fabricated fear of the Communist bogey' and the French middle class were prepared to accept a compromise with Hitler rather than risk a revolution of the left.[1] Looking back to her last pre-war visit to France with Louis in summer 1939, she recalled how their reception from old friends had been distinctly chilly – they did not want to be dragged into England's conflict. And again, in February 1940, when she was putting the finishing touches to her hospital, her old Parisian friends had demonstrated their lack of interest and tried to make her understand that things were different this time. 'Now I am afraid to ask what became of that charming group when the monstrous thing happened', she wrote in her memoirs. 'Because they were friends, I cannot pry into their secrets … we used to be intimate … It used to seem almost as if we belonged to the same race. Now we are strangers. It may be that I shall meet them again in the streets of Paris or London: if I do, if they speak and smile to me, it will not alter the fact that I have lost them.'[2]

As a chronicler of the events of June 1940 she is unforgiving, and her attitude unsoftened by time, but in happier contrast, *Journey* charts her deepening friendships with the band of English nurses and drivers she grew to know 'better perhaps than I know anyone in the world', and her affection for the people of Syria and Lebanon, whose countries had come to occupy a special place in her heart and where she still yearned to be 'in body' as she was 'in spirit'.[3] Tobruk, too, is recalled with wistful longing. The 'heroism of its siege' and its 'perilous harbour' became imprinted upon her inner landscape: 'Always as long as I live I shall be aware of its men who are buried below the escarpment, and the men who went down and still seem to be waiting, beside their ships under the waters of the still harbour, to be raised by the sound of a trumpet blast.'[4]

The exercise of writing her war memoirs was undoubtedly cathartic, and the result is an erratic mix of fascinating material and insights, juxtaposed with curiously inconsequential and indiscreet detail, with odd grievances thrown in, and the reader taken off at tangents. But if the book feels haphazardly constructed in parts, this is compensated for by its descriptive power as she vividly brings to life the drama of the events she witnessed during the Fall of France and Middle East campaign. When *Journey Down a Blind Alley* was published in the autumn of 1946, it was immediately recognized as an absorbing inside account of war. It was praised for its insights into the Franco-Syrian crisis, and for its contribution to public knowledge about the aloof de Gaulle, as well as its candid close-ups of other prominent wartime figures of the Middle Eastern theatre such as Koenig and Catroux. One critic wrote that May's experience in both diplomacy and battle make it the raw stuff of history, others admired her novelist's awareness of human motives and actions. Harold Nicolson, reviewing the book for the *Daily Telegraph*,[5] referred to the description of the invasion of France as the most vivid and beautifully told he had read.

For some of her French friends, though, May's study of their country made painful reading: 'I suffer at growing old during the decline of France which you have shown in a somewhat cruel way', wrote the Countess of Chambrun in a letter.

Reviewing the book for the *Observer*, Elizabeth Monroe felt it was May's unhappy relationship with de Gaulle that lay at its core, and that the blind alley of its title was 'the road to de Gaulle's heart'.[6]

The events of the war had left Louis, too, with a sense of bitterness and he was relieved to resume his parliamentary duties, which he found more rewarding than those of a diplomat. May's first task on arriving back in England in June 1945 was to help him prepare for the first post-war general election in his constituency in Carlisle. She had always intended to be there at this important time as all her husband's plans and ambitions for the future depended upon keeping his seat at Westminster. To offset the unpopularity of the Conservatives in his constituency, Louis called himself the National Candidate which identified him with Churchill and the disbanded national government. [7] His chances of winning were slim but he was nevertheless hopeful, and it was a great blow when he lost to a Labour majority. Disappointment followed disappointment, with all his attempts to find another constituency being unsuccessful.

But his appointment as chairman of Ashanti Goldfields, a company which had its head office in London, opened up new opportunities. In November 1945 he went on his first trip to the mine at Obuasi, on the Gold Coast (now Ghana), where he was taken down into its deepest part, and was appalled that men had to work in such intolerably hot and airless conditions. He saw changes to working practices as essential and was determined to instigate improvements. He knew little about the technical side of running a mine, but he felt that his strengths lay in his political and diplomatic experience which, with African nationalism swiftly boiling up, could be of use in calming instability, and he wasted no time in becoming versed in local politics.

May was only too glad to join Louis on his next visit and a trip to the Gold Coast became an annual event, timed to escape the English winters. She relished the chance to abandon 'the dismal discomfort' of life at home for a land that looked like 'some vast botanical garden', in which the people seemed so much happier. As she described her first impressions in the *Daily Telegraph*:

> It had been snowing when I left London, the skies were grey, my house was dark and cold, its larder bare save for some oddments in tins and a bit of cheese as big as your thumb, and the faces of the people in the street had a pinched, patient, dogged look. Now after three days in the air, West Africa rose out of the limbo of my ignorance to meet me, a great exuberant wave of colour.[8]

Accompanying Louis each year, May found a country to embrace as she had Beirut and Syria, and one in which instead of racial discordances she believed there was harmony. She wrote: 'The Africans of the Gold Coast are our friends. The white man and the black man meet there on a basis of race equality. With no colour bar between them as in South Africa; and I suspect that we are more akin to them than to any of the nations of Europe.'

A few days later this altogether glowing piece about the Gold Coast earned her a vitriolic response from a reader which began: 'I hope you will excuse my impudence in writing this letter, for even a slave is sometimes allowed to slip in a word or two on his master's opinions.' The sender accused May of pretending not to notice evidence of discrimination and of demonstrating the 'ideology of the superiority of the white race'.

She and Louis certainly enjoyed a privileged European existence in the Gold Coast during their two-month visits each year, with all the benefits which came with the position of chairman – flying first class to Accra, chauffeured about in an Armstrong Siddeley limousine, and staying in a comfortable house in the capital belonging to the company's representative where they were looked after by numerous servants. Louis assumed the role of the big white bwana, and partly through the sheer force of his character, lorded over Ashanti as if it was his personal kingdom. His attitude towards the Obuasi employees was paternalistic and although critics felt he could have done more, he was proud of the company's achievements in building houses, schools and clinics. May carved out her own responsibilities, working energetically to promote and support education: she and Louis integrated with the people, showing courtesy and concern,[9] and earned the genuine gratitude and affection of many with whom they came into contact.

May still retained her loyalty to the Arab people; in 1948 she was involved in setting up the Anglo-Arab Relief Fund to help Palestinian refugees, showing a particularly perspicacious grasp of the situation. In a strongly worded letter of appeal, published in many of the British newspapers, she warned that 'the troubled story of Palestine is not finished. We are watching from our comfortable distance, not the end, but the beginning of a tragedy that is going to affect the history of the world.'[10]

She had lost none of her dynamism as a commentator on issues of public concern. Indeed, her mental vigour seemed scarcely diminished and her hunger for knowledge and understanding unabated as she kept on the go with whatever caught her attention. Her journalistic output was prolific, as she provided commentary on anything from the wedding of Princess Elizabeth – an occasion she celebrated for the collective cheer it brought to the streets in the face of 'dreariness and depression' – to discussions on matters of the day both small and large. Her absorption in international politics led her to report on elections around the world for different daily newspapers, simultaneously enjoying the chance to travel. Besides her two months a year spent in the Gold Coast and usually another two in America, she made various trips abroad for work and for enjoyment, often combining the two.

There were slightly longer gaps between books now, and it was not until 1949 that she published her first post-war novel, *2 Shovel Street*. The title refers to a 'bijou residence' in the heart of Mayfair, which Millicent Pryde, a widow, has struggled to buy for the sole reason that her daughters, Diane and Susan, can be launched into the debutante season and married off to financial security. The Second World War scuppers these plans and when it is over, life does not relapse into the old ways Millicent expects; instead she finds herself at sea in a changed society, and with daughters with whom she feels out of step. Besides capturing the sense of dislocation in England after the war, the story allowed May to use her experiences in the Western Desert, where Susan goes to work as a nurse. Like the author, she finds it hard to settle when she returns to London – where once she had longed for 'fog, rain, a damp blustering English wind', she instead longs to be back in the desert, and for 'the freedom, the danger and discomfort, the horror and the exhilaration of the war.[11]

Into the novel May also brought the political scene in new socialist England, with Atlee, Churchill and Eden all making appearances.

Her observations on public life were for general consumption, but her private life remained exactly that and she bore Nancy Maurice's baleful presence in her life with silent indignity. Nancy's extraordinary possessiveness of Louis was no less tenacious after the war than it had been before, and she still competed relentlessly for his attention, using the pretext of work to spend as much time with him as possible.

To the public world, May and Louis presented a genial front, which was not by any means all a pretence, for in spite of rocky patches and the volatile nature of their relationship, they were bonded by many shared interests and could still enjoy each other's company. To the majority of people who knew them, they had a complementary marriage and together made a good team. This was certainly so when it came to giving grand dinner parties at their house at 12 Strathearn Place, a tall, gloomy building fronting on to the main taxi-route to Paddington Station. To these frequent gatherings they invited a mixture of famous and influential people, including politicians, businessmen and diplomats, for Louis relied on May's help with promoting his business work in this way, and she was always the life and soul of the party, charming, witty and unfailingly gracious.

By the end of the war May had some catching up to do for she was by then a grandmother to six – three on either side of the Atlantic. In Maine, her daughter Mary (always known as Emmy) had three children, and in July 1943, Comfort and Rupert had their third child Adam. In a strange repetition of Comfort's own childhood, a tug-of-war threatened to keep her older children from her after she left them in the care of her childless aunt Joyce to return to Rupert in London during the war. When it seemed safe enough to bring them back to the family nest, Joyce, having become very attached to them, tried to prevent them leaving, arguing it would be a risk for them to make the journey. When this protest failed, she managed to have a doctor say they were unfit to travel; the children were told they had tuberculosis and high fevers and were confined to their bedroom where they puzzled over their diagnosis for they felt perfectly normal, although they were soon infected with an outbreak of dreadful boredom, and also of insomnia through lack of exercise, leading to marathon all-night games of gin rummy. The situation was only resolved when Rupert, having obtained compassionate leave from the army, arrived in Camden to insist on taking his children home, whereupon Joyce accepted the parting could not be avoided and backed down with good face.

Ties between the American and English branches of the family remained close and whenever May finished a novel and was required by her American publishers to carry out a publicity tour of the country, she relaxed at the end of it with a holiday in Camden where she stayed with Emmy and her children. She looked forward to these trips back to the place where she had spent happy holidays with her own parents and which brimmed with childhood associations; in these peaceful surroundings, May and her sister had a fresh chance to get to know each other in a way that circumstances had never before allowed.

Another source of conflict between May and Louis was their son Peti who appeared painfully shy to all who knew him. As a child he had brought his father unrivalled joy, but now that he had grown up their relationship was an uneasy one. His job at the Foreign Office had led nowhere, and he was financially dependent upon his parents. Louis, having held high expectations for him, found it bewildering that his son did not share the same ambitions or values. When Peti was due to stay with Joyce and Zlatko in France, Louis sent a letter asking for their help in pointing him in the right direction:

> I should be personally grateful if, as and when the opportunity offers, it could be gently pointed out to him that it would be to his own great advantage to be a little more careful of his dressing and to keep his hair tidy. He really does handicap himself unnecessarily by so neglecting his appearance, and he can look quite nice and tidy if he chooses, but he seldom takes the trouble and never keeps it up. He seems to be letting his hair look like a cockatoo. All this is much more important than he realizes for he cuts himself off from his contemporaries, the lads with whom he was educated. He ends up feeling himself strange and different and so shuns their company. He is, for instance, a member of a very good London club to which I had him elected a good many years ago but he never by any chance sets foot there.[12]

Louis blamed May for being too soft with Peti, although he understood her reasons: 'She cannot bear to cross him', his letter to Joyce continued. 'She feels, truly enough, that he has had such disabilities in life that nothing should be done to increase his sense of inferiority. This is a vicious circle and his appearance by cutting him off from his friends increases that very sense which one would like him to combat.'

Even to his extended family Peti was something of an enigma and hard to know well, but in 1950 he met and married a divorcee called Margery Eynon, and they ran a fruit farm together in Kent. Nurse Lamb approved of the marriage and felt Peti had found someone who understood his quiet nature but, in truth, they had little in common and were temperamentally unsuited. Margery was a larger than life character – formidable and strong-minded, and far too dominating a force for Peti, and after two years they separated. Peti stayed on at the farm, and although country life suited him better than London, he was often to be found sitting by himself at the bar of the local pub, chain-smoking and exuding an aura of unhappiness. His inertia caused May great sadness and dragged her spirits down.

No matter what was going on in her life, however, she was still revived and energized by ideas for novels, which, having coalesced and fermented in her mind over time, could suddenly take form with irresistible effect in transforming moments of intense mental excitement – as with *For the Record*, published in 1950 (as *Catspaw* in America). In April 1949 she reported on the forthcoming Italian election for the *Sunday Graphic* from Rome where she joined a crowd of some twenty thousand people gathered together at a communist open-air meeting to listen to the leader Togliatti, and on Easter Sunday, she joined another huge crowd in front of St Peter's to hear Pope Pius XII speak. In a rousing attack on communism he uttered the words 'the hour has struck for Christendom', which was the catalyst May needed for a story she had been trying to piece together. Suddenly her ideas caught fire in an 'explosive' eureka moment: 'I had a sensation of such stimulus that I could almost hear and feel the various parts of my drama rushing together in my brain,' she wrote:

> The powers of Light and the Powers of Darkness, or in less exalted terms, the worship of the State against the individual human being's right to think, search and act for himself. Since the end of the war I have been obsessed by the struggle of these two ideologies on the one hand to capture, on the other to set free the minds of men. There in the great throng outside St Peter's I realized anew that the issue would be decided by the faith of Christendom. If that faith failed, if the Western nations no longer believed with fervour and conviction in their own ideals, then humanity as one knew it was doomed.[13]

The outcome of this epiphany was a book about the communist infiltration of a small independent country in Central Europe – a story which grew out of her horror at Soviet imperialism, based in part on events in Czechoslovakia and other recent incidents behind the Iron Curtain, including the death of Louis' friend Jan Masaryk, who fell from a window in Prague in mysterious circumstances. It was a book she felt 'obliged' and 'compelled' to write.

Although its genesis had been compulsive and exhilarating, May found her research far more taxing as she waded through communist literature; texts such as Stalin on Lenin she found laborious and heavy going but believed they were essential if she was to enter the mind of an 'ardent young communist'. Alex, the narrator, is a Soviet secret agent through whom May wanted to communicate the 'powerful appeal' of communist ideology 'to the unhappy youth of the world in search of salvation' – his self-revelations of subterfuge turning into tortured disillusion with his mission to help instigate a revolution. Her efforts were anyway appreciated by the *Sunday Times* which thought it an 'important book', and the *Daily Telegraph* rated it 'extremely clever'.

Meanwhile another novel was simmering as she pondered the question of how the 'modern so-called Christian world' would react to Jesus Christ if he was born in the present day, bringing her to the conclusion that he would be treated in much the same way as he had been two thousand years earlier. She had found another compelling idea and with enthusiasm and excitement, immersed herself in the task of reinterpreting the Gospels as a contemporary tale. She set the story in England where the eponymous hero, Martin Merriedew, is the son of a country doctor. His journey from boyhood to spiritual leader is observed by Barbara Patche, the narrator, who, as the squire's daughter, grows up in the same village and is both repelled and drawn by his unconventional behaviour that sets him apart. During the Second World War, Martin joins the Red Cross as an orderly in a field hospital in North Africa, where he is attached to the 10th corps of the Eighth Army, allowing May to draw on her own war experiences. There is more than a little of her old Quaker colleague Nick Alderson in the characterization of her hero; he is a conscientious objector whose brother comes to understand that although he does not share Martin's pacifist beliefs, 'there was more than one kind of courage', an observation lifted straight from the pages of May's autobiography and an apologia and tribute to a young man she felt she had once unfairly judged.

Perhaps wishing to repeat the huge success of *Action for Slander* she turned the last part of the novel into a courtroom drama, in which Martin is accused of being a dangerous social agitator and a traitor to his country for allowing German prisoners to escape from his care during the war and for encouraging British soldiers to lay down their arms. Barbara's husband is the judge presiding over the case, and the two of them represent Pilate and his wife. Other biblical parallels are there in the people Martin befriends and in the language used during the trial, with some lines taken almost directly from the Gospels.

Moral dilemmas, as much as religious belief, were the novel's driving force and, once more, May felt compelled to write it, but when she sent her son-in-law, Rupert, the proofs of the first chapters, he had strong reservations about their literary merit; in particular he felt that the character of Martin was too shadowy – a criticism backed up by David Garnett, who also saw the manuscript. May's response to his comments was typical in both its honesty and steadfastness: 'I cannot deny that your letter was a blow & quite staggering at first impact', she wrote. 'But now I feel more pugnacious than despairing.' She was 'exceedingly glad' that Rupert had read the book and given her his truthful and 'drastic criticism', which she felt was right 'up to a point'.[14] Although she wished to keep an element of mystery about her hero, she needed him to be believable and had to find a balance between the two.

The book was published in England in autumn 1952, and reviewers described it as thought provoking and 'a tale told with consummate skill'. The *Daily Mail* selected it as its Book of the Month. In Melbourne it was chosen as the book of the week, and in America, where it was published by Longman's Green under the title *You, the Jury*, it was selected for the Book of the Month Club along with Hemingway's *Old Man and the Sea*. Its overall success prompted May to turn it into a screenplay, but Rupert's worries were not altogether unfounded – some critics found the earlier chapters slow, preferring the court-room scenes in the latter part of the novel where Martin Merriedew is given a greater presence, and the reader is asked to decide whether he is guilty as charged.

May's fascination with religious themes, which had fuelled so much of her work, was far from exhausted. In fact it was becoming more pressing with her need for a definitive resolution to her questioning agnosticism. As she approached her seventieth birthday, she retained a passionate belief in life and a love of the world which made it difficult to contemplate its end, and yet neither could she make the necessary leap into faith. As she put it herself, 'I lacked the gift of belief and yet I was unwilling to believe that all life was an accident, or that I would one day cease to exist.'[15] In *Martin Merriedew* Barbara reflects that 'if one could be certain about God' one would be safe – a remark which clearly has strong autobiographical resonances. For most of May's life she had been reacting against her evangelical upbringing but her scepticism was increasingly in conflict with a longing for religious comfort. 'I was in a jam', she wrote wryly of the dilemma this presented, making light of what was in truth a deeply preoccupying ambivalence.

An unconscious search for a solution sent her delving into book after book about the physical universe. What she wanted was a rational approach to God, 'an authoritative statement by a master mind arriving at its conclusions by pure reason that God was the Y of the great equation'. The scientist, Albert Einstein, whose own thoughts on the subject of spirituality she had come across in the process of her reading, seemed to offer her some comforting enlightenment.

A desire to meet him took hold, and during a visit to America in late summer 1954, she enlisted the help of a mutual friend to arrange an introduction, and was invited to his home on Mercer Street, in Princeton, New Jersey. She had anticipated this moment for a long time, but when she came face to face with the great scientist, she was rendered awestruck, and all that she had planned to ask him vanished from her head. Instead she found herself babbling like a child, and somewhere in the stream of words that gushed forth, she heard herself asking him if he believed in God. 'Yes,' he replied, 'but God is a concept that I cannot explain and I have no proof. You understand, there is no proof, you can never be sure. You can only say that you are not sure.'[16] He was more emphatic about why time seems to speed up as one gets older, for which he had a very simple explanation: 'When one grows old one remembers less of the past – one forgets the details of what happened during the year and so the year is shortened.'

Einstein may not have given May the proof she was looking for, but she found her meeting with him greatly consoling. Since her father's death, she had often looked for substitutes in venerable and learned men who could teach her about life, and, as she grew older, who could perhaps bring her spiritual enlightenment. This need had sent her to consult Canon Streeter when she was researching her religious trilogy, and now she bestowed upon Einstein elements of a divine presence: 'In his great wisdom and utter innocence, he seems to be an expression of the spirit of God.'[17]

This latest trip to America had seen the launch of her new novel, *Margin of Error*, which centres on a transcontinental flight from London to a colony in West Africa, on Christmas Eve, 1948, which is forced to make a crash landing on the edge of the Sahara. On board are several Members of Parliament sent to investigate an uprising in the colony – a synopsis which allowed May to deliver an ironic commentary on the world of Whitehall and to use her knowledge of the Gold Coast and her observations of its political scene, with the rise of nationalism and the subsequent elections in 1951. It is not just politics that interested her but how the threat of imminent death affects the various passengers – not all of whom will survive.

Her children grown up, May had chosen to write in strict seclusion, shutting herself away in her study at St Michael's Grange, and anyone who disturbed her was severely admonished. Louis was also writing and in 1954 Heinemann published his account of his experiences in the Second World War in two volumes under the title *Assignment to Catastrophe* which earned him enthusiastic accolades. Yet their combined earnings, including Louis' six thousand pounds a year from Ashanti, were scarcely enough to pay for their lavish entertaining, or for the luxuries they were reluctant to go without, and every now and again May would feel concerned enough about their finances to insist on cutbacks. Budgeting was never her strong point and she showed surprising vagueness over where the money went - during one belt-tightening exercise she was horrified when she added up the cost of their laundry bill.

When May was seventy, she wrote *The Hungry Leopard*, a psychological thriller in which the biographer of an enigmatic writer who has gone missing behind the Iron Curtain, discovers some letters he has written since his disappearance, initiating a desperate mission to obtain them. As a literary thriller of sorts, the novel includes observations on the publishing world, territory that May had not ventured into before. It sold well, with both the *New York Times* and *The Times* finding it a fascinating work written in the author's 'usual polished style'. But it was to be her last novel. After writing twenty-two books of fiction she had finally had enough, for as she later told her grandson's wife, she felt she had nothing more she wanted to say.

For a brief time it seemed that Peti had found a companion with whom he had a real chance of a compatible relationship. She lived locally and their paths crossed when she went fruit picking on his farm. Like him, she was an intellectual with a quirky and unconventional outlook on life, brought up by her mother and grandmother in a somewhat sheltered and over-protective Irish Catholic household. Her name was Jennifer Aldington, the niece of the war poet who had encouraged her love of literature, a subject which she and Peti discussed animatedly and which helped break through shyness on both sides. The relationship had progressed enough for May to visit her family at their house – which perhaps set warning bells going for they were devout in their religious convictions and there could be no future in a relationship with a man who was already married. Indeed, the threat of Jennifer being cited in a divorce case was so alarming that she was made to break off the friendship altogether.

Peti returned to London where he became increasingly reclusive and withdrawn. May acted as a buffer between father and son when Louis's disappointment showed itself too strongly, but her tendency to fuss and overprotect Peti was something

Michael (back row, second right) with Jennifer Aldington (front row, left) and members of her family at a party in Folkestone, Kent

he found maddening, provoking him into irritated silence. Her relationship with Comfort, at least, was uncomplicated, and her children more appreciative of her attention. Duff Hart-Davis remembers May coming to take him out for tea when he was at Eton – a treat that he nonetheless anticipated with some trepidation because of her terrifying driving at high speed down the narrow country lanes.

As a substitute to writing fiction, May poured her creative energy into painting, and took it seriously enough to exhibit her work. Her subjects included landscapes, still-life and portraits in which she captured good likenesses of grandchildren and family (one she made of Louis is held at the National Portrait Gallery). During her long periods on the Gold Coast she painted a number of portraits of local men and women – two of Ashanti employees, including one of a 6 foot gold-miner, adorned the walls of the London offices of the corporation. Her portraits of West African natives, often concentrating on close-ups of faces, have a moving and authentic quality which reveals much about her abiding and compassionate interest in humanity.

She also engaged enthusiastically in criticism of the visual arts. When her positive endorsement of the modernist tradition received spiky putdowns from Sir Alfred Munnings at the Royal Academy, among others, she found herself exposed to a public sparring match, and retaliated, with sardonic rebuke, with a letter to the *Daily Telegraph* in which she made her point in defending 'our young experimentalists' against 'old venerable men who are a little too intolerant of the young'.

She gave encouragement and support to young artists and writers, and anyone else she felt able to help by using her extensive contacts in the world of theatre and the arts. Noël Coward remained a dear friend and she admired his work tremendously, but she never held back from saying what she believed was wrong when she wrote to give her thoughts after seeing his plays or musicals.

As she grew older she seemed increasingly drawn to America, telling Louis that she found it a far more exhilarating and pleasanter place to live than England, and through her nephew-in-law, Adlai Stevenson, the twice-unsuccessful Democratic presidential candidate, she had her finger on the pulse of American politics, even helping him with his speech-writing and other campaign work. She adored him like a son, and their closeness was a great consolation to her when other relationships were burdened by troubles. The situation with Nancy had reached crisis point in the summer of 1955 when Louis had extended a business trip with her into a holiday in the Adriatic, at a time when May needed his support with Peti who was causing her grave concern. 'How far you travelled together is of no consequence. It is enough to

May found great pleasure in painting. (Above) One of her granddaughters poses for her. (Below) a portrait by May of a Ghanian chief

know that when my deepest feelings run counter to her wishes and convenience, I am not worth considering', she wrote to Louis. 'She has got everything she wanted except your name. I am a cipher.'[18] The thought of a separation weighed heavily upon her. Once and for all she wanted a resolution: 'I await your suggestions and I dread your return.' But the outcome was a continuation of the status quo.

It was hardly surprising that May found respite in America, and supporting Adlai gave her purpose. She was fully engaged in the excitement of the presidential election in summer 1956 when she received the news that Peti had suffered a brain haemorrhage and had fallen into a coma. Rushing back to England, she learned from the doctors treating him at the Middlesex Hospital that he had little chance of recovery, and that if he did regain consciousness, he could be permanently brain-damaged. Comfort came to support her mother, alternating her time between the hospital and Strathearn Place.

The agonising bedside vigil lasted a month before Peti came out of his coma. Eventually he was allowed home, where May looked after him round the clock, and Louis became increasingly concerned for her own health as she showed the immense strain she was under. Then Peti caught pneumonia and had to be taken to hospital by ambulance, before embarking on another long period of convalescence. In a letter to Joyce, Louis wrote of how May was 'tearing herself apart over Peti' and 'so terribly thin and goes on losing weight … she is incredibly diminished in every way'. She herself told Louis 'that her heart was broken' and he believed this to be true. 'As to whether there is anything organically the matter with her, one cannot be certain since she absolutely refuses to have the thorough examination her doctor demands. Beg as I will, she will not have it, although she does recognize that her health is of vital importance to the boy.'

When Peti was stable enough to move back to his flat, May found it hard to relinquish responsibility for him, and still felt desperate with worry and sadness. On top of this, her relationship with her youngest daughter, Emmy, had become fraught – in Maine she and her husband had parted ways after an increasingly destructive relationship fuelled by heavy drinking, and as Emmy spiralled into depression and alcoholism, she became progressively hostile towards her mother.

Duff remembers May as having an air of doom and tragedy about her during the latter years of her life as she struggled to cope with many difficulties. But when Adlai Stevenson stayed with her in 1958 he felt she seemed more serene and happy than she had in a long while.

Through her seventies and into her eighties she retained her sense of style and glamour, making an effort with her appearance whenever she went out or received company – even if it was only family visiting. Cyril Connolly described her as being like an exotic bird, and photographs of her in older age show her chicly dressed with her slim legs neatly crossed, and tiny feet in trim high-heeled shoes, fingernails painted with bright red varnish, and brown eyeliner around her startlingly large blue eyes. In her hand, a cigarette is invariably held between languid fingers. She retained her American accent, speaking with a very slow, measured, deep drawl, exaggerated by years of incessant smoking. She was still a wonderful raconteur and kept her dinner guests spellbound with her stories, but they would have to wait patiently during her long drawn out pauses. When Louis interrupted or tried to take over, she would appeal to him along the table, 'Let me tell this one B.' There was always a competitive edge to their relationship, but together they could energize a room, sparking off each other when they were not fighting. Both loved to debate and argue a point and May enjoyed throwing out provocative comments for the sake of a lively discussion, with a humorous glint in her eyes.

***

The fact that May stayed with Louis puzzled many friends

who were infuriated by his obtuse disregard of her feelings over Nancy, but others recognized the solid foundations of their marriage that held together through thick and thin. The fact was that May remained unfailingly devoted to Louis and proud of his strengths while accepting his weaknesses. In his own uncompromising way, Louis loved May too and was hugely proud of her achievements and strength of character. When Nancy once complained about ill health to him, he sharply reprimanded her and drew a comparison with May's fortitude when ill. In spite of Nancy's continuing hold on him, they persistently weathered the effects to renew their closeness time and again. Those who knew them well saw that a vital reparative element in their marriage was a core of deep affection and mutual dependence which endured into old age.

'I must say it is quite extraordinary how so small a person can leave so big a gap,'[19] Louis wrote to her in 1964 from Corfu where he was staying on his own. He worried about her chest pains, and thought of her constantly: 'I really think I am with you practically all day, see you off to bed & then imagine you safely in your chair when you get up.' They had exchanged letters for nearly fifty years, from the early ones sent from the front to those scribbled in old age in shaky handwriting: 'I must say – & this without reproach – that you telling me my letter was almost illegible was written in a letter I could hardly read', scribbled Louis with affection. 'I smiled a rather wry smile at the thought of us so anxious to write to each other but finding it hard to do so owing to a lack of a mutually comprehensible medium – tonight I am writing fairly well I think.'[20]

He was working on a book about the Syrian campaign, which prompted him to recall the time when May had been so ill with her infected shoulder which had taken up a 'disproportionate' amount of his time and energy 'when so much was at stake', leaving him to muse that 'it is remarkable how often in times of national crisis this has been the case.'[21]

***

By 1964 May was a great-grandmother, which gave her pleasure, but life still had more shattering shocks in store for her. On 14 July 1965, Adlai Stevenson, over in England in his role as United States Ambassador to the United Nations, collapsed of a heart attack in a London street and was pronounced dead; just three days earlier he had enjoyed a relaxing lunch with May at St Michael's Grange. She once told a friend that Adlai was 'the very breath of life' to her and she mourned his death at the age of sixty-five most profoundly. Although she was in poor health, she escorted his body back to America in the presidential plane with his sons.

Back in England she began to take life at a quieter pace, preferring the solitude of the countryside. She and Louis were looked after by their housekeeper, Mrs Reichart, a German refugee who, since coming to work for them in 1957, had become a devoted part of the family.

May had more or less stopped writing, but when she was eighty, ten years after her last publication, fresh interest in her work came from the country of her birth. The director of the new Mugar Memorial Library at Boston University, Howard Gothlieb, believed May's work would stand the test of time, and in recognition of this he asked her to denote her manuscripts and papers to the collection. (She had shown scant concern for their survival, storing them in an outbuilding and the granary at St Michael's Grange, where they had been attacked by mice.) In October 1966, she was asked to be an honorary fellow. She was too frail to make the journey to attend the celebratory dinner, but speaking by telephone, in a shaky voice, she gave her acceptance and thanks, and spoke poignantly of her desire to return to her roots once more. She was often aware of being an exile, she said, and although she loved England and believed in the British people – 'stalwart, unbeatable when roused' – after trying to understand them for forty years, they remained baffling to her. 'The truth is I am not at home here. My home is on your side

May with Howard Gothlieb (right)

of the Atlantic and I need to come home to renew my youth'.[22] In spite of her tremendously long adult expatriation she never severed her roots, or transcended them with a wholehearted sense of Englishness, or even that of a European; she remained at heart an American and now, more than ever perhaps, that old periodic homesickness, which she used to appease by watching cowboy westerns, made her pine but, alas, ill health prevented May from crossing the Atlantic again.

She had not finished with travelling, however, and in January 1968 she felt strong enough to accompany Louis on his annual trip to Ghana. While visiting the mine at Obuasi, she fell and broke her hip, bringing her holiday to an abrupt and painful end, but she demonstrated her stoic side, refusing to take the strong painkillers offered to her for fear they would make her feel confused when she wanted a clear head for saying goodbye to the Ashanti employees. She was airlifted to Accra and from there flown back to London where she underwent an operation for an artificial hip. Afterwards she moved into Strathearn Place where she was looked after by two trained nurses.

Louis spoke of her tremendous courage as she battled towards recovery and overcame the difficulties of learning to walk with the aid of two sticks. In March they celebrated their golden wedding anniversary and May confided to an old friend that she felt closer to him than she had for a long time – something that others observed for themselves.

She was always cheered by visits from friends who found her as good company as ever, her brain no less sharp, and still with the same dry humour. But the accident left her physically and emotionally frailer and by the end of the year she was sinking rapidly. Even so she was looking forward to returning to Ghana in the New Year, having been given permission by her doctor to do so. She appeared both serene and mentally lively to those who saw or spoke to her in her final days as she continued to take note of events both domestic and public, and made telephone calls to friends and family. Her abiding philosophy had always been to live life to the full until she dropped and even when she was too debilitated to get out of bed, she retained her ardent interest in living, with her thoughts dwelling not so much on the past, but of all that she wanted to do if given another life.

On 2nd December 1968, at St Michael's Grange, she finally let go of the world she had loved and been a part of for eighty-two years. Louis was at her side, her hand held in his. He felt hers was a peaceful death, but afterwards he could not contain his own shock and despair, and collapsed on the floor, prostrate with grief. Her finite absence from his life left a far bigger gap now, and although Nancy seized her chance to fill it, her own importance to Louis was undermined by the profoundness of his sense of loss. May had sometimes feared that he might leave her for Nancy, but ironically she had provided a safeguard against any obligation to commit to her this way. As it was, Louis survived May by just over five years – after one of these finally giving in to Nancy's domineering pressure to marry her.

On 12 January 1969, just over a month after his mother died, Peti followed her and their ashes were buried together in the churchyard at Warfield.

Epilogue

When the news of May's death was made public, a flood of letters of love and tribute revealed the huge impact she had made on people's lives around the world. Many spoke of her as a truly remarkable person who had lived a brilliant life dedicated to the good of others. The same qualities were saluted again and again: the combination of a strong character with warmth, gentleness and deep insight into human nature – as shown in her writing and deeds – her vitality, humour and intelligence. It was 'a delight to be torpedoed by her wit', wrote one friend, summing up the view of many. Cyril Connolly wrote of how 'exceptionally kind & generous' she had been to him when he was young, echoing the appreciation of others whom she had helped in their youth. Noël Coward remembered a 'very valued friend' who always 'enchanted while she talked' and never failed to impress him with her views and deductions: 'she was wise – and understanding & kind and intelligent – balanced in her judgements and wonderfully unprejudiced'.

She was also celebrated for her courage and bravery in both personal and professional spheres, reflecting the different dimensions of her eventful life. In a moving obituary in the

Revue de la France Libre, Vernier recalled the devotion she inspired in her staff, and General de Gaulle wrote of her achievements during both world wars, while *The Times* obituary compared her novels to those of Edith Wharton.[1]

Once, to ensure the attendance of celebrated guests at her birthday party, May had found it necessary to invoke the Queen of Scots. By the time of her death she needed no such enticement, having become a prominent figure in her own right and in more than one capacity. On 7 January, at St Paul's Church, Knightsbridge, a very well-attended memorial service gave her a send-off that would no doubt have surprised and touched her. In attendance, in full military regalia, were twenty-five soldiers from the division to which her ambulance unit had been attached, sent over by the French Minister of Defence. The British Field Marshals Alexander and Templer were there, and the widow of General de Larminat. Members of the Hadfield–Spears Unit were there, including many of May's 'English girls', the nurses and drivers with whom she had forged such special friendships. The ambassadors of the United States, France, Switzerland, Turkey, Lebanon and Saudi Arabia and Kuwait were also in attendance, and Lord Boothby gave the address.

When May was a young child she wrote down her hopes for the future on a piece of paper which she then folded and placed in an envelope for posterity. Her words were remarkably prescient: I would like to be a help to God. I would like to be honest, brave and kind, I would like to help the soldiers in war. I would like to do something for my country.'

Acknowledgements

I first became aware of May when I came across her poetry and prose written from behind the lines during the First World War. Nearly a century after its composition, her war writing still has the power to shock and inform. From my first excited reading of this powerful body of work, May began to haunt my imagination, and all the more intensely because I could discover little about her. The desire to know more sent me on a compulsive detective hunt, and although I did not know it then, the biographer's muse had possessed me.

Sometime during the early weeks of this possession, I discovered that May's much-adored only son, Michael, had lived in the village next to the one where I grew up and had had a brief romance with my cousin. There was even a photograph of them together in an old family album, taken with my parents and aunt at a Kent ball (see page 304). As a young child I had been fascinated by the photograph for it was rare to see my parents dressed in such glamorous clothes, and I wondered about the identity of the young man standing next to my father. This uncanny coincidence sent a shiver up my spine and made it seem that my discovery of May was predestined. Enrolling for an MA in Life Writing at King's College, London, under

Professor Max Saunders, I was given the opportunity to write a short biography of May, and had a legitimate reason for making contact with her grandson, Duff Hart-Davis. After an exchange of letters, he invited me to his farmhouse in Gloucestershire and was generous and trusting enough to send me back to London with an old dusty trunk of May's, retrieved from his attic. I could hardly believe my good fortune when I discovered a veritable treasure chest containing May's letters from boarding school and university, unpublished poems and other kinds of personal materials. All the qualities that made her the boundary breaker she became radiate from May's early letters, and this intimate contact with her deepened the imaginary ties between us. There seemed no turning back, and with deceptive ease I found myself embarking upon a full-length biography. There were many times when I felt overwhelmed by the task of writing it, but May's formidably determined spirit inhabited my consciousness and I would hear her dismiss defeatist talk with a stern, no-nonsense ticking-off. And the more I unearthed about her life, and realized how much she had achieved, the more I wanted to put her back in the public eye.

Besides my gratitude to May for taking me on this journey, I owe an inestimable amount to her executors without whose kindness and encouragement I would never have started this book, let alone finish it. Duff Hart-Davis could not have been more generous with his help and time, and his experience and wisdom have been a great inspiration and comfort. I am very grateful to him for reading my manuscript at various stages and for somehow always knowing the right thing to say and do to keep a novice biographer's spirits up. I also give many thanks to his wife Phyllida for feeding me so well on my visits, for her memories of May, and for dismissing my doubts about being up to the task ahead by telling me just to 'follow my nose'. Colonel Aylmer, Spears's godson, and his wife Shaunagh have also been endlessly kind and supportive, and in whose welcoming house I spent several days going through papers with May's coffee pot beside me on a tray, thoughtfully refilled at frequent intervals by my hospitable hosts. I am grateful to other family members who have talked to me about May. In particular, I thank May's granddaughters Lady Silsoe, and in America, Mary Bok, who had me to stay for several days in her house in the hills of Camden, Maine, where I slept in the room May always used on her visits, and in the bed hand carved by her brother William. I thank May's niece, Courtney Cazden, for meeting me in London and Elizabeth Hall for her emails sharing stories about May and Louis. These meetings and communications with May's extended family have been the joyful rewards of my research for this book and made it all worthwhile.

I also want to thank my tutors at Middlesex University, in particular Patrick Campbell, for first persuading me to pursue my interest in May, and Max Saunders who I was fortunate enough to have as my supervisor at King's and who long after I completed my MA has continued to help and encourage me way beyond any call of duty. David Atkinson has been a constant source of help to me from the very outset, and I am particularly grateful to him for reading my manuscript and for all his candid suggestions. I also thank my other early readers for their thoughts and suggestions, my mother, Hope Osborne, my aunt, Penel Forbes Adam, and Catherine Atkinson.

There are many others who have shown me great kindness and practical support: Max Egremont, who gave me valuable information about sources and archives, having travelled the path before me with his biography of May's second husband Edward Spears entitled *Under Two Flags*; Jeremy Lewis for his time and publishing advice; Sheridan Morley, Literary Adviser to the Coward Estate, for giving me permission to consult May's letters at University of Birmingham Special Collections; my cousin, Jennifer Aldington, for sharing with me her memories of Michael, as did Marjorie Heritage; Anne Powell who found me my copy of *The Forbidden Zone* and who has shared many long encouraging talks with me over the years; Mr Lunn, May's gardener; Katie Millet and Annie Mackenzie for permission to use material from their mother's autobiography; my niece Wendy Conway Lamb for her help with French translations; Paul Hamilton and Andrew Heritage for their thoughtful advice; Dominick Jones and Rosalind Michahelles for putting me up on my visits to Boston, and to their friend, Andrew Cunynghame, who they brought to dinner one evening at the exact time I was researching May's work with Alexander Korda. By another strange coincidence, the famous film director turned out to be Andrew's godfather, and his own father, Korda's business associate, and this chance introduction led to him kindly giving me access to his father's diaries. I also thank all my friends who have taken such an interest in my book, especially Ann Bouza for her wonderful and boundless enthusiasm, Harriet Price, for listening to my worries, and Deborah Asher, Bob Boynton and Heather Johns, for their practical help in various ways.

The following institutions and their librarians and archivists have all been enormously helpful: Alex Rankin at the Mugar Library, Boston; Sophie Bridges and the rest of the team at the Churchill Archive Centre, Cambridge; Willa McCarthy, Director of Alumnae/Alumni at Vassar University; Patrick Stevens at Cornell University; and the staff at both the British Library and the Newspaper Library at Colindale.

Finally, I thank my husband, Steve, and my children James, Dominic and Sophy who have shared my one-track-minded obsession with May without complaint, welcoming her into our family and looking after her even when at times I failed to, never for one moment losing faith that I would complete and publish the story of her remarkable life.

Sources

Mary Borden's papers are mainly divided between the Mugar Memorial Library at Boston University, and Churchill College, Cambridge, where they are catalogued under Spears. Unpublished poems are included in both archives although the Mugar holds the majority of May's literary manuscripts, including the original version of *The Forbidden Zone*. For most of her life May did not keep a diary, although she kept an intermittent one during both world wars and these are kept at Churchill College with other papers relating to war, as well as her personal life, including the correspondence between her and Louis, spanning fifty years.

Private collections are also split between America and England. May's grandson, Duff Hart-Davis (abbreviated DH-D in the notes), and her granddaughter, Mary Bok, both hold letters, photographs and other documents, and Spears's godson, Colonel Aylmer, has a fascinating collection of artefacts and scrapbooks.

Notes

Chapter 1: A London Party

1. Ford Madox Ford, *Return to Yesterday*, pp. 432–3.
2. *The Selected Letters of E. M. Forster 1879–1920,* ed. M. Lago and P. N. Furbank, vol. 1, p. 211.
3. *The Mistress of Kingdoms,* p. 4.
4. DH-D Papers, undated.
5. DH-D Papers, undated.
6. DH-D Papers, undated.
7. DH-D Papers, Vassar letters.
8. DH-D Papers, Vassar letters.
9. DH-D Papers, undated.

Chapter 2: Collision

1. *The Selected Letters of E. M. Forster 1879–1920,* ed. M. Lago and P. N. Furbank, vol. 1, p. 156.
2. See entry for Mary Borden in *Oxford Dictionary of National Biographyy*
3. *Selected Letters of E. M. Forster,* vol. 1, pp. 150–1.
4. DH-D Papers.
5. H. Taylor, *Borden of Yale,* p. 167.
6. *The Mistress of Kingdoms,* p. 5.
7. J. Meyers, *The Enemy,* p. 72.
8. W. Lewis, *Blasting and Bombardiering,* p. 56.
9. Cornell University, Wyndham Lewis Collection, undated.
10. Ibid.
11. J. Meyers, *The Enemy,* p. 84.
12. Wyndham Lewis Collection, undated.
13. Ibid.
14. Wyndham Lewis Collection, 13 July 1914.
15. Wyndham Lewis Collection, undated.
16. Ibid.

Chapter 3: Croix-Rouge

1. M. Gilbert, *The First World War*, p. 23.
2. Cornell University, Wyndham Lewis Collection, 12 December 1914.
3. Wyndham Lewis Collection, 31 December 1914.
4. *The Forbidden Zone*, p. 46.
5. Ibid., p. 47.
6. *Journey Down a Blind Alley*, p. 7.
7. Wyndham Lewis Collection, 23 June 1915.
8. P. O'Keefe, *Some Sort of Genius: A Life of Wyndham Lewis*, p. 171.
9. *The Letters of Ezra Pound and Wyndham Lewis*, ed. T. Materer, p. 56.

Chapter 4: Behind the Lines

1. *Brooklyn Life* (1916).
2. Ibid.
3. Ibid.
4. *Journey Down a Blind Alley*, p. 10.
5. Ibid.
6. *The Forbidden Zone*, pp. 144–5.
7. Ibid., pp. 143–4.
8. Ibid., p. 154.
9. Ibid., p. 117.
10. Ibid., p. 149.
11. Ibid., p. 151.
12. *Journey Down a Blind Alley*, p. 10.
13. *Sarah Gay*, p. 39.
14. D. Franck, *The Bohemians: The Birth of Modern Art, Paris 1900–1930*.
15. G. Stein, *The Autobiography of Alice B. Toklas*, p. 185.

Chapter 5: Love Letters from the Front

1. *The Romantic Woman*
2. *Selected Letters of E. M. Forster 1879–1920,* ed. M. Lago and P. N. Furbank, vol. 1, p. 239.
3. Churchill College, Spears Papers, 2/29, 27 May 1917.
4. Spears Papers, 2/29, 26 May 1917
5. Ibid.
6. Spears Papers, 2/29, undated.
7. *New York Herald*, July 1917.
8. Spears Papers, 2/29, 18 June 1917.
9. Spears Papers, 2/29, undated.
10. Spears Papers, 2/29, undated.
11. Spears Papers, 2/29, undated.
12. Spears Papers, 2/29, 2 August 1917.
13. Spears Papers, 2/29, 9 August 1917.
14. Spears Papers, 2/29, 25 August 1917.
15. Ibid.
16. Published in *English Review* (December 1917).
17. Spears Papers, 2/29, 11 August 1917.
18. Spears Papers, 2/29, undated.
19. Spears Papers, 2/29, 9 September 1917.
20. Spears Papers, 2/29, undated.

21. Spears Papers, 2/29, 18 September 1917.
22. Spears Papers, 2/29, 21 September 1917.
23. Spears Papers, 2/29, 19 September 1917.
24. Spears Papers, 2/29, 20 September 1917.
25. Spears Papers, 2/29, 21 September 1917.

Chapter 6: The Trauma of Parting

1. Churchill College, Spears Papers, 2/29, 2 October 1917.
2. Spears Papers, 2/29.
3. Spears Papers, 2/29, 8 October 1917.
4. Ibid.
5. Spears Papers, acc. 1048.
6. Spears Papers, 2/29, 17 February 1918.
7. Spears Papers, 2/29.

Chapter 7: Trouble on the Horizon

1. *Journey Down a Blind Alley*, p. 6.
2. Churchill College, Spears Papers, Box 4, Diary, 20 January 1919.
3. Ibid.
4. Ibid.
5. Spears Papers, Box 4, Diary, 11 April 1919.
6. Derby diary 28/1/4, cited in Max Egremont, *Under Two Flags*, p. 84.
7. Egremont, *Under Two Flags,* p. 84.
8. Spears Papers, 1/76, 1 November 1919.
9. Spears Papers, 2/29, 31 August 1920.
10. Ibid.
11. Egremont, *Under Two Flags*, p. 91.
12. Spears Papers, 2/29, 20 October 1920.
13. Spears Papers, Custody Case Papers.
14. Spears Papers, 2/4, March 1921.
15. Spears Papers, Custody Case Papers.
16. Spears Papers, 2/4, Diary, 5 July 1921.
17. Spears Papers, 2/4, Diary, 31 December 1921.

Chapter 8: A Welcome from the Windy City

1. Noël Coward, *The Autobiography of Noël Coward*, p. 11.
2. *Daily Telegraph*, 1 April 1924.
3. *Daily Sketch*, 2 April 1924.
4. Ibid.
5. Ibid.
6. *Washington Star*, 7 September 1924.
7. Churchill College, Spears Papers, acc. 1048.
8. *Sacramento [Cal.] Union*, 18 September 1932.
9. *The Queen* 5 March 1924.
10. *Sacramento [Cal.] Union*, 18 September 1932.
11. Spears Papers, acc. 1048.
12. Ibid.
13. Spears Papers, August 1924
14. *New York Town Topic*, 2 October 1924.

Chapter 9: An Extraordinarily Stirring Story

1. *Three Pilgrims and a Tinker*, p. 312.
2. Churchill College, Spears Papers, acc. 1048, Box 4, 6 April 1924.
3. Ibid.
4. Joyce Borden Baloković, *Singing Wings*, p. 27.
5. C. Headlam, *Parliament and Politics in the Age of Baldwin and MacDonald*, p. 122.

Chapter 10: The Forbidden Zone

1. *Flamingo*, p. 9.
2. Ibid., p. 87.
3. Ibid., p. 19.
4. Ibid., p. 78.
5. Ibid., p. 8.
6. Ibid., p. 89.
7. Ibid., p. 83.
8. Ibid., p. 85.
9. Ibid., p. 95.
10. Ibid., p. 93.
11. D. Pryce-Jones, *Cyril Connolly*, pp. 264–5.
12. Mary Borden, 'Personal Experience and the Art of Fiction', p. 91.
13. *Flamingo*, p. 80.
14. Mugar Library, Mary Borden Collection, Box 23, 8 April 1927 (scrapbook vol. 2).
15. D. Pryce-Jones, *Cyril Connolly*, pp. 171–2.
16. Mary Borden Collection, Box 9, July 1928.
17. *Southport Guardian*, 23 November 1929.
18. *The Sphere*, 7 December 1929.

Chapter 11: Family Matters

1. Mugar Library, Mary Borden Collection, Box 23, 1 May 1930 (scrapbook).
2. DH-D Papers, 14 October 1931.
3. DH-D Papers, 25 September 1931.
4. DH-D Papers, 12 October 1931.
5. Ibid.
6. Max Saunders, *A Dual Life*, vol. 2, p. 377.
7. 'Man, the Master: An Illusion', p. 12, in *Man Proud Man*, ed. Mabel Ulrich.
8. University of Birmingham, Noël Coward Collection, 13 September 1932.
9. *The Technique of Marriage*, p. 144.
10. Ibid., p. 296.
11. Ibid., p. 131.
12. Ibid.
13. Ibid.
14. Philip Ziegler, *Rupert Hart-Davis Man of Letters*, p. 84.

Chapter 12: A Catholic Commotion

1. Mugar Library, Mary Borden Collection, Box 6, 23 November 1933.

2. Mary Borden Collection, 28 November 1933.
3. Mary Borden Collection, 14 November 1933.
4. Mary Borden Collection, 8 December 1933.
5. Mary Borden Collection, 25 January 1934.
6. David Pryce-Jones, *Cyril Connolly*, London, p. 265.
7. Ibid.
8. Mary Borden Collection, Box 9, 12 February 1935.

Chapter 13: Censored

1. Mugar Library, Mary Borden Collection, Box 9, 6 March 1935.
2. Ibid.
3. Mary Borden Collection, 7 March 1935.
4. Ibid.
5. Mary Borden Collection, 15 April 1935.
6. Charles Drazin, *Korda: Britain's Only Movie Mogul*, p. 118.
7. Mary Borden Collection, Box 9, 19 February 1937.
8. University of Birmingham, Noël Coward Collection, undated.
9. Max Saunders, *Ford Madox Ford: A Dual Life,* vol. 2, p. 377.
10. Max Egremont, *Under Two Flags*, p. 127.
11. Ibid.
12. *The Technique of Marriage*, p. 131.
13. Mary Borden Collection, Box 20, Diary during the Crisis. 8 October 1938.
14. Mary Borden Collection, Diary during the Crisis, 26 September.
15. Churchill College, Spears Papers, Box 6, Diary, 4 October 1939.
16. Spears Papers, Box 6, Diary, 25 September 1939.
17. Spears papers, Box 6, Diary, 7 October.
18. Spears Papers, Box 6, Diary, 6 October.
19. Ibid.
20. *Journey Down a Blind Alley*, p. 15.

Chapter 14: Journey Down a Blind Alley

1. *Journey Down a Blind Alley*, p. 15.
2. Edward Spears, *Assignment to Catastrophe*, p. 90.
3. *Journey Down a Blind Alley*, p. 36.
4. Churchill College, Spears Papers, Box 6, Diary, 17 May 1940.
5. Spears Papers, Box 6, Diary, 19 May.
6. Spears Papers, Box 6, Diary, 28 May.
7. *Journey Down a Blind Alley,* p. 45.
8. Spears, *Assignment to Catastrophe*, p. 412.
9. Ibid., p. 406.
10. Ibid., p. 382.
11. *Journey Down a Blind Alley*, p. 64.
12. Ibid., p. 64.
13. Ibid., p. 71.
14. Ibid., p. 60.
15. Ibid., p. 89.

Chapter 15: A New Beginning

1. *Journey Down a Blind Alley,* p. 113.
2. Churchill College, Spears Papers, Box 6, Diary, 2 October 1940.

3. Spears papers, Box 6, Diary, 5 October.
4. Spears papers, Box 6, Diary, 8 October.
5. *Journey Down a Blind Alley,* p. 122.
6. Ibid.
7. Spears Papers, Box 6, Diary, 29 January 1941.

Chapter 16: Doubt and Disillusion

1. Churchill College, Spears Papers, Box 6, Diary, 16 March 1941.
2. Spears Diary, 24 May 1941, cited in Max Egremont, *Under Two Flags,* p. 224.
3. Spears Papers, Box 6, Diary, 22 May 1941.
4. *Journey Down a Blind Alley,* p. 127.
5. Ibid., p141.
6. Ibid., p139.
7. Ibid., 141.
8. Ibid.
9. Spears Papers, Box 6, Diary.
10. *Journey Down a Blind Alley,* p. 143.
11. *Noël Coward Diaries,* p. 664.
12. *Journey Down a Blind Alley,* p. 149.
13. Spears Papers, Box 6, Diary, 11 September 1941.
14. *Journey Down a Blind Alley,* p. 154.
15. Ibid., p. 149.
16. Ibid., p. 153.
17. Spears Papers, Box 6, 23 December 1941.
18. Ibid.

Chapter 17: Factions in the Desert

1. *Journey Down a Blind Alley,* p. 155.
2. Churchill College, Spears Papers, Box 6, Diary, 20 January 1942.
3. *Journey Down a Blind Alley,* pp. 157–8.
4. Ibid., p. 158.
5. Ibid., p. 159.
6. Ibid., p. 164.
7. Ibid., p. 171.
8. Ibid., p. 169.
9. Ibid., p. 173.
10. Spears Papers, Box 6, Diary, 2 January 1942.
11. *Journey Down a Blind Alley,* p. 174.

Chapter 18: Two Centres of Gravity

1. Rachel Millet, *Spearette,* p. 15.
2. Hermione, Countess of Ranfurly, *To War with Whitaker,* p. 147.
3 *Journey Down a Blind Alley,* p. 188.
4. Jacques Duprey, *Memoirs of the Hadfield–Spears Unit* (translated summary).
5. Millet, p. 21.
6. *Journey Down a Blind Alley,* p. 190.
7. Duprey.
8. *Journey Down a Blind Alley,* pp. 199–200.
9. DH-D Papers, Memories of Damascus.
10. *Journey Down a Blind Alley,* p. 204.

11. Ibid., p. 206.
12. Churchill College, Spears Papers, Diary, 19 Febuary 1943.
13. Spears Papers, Diary, 11 March.
14. Spears Papers, Diary, 29 April.
15. Spears Papers, Diary, April 23 1943.
16. Spears Papers, Diary, 6 November 1943.
17. *Journey Down a Blind Alley,* p. 220.
18. Max Egremont, *Under Two Flags,* p. 254.
19. Spears Papers, Diary, 30 November 1943.
20. Spears Papers, Diary, 11 December 1943.
21. Egremont, p 256.
22. Ibid., p. 257.
23. Rachel Millet, *Spearette,* p. 98.
24. *Journey Down a Blind Alley,* p. 247.
25. Ibid., p. 249.
26. Ibid., p. 246.

Chapter 19: Demobilization

1. *Journey Down a Blind Alley,* pp. 252–3.
2. Ibid., p. 264.
3. Ibid., p. 281.
4. Ibid., p. 289.
5. Ibid., p. 187.

Chapter 20: Home is in the Heartland

1. *Journey Down a Blind Alley* , p. 13.
2. Ibid., p. 21.
3. Ibid., pp. 143–4.
4. Ibid., p.170.
5. *Daily Telegraph,* 1 November 1946.
6. *Observer,* 24 October 1946.
7. Max Egremont, *Under Two Flags,* p. 272.
8. *Daily Telegraph,* 26 May 1947.
9. Egremont, p. 308.
10. *Daily Telegraph,* 25 August 1948.
11. *No. 2 Shovel Street,* p. 36.
12. Churchill College, Spears Papers.
13. DH-D Papers.
14. Ibid.
15. Mugar Library, Mary Borden Collection, 'A Moment with Doctor Einstein'.
16. Ibid.
17. Ibid.
18. Spears Papers, 2/29, 18 August 1955.
19. Spears Papers, 2/29, 16 October 1964.
20. Spears Papers, 2/29, 7 October 1964.
21. Spears papers, 2/29, 3 August 1964.
22. Spears Papers, acc. 1048, Box 8.

Bibliography

Books by Mary Borden

Mistress of Kingdoms (under pseudonym Bridget Maclagan) (London: Duckworth, 1912).

Collision (under pseudonym Bridget Maclagan) (London: Duckworth, 1913).

The Romantic Woman (under pseudonym Bridget Maclagan) (London: Constable, 1916; reissued under the name of Mary Borden, 1924).

The Tortoise (New York: Alfred Knopf, 1921).

Jane Our Stranger (London: Heinemann, 1923).

Three Pilgrims and a Tinker (London: Heinemann, 1924).

Jericho Sands (London: Heinemann, 1925).

Four O'Clock and Other Stories (London: Heinemann, 1926).

Flamingo (London: Heinemann, 1927).

Jehovah's Day (London: Heinemann, 1928).

The Forbidden Zone (London: Heinemann, 1929).

A Woman with White Eyes (London: Heinemann, 1930).

Sarah Gay (London: Heinemann, 1931).

Mary of Nazareth (London: Heinemann, 1933).

The Technique of Marriage (London: Heinemann, 1933).
The King of the Jews (London: Heinemann, 1935).
Action for Slander (London: Heinemann, 1936).
The Black Virgin (London: Heinemann, 1937).
Passport for a Girl (London: Heinemann, 1938).
Journey Down a Blind Alley (London: Hutchinson, 1946).
No. 2 Shovel Street (London: Heinemann, 1949).
For the Record (London: Heinemann, 1950).
Martin Merriedew (London: Heinemann, 1952).
Margin of Error (London: Heinemann, 1954).
The Hungry Leopard (London: Heinemann, 1956).

Other publications by Mary Borden
'The Gift of Forgiving Gods', *Atlantic Monthly* , February 1910.
'Mr John's Miss Best', *Atlantic Monthly*, March 1910.
'Man, the Master: An Illusion', in *Man Proud Man*, ed. Mabel
    Ulrich (Hamish Hamilton, 1932).
'Personal Experience and the Art of Fiction' (Royal Society of
    Literature lecture, 19 April,1956), *Essays by Divers Hands*, 29
    (1958).

Secondary Sources

Baloković, Joyce, *Singing Wings* (privately printed).

Beauman, N, *A Very Great Profession: The Woman's Novel* 1914–39 (Virago, 1983)

Borden, J., *The Cruise of the Northern Light* (Macmillan, 1928).

Coward, Noël, *The Autobiography of Noël Coward* (Methuen, 1986).

Cardinal, A., D. Goldman, and J. Hattaway, *Women's Writing on the First World War* (Oxford University Press, 2002).

David, Hugh, *Fitzrovians: A Portrait of Bohemian Society* (Michael Joseph, 1988).

Dell, Ethel, *The Way of an Eagle* (George Newnes, 1912).

Dell, Floyd, *Moon-Calf* (Heineman, 1922).

Diver, Maud, *The Englishwoman in India* (William Blackwood & Sons, 1909).

Drazin, C., *Korda: Britain's Only Movie Mogul* (Sidgwick and Jackson, 2002).

Dunn, J. C., *The War the Infantry Knew 1914–1919* (Abacus, 1987).

Duprey, J., *L'ambulance Hadfield–Spears, ou la drôle d'équipe* (1953).

Egremont, Max, *Under Two Flags* (Weidenfield & Nicolson, 1997).

Ford, Ford Madox, *Return to Yesterday: Reminiscences 1894–1914*

(Gollancz, 1931).

Forster, E. M., *The Selected Letters of E. M. Forster*, vol. 1, 1879–1920, ed. M. Lago and P. N. Furbank (Collins, 1983).

Franck, D, *The Bohemians: The Birth of Modern Art, Paris 1900–1930* (Phoenix, 2002).

Gems, G., *Windy City Wars: Labor, Leisure, and Sport in the Making of Chicago* (Scarecrow Press, 1997).

Gilbert, M., *First World War* (Harper Collins, 1995).

Goldman, D., *Women Writers and the Great War* (Twayne, 1995).

Headlam, C., *Parliament and Politics in the Age of Baldwin and Macdonald: The Headlam Diaries*, ed. S. Bell (1992).

Higonnet, M., ed., *Nurses at the Front: Writing the Wounds of the Great War* (Northeastern University Press, 2001).

Huxley, J., *Leaves of the Tulip Tree* (John Murray, 1986).

La Motte, E. N., *The Backwash of War* (Putnam's, 1916).

Lewis, J., *Cyril Connolly: A Life* (Jonathan Cape, 1997).

Lewis, Wyndham, *Blasting and Bombardering* (Calder & Boyars, 1967).

Lindberg, Richard, *Chicago Ragtime* (Icarus Press, 1985).

Marlow, Joyce, *Women and the Great War* (Virago, 1998).

McLaren, E., ed., *A History of the Scottish Women's Hospitals* (Hodder & Stoughton, 1919).

Materer, T., ed., *The Letters of Ezra Pound and Wyndham Lewis* (Faber, 1985).

Miller, Donald, *City of the Century* (Simon and Schuster, 1996).

Millet, R., *Spearette: A Memoir of the Hadfield–Spears Ambulance Unit* (Fern House,1998).

Montefiore, J., *Men and Women Writers of the 1930s* (Routledge, 1996).

Myers, J., *The Enemy* (Routledge, 1980).

O'Keefe, Paul. *Some Sort of Genius: A Life of Wyndham Lewis* (Jonathan Cape, 2000).

Onions, Maude, *A Woman at War* (C. W. Daniel, 1929).

Powell, Anne, *Women in the War Zone* (History Press, 2009).

Pryce-Jones, D., *Cyril Connolly: Journal and Memoir* (Collins, 1983).

Ranfurly, Hermione, Countess of, *To War with Whitaker: The Wartime Diaries of the Countess of Ranfurly 1939–45* (Heinemann, 1995).

Robertson, D. *The Chicago Revival: Society and Revivalism in a Nineteenth Century City* (Scarecrow Press, 1989).

Rose, W. K., ed., *The Letters of Wyndham Lewis* (Methuen, 1963).

Saunders, M., *Ford Madox Ford: A Dual Life*, 2 vols (Oxford University Press, 1996).

Shone, R., *The Art of Bloomsbury* (Tate Publishing, 1999).

Spears, E., *Liaison 1914* (London, 1930).

—, *Prelude to Victory* (London, 1939).

—, *Assignment to Catastrophe*: vol. 1 *Prelude to Dunkirk*; vol. 2 *The Fall of France* (1954).

Stein, G., *The Autobiography of Alice B. Toklas* (Penguin, 1966).

Sullivan, R., *Goodbye Lizzie Borden* (Chatto & Windus, 1975).

Taylor, H., *Borden of Yale* (China Inland Mission, 1952).

Travers, S., *Tomorrow to be Brave* (Bantam, 2000).

Willmott, H. P., *First World War* (Dorling Kindersley, 2003).

—, C. Messenger, and R. Cross, *Second World War* (Dorling Kindersley, 2004).

Ziegler, P., *Rupert Hart-Davis: Man of Letters* (Chatto and Windus, 2004).

Index

Forster, E. M., 3, 24, 30–1, 65
Forum Theatre Guild, 135
Franco-German armistice, 207, 209–10, 213
Freetown, 224
Freiburg, 6
Friends' Ambulance Unit (FAU), 216, 238–9, 243, 250, 252–3, 262–4, 266–7, 273
Fruchaud, Colonel, 217, 226, 228, 233–4, 246–8, 250–1, 254–5, 262
Fry, Roger, 33
Fulroth, Evelyn, 217, 270

Galilee, 162
Galsworthy, John, 131
Gamelin, General Maurice, 189–91
Gannat, 208
Garigliano, river, 276
Garnett, David, 300
Gauguin, Paul, 262
Gazala Line, 250–1, 254
General Strike, 146
Geneva, 125
George V, King, 92
Germany, 289
Ghana, 291, 311–12
Glasgow, 24, 222, 281
Glenwild estate, 13, 128, 158
Gold Coast, 291–3, 302, 304
Goldstein, David, 168–9
Gollancz, Victor, 158
Gordon, Jessie, 68, 80
Gosset, Jean, 192, 195, 197, 199, 201, 205, 208, 211
Gothlieb, Howard, 310
Graham, Barbara, 201, 203, 217, 223, 228–9, 234, 246, 252, 254, 260, 269–70, 273
Grand Canyon, 124
Great Lakes, 7
Greece, 224
Gretton, Hugh, 99, 102–3, 105
Gretton, Mrs, 99–101, 103, 105, 109, 121
Grey, Lady Jane, 18
Guénin, Dr, 204, 206, 210
Guerin (orderly and priest), 76
Guerriac, General, 284
Guigny, 205
Gulmarg, 25

Guta, 281

Hack, Lucy, 66, 113–14
Hack, Melicent, 66
Hadfield, Lady, 189, 192–3, 215
Hadfield–Spears Unit: and fall of France, 191–212, 230; and Middle East, 213–35, 238–57, 261–8, 272–4; de Gaulle's endorsement, 221, 228, 239; and permanent clinics, 263–4, 280; and Italian campaign, 275–8; and French campaign, 277–8, 280–5; name changes, 277, 282, 284–5; disbandment, 285–7; and May's memorial, 315
Haig, Field Marshal Douglas, 79
Haig offensive, 73, 75
Hajali (cook), 252
Halfaya Pass, 244
Hamilton, Hon. Rowan, 166
Hamish Hamilton (publishers), 159
Harrison, Mrs, 60
Hart-Davis, Adam, 295
Hart-Davis, Bridget, 183
Hart-Davis, Comfort (née Turner), 25, 74, 198, 241, 295, 304, 307; and custody battle, 99, 102, 104–11, 121–2; education, 143, 154; courtship and marriage, 161, 183–4, 186; and sister's suicide, 172–3
Hart-Davis, Duff, 184, 304, 308
Hart-Davis, Rupert, 161, 168, 183–4, 186, 199, 241, 295; and *Martin Merriedew*, 299–300
Hartley, L. P., 142
Hastings, Battle of, 5
Hawes, Lady Millicent, 94, 100, 103
Headcorn, Kent, 4–5
Headington School, 99, 104–5
Headlam, Cuthbert, 138
Heidelberg, 6
Heinemann (publishers), 118–19, 129, 146, 158, 161, 173, 178
Heliopolis, 256
Helleu, Jean, 271
Hemingway, Ernest, 150, 300
Herald-Tribune, 165
Herbert, A. P., 123, 148
Highgate, 184
Hitler, Adolf, 186–7, 289

This book is available through:

www.maryborden.com